A Glass of Crazy

Tina Laningham

A Glass of Crazy © 2014 Tina Laningham

This is a work of fiction.
Names, characters, and incidents are the product of
the author's imagination or are used fictitiously.
Any resemblance to actual persons, living or dead,
organizations, or events is entirely coincidental.

ISBN-13: 978-1495494734
ISBN-10: 149549473X

Special thanks to
Tracy Muras and Sandi Simon
for insightful critiques and constant encouragement.

For my father,
the best short story writer ever.

— 1 —

This is not the story I wanted to write when I turned fifteen. If your parents are still married, put down this book and walk away while you still have your innocence. If your parents have told you they're getting a divorce, keep reading. You're going to need some help.

My name is Abby Alexander and I almost didn't survive my parents' divorce. I mean this literally, not figuratively. I actually almost died. And no, I did not try to kill myself. Unfortunately, the lessons I learned are not taught in school and believe me, when your parents are going through a divorce, they can't stop their own insanity long enough to teach these skills to you at home. Basically, you're on your own.

It doesn't matter how you find out. Some parents actually sit their children down and talk to them like normal people. Other kids find out by overhearing an all night scream-a-thon. Or if you're like me and your parents are famous, you find out with the rest of the world on the six o'clock news.

No matter how you find out, you're going to have a mental break from reality. This is normal. After all, the reality you once knew doesn't exist anymore and who knows what frightening step monsters lurk ahead? But don't worry about that just yet. The only thing you need to understand now is that a mental break will occur and there's nothing you can do to stop it.

I know. It happened to me.

Obviously some pathetic joker used a cheap cell phone to capture Dad with his secret girlfriend. The low quality video played for the ninth time, in case anyone missed the first eight broadcasts and for those who had their TVs on mute, the scrolling news feed at the bottom of the screen read, *U.S. Senator John Alexander has extramarital affair.* I couldn't stop watching because every kid at Marconi High School was probably watching it, too and tomorrow was the first day of school. My hand covered my wide open mouth and when a text bleeped on my phone, I didn't even blink.

Rafa: u watching this?

My thumbs blazed over the mini keyboard.

Abby: is anyone NOT watching this???

Seeing Dad on the news wasn't the issue. He was on TV a lot, usually about some new law he wanted to get passed. Wasn't the news supposed to be about stuff like that? I shot a text to Megan:

Abby: omg!!! Come over NOW!!!

The TV screen went blank and Mom tossed a remote on the black leather sofa that wrapped halfway around the African safari-themed parlor.

Ohmygod. This was one thing the Queen of Control couldn't deny. Did Mom find out the way I had—on TV with millions of other people? Not that it mattered. The only thing that mattered now was that Mom knew, but what was she thinking? No, what was she feeling? Mom never had a feeling in her life, but I was pretty sure she was having one now.

"Put your phone on mute," Mom said and peeked through the zebra patterned drapes. Then Mom put herself on mute. No surprise there.

Still nothing from Megan, but she was on her way. I didn't need a text to tell me that, since we could practically read each other's minds.

While Mom collapsed in a chair and massaged her temples, I clicked the TV back on. HER name was Katrina and she looked like a high school senior, but according to a television reporter, she started working at Dad's Washington D.C. office right after graduating from college.

She must've used red food coloring to dye her hair. Parted perfectly in the middle, it waved up and around black cat-eye glasses and curved back in, touching just beneath her chin like a giant red heart. But that's not the first thing I noticed. It was kind of hard to miss all that cleavage. If the phone hadn't bleeped, twice this time, I might've actually heaved.

Rafa: looks like a cat woman

Rafa: OMG her name!! She is a KAT woman!!!

I powered off the TV, but the video still streamed in my mind. There was no power button for that. Who was this woman? This complete stranger stealing the show. The tightly produced show with Mom directing every move. The well performed, Perfect Family Show created for the public's viewing pleasure. The Alexander family, which up until this moment consisted of John and Doreen Alexander and their daughter, Abby. So who was Kat? The family pet? The bizarre creature Dad was bringing home that nobody else in the family wanted?

The weird creature took center stage and had the audience's full attention. An intruder no one in the family had ever met—well, obviously Dad had met her, several times. It had to be the Kat creature's fault. Dad was framed. I closed my eyes and replayed the video in my mind. No one held a gun to Dad's head and forced him to walk with the creepy lady out of the hotel. He went willingly. Happily.

Without thinking, I reached to hug Mom, but stopped because it wasn't something we normally did. Part of me wanted to be the grownup and comfort her; the other part wanted to be held like a baby and told everything was going to be all right—like that would ever happen. The hugger in the family was Dad, when he was home.

My eyes welled up and I tried not to blink, but a teardrop smacked my arm and it hurt more than anything the reporters had said because one thing I knew about myself was that I didn't cry. Now nothing made sense.

Mom peeked out the window again. "We have to be

strong," she said, "for your father."

I bolted to the foyer and took the stairs three at a time as if running hurdles for the school track team. I needed to run and run and keep on running. Not toward anything but away. Away from the La-La Land Queen Doreen built around herself a long time ago.

To shut the bedroom door, I lifted the antique glass doorknob ever so slightly. Mom had the hundred and something year old house listed as a Texas Historical Site, which meant like everything else in my life, my bedroom was open to the public. Every year during the Historic Houses Tour, anyone willing to buy a ticket could parade through my room—the only place where I could be alone—and gawk at my personal stuff.

Even though the Asian themed bedroom represented Queen Doreen's obsession with décor and what other people thought, it also represented Mom's one and only act of rebellion. While neighbors filled their Victorian homes with nineteenth century furniture, Mom pioneered a movement of younger historic homeowners to break away from that cobwebby tradition and create something new. To meet the requirements of the Historical Society, homeowners had to maintain the architectural integrity of the *house*, not its furniture. Mom discovered this loophole and went all avant garde on everyone by establishing the Society of Modern Victorian Women.

Rafa labeled Mom's interior design "Décor de United Nations," but quickly pointed out Mexico wasn't included. Mom argued that Mexico was represented under Spain, but Rafa took that as a double insult and went all emo on Mom, saying Mexico won independence from Spain two hundred years before. Mom said she didn't need a history lesson from Rafa, but I admired his courage to argue with her in the first place.

If they gave an award for pretending, it would go to Mom for giving each room in the house its own cultural theme and pretending she had been born an international aristocrat. But in the reality outside La-La Land, Mom came from a one stoplight town known mostly for its swap meets. Still, rebelling against the Historical Society was the tiniest morsel of something courageous I could find in Mom and it gave me a reason to admire her. This opened the door, just a crack, for me to love her as much as I needed at any given time.

But right now I needed Megan. Why wasn't she checking her phone? All I could say was she'd better have an actual excuse, like getting kidnapped and taken to some remote island with no phone signals.

Through Chinese silk sheers, I studied the hungry pack of reporters who had set up camp in front of the house wearing multi-pocketed vests and carrying cameras with foot-long lenses. Some stood around waiting, others snooped like hound dogs, and I couldn't figure out why any of this surprised the media since Galveston Island was a magnet for people with a past.

The locals always joked how everyone here was either wanted or not wanted. Like three years ago, they arrested the mayor because he had embezzled a million dollars from some church in Denver. After getting caught, he'd faked suicide, changed his name and moved to Galveston where he ran for public office. Eventually he went to prison and when he came back, everyone welcomed him with open arms. That's the last time Galveston was on the news for a scandal, but this was different. This was Dad.

It was probably just a weird coincidence, but over the past couple of weeks, I'd been obsessing about how cool it would be to have the paparazzi follow me around, but this was definitely more creepy than cool. Clearly I needed to rethink my one and only goal in life, because if I were to win the Teen Fantasy Writers' first novel contest, the paparazzi would be at my door forever. Of course I could always use a pen name, like Nancy Nobody.

Megan. Ohmygod, come on. I touched her number, but it went straight to voicemail after only one ring. I screamed at the phone, "Turn on the TV! No, get over here, NOW!" and threw the phone on the bed. Not even making out with Brad could be more important than this. Except this is Megan we're talking about.

From gingerbread porches, neighbors watched like spectators at a tennis match, turning their heads back and forth not wanting to miss anything. Reporters swarmed the ones who dared to open their white picket fences and shoved microphones in their faces, but what could they possibly be saying?

I clicked on the TV and Mrs. Busybody next door was going on and on about her shock and disappointment in "John." The scrolling ticker below now read, *Confirmed: U.S. Senator John Alexander (TX) Commits Adultery.* While

Mrs. Busybody babbled on about how well she knew Dad, which was a lie, the camera panned the street and caught Rafa strolling up the sidewalk unnoticed.

I lunged to the window as Rafa slipped over a neighbor's fence and I nearly took Mom out dashing downstairs to let him in the back door. "Hurry!" I whispered.

Rafa sneaked in. "You ignoring me?"

I couldn't figure out why he was yelling until I spotted wires from his ears to a phone perched in the pocket of his white shorts.

I twisted the deadbolt. "This isn't about you."

Rafa fixed his flip flop and slid his foot back in. "How's the queen of La-La Land taking all this?"

He said it loud enough for Mom to hear, not that it mattered since nothing ever registered in Mom's mind that didn't fit into her fantasy world of bliss and perfection. I yanked the wires out of his ears and hurried upstairs with Rafa following close behind.

"What are kids saying?" I asked, squeezing the bedroom door shut.

Rafa scrolled through messages. "Uh, you don't want to know."

I sat on the bed and cupped my head in my hands. "Please tell me I'm asleep."

Rafa wrapped his skinny arms around me. "It's real," he whispered.

My lip trembled.

A siren shrieked and I nearly jumped out of my body. We shot to the window and watched a circle of news vans block the street.

"I hope they get arrested," Rafa said. "Blood thirsty animals."

The room started spinning and I took a deep breath, trying to get it to stop. One by one, pieces of me started shutting down. Since my body didn't want to move anymore, I lowered myself into the Asian throne in the corner and stared straight ahead at nothing. Numbness was good.

Rafa snapped his fingers. "Abby? Abby?"

I wanted to answer, but nothing came out. I was in safe mode.

Rafa pulled blankets and pillows out of the closet and made a bed for himself on the floor. I closed my eyes. I was tired of thinking about it. The faint sound of Rafa snoozing on the floor made me sleepy, but my mind was still reeling. I finally gave up and let my thoughts run wild, hoping my mind would eventually wear itself out. I guess it finally did because I shot up and gasped to the sound of the alarm blasting and according to the clock, it was six in the morning. Rafa was gone and so were all the blankets and pillows he had put on the floor. He must've set the alarm and slipped out in the middle of the night.

Or maybe it was a dream—a dark, twisted dream. Dad, the Kat creature. The whole thing was too bizarre to be real. I clicked on the TV and like a bad rerun, they were leaving the hotel. Oh, and Dad was happy.

Mom appeared in the doorway clapping, like she'd resigned from our sleazy reality show to star in a better one. "Today's the first day of school. Up, up!"

"You're joking, right?"

Mom had that I'm-completely-serious look on her face. "How would it look if Abigail Alexander didn't show up on the first day of school?"

It was so annoying the way she talked to me in the third person. I rubbed my eyes and tried to think. "Ohmygod, you set the alarm." Even though Mom's frozen eyes revealed she didn't care, I continued. "It had to be you, because Rafa would know that going to school is definitely not a normal thing to do in this situation."

But suddenly going to school sounded better than staying home all day with Mom. For one thing, Megan would be there. New school, new teachers, lots of things to take my mind off Dad. For once, I mean truly for once, maybe Mom was right.

I rolled out of bed and headed for the bathroom. If my freshman year was starting off like this, things couldn't possibly get any worse.

— 2 —

Mom had the engine running in the white Mercedes when I slipped out the back door. By driving through the alley, we tricked the few media hounds who had returned at some obnoxious early morning hour. Mom didn't say a word the entire way to school, but judging by her wrinkled forehead, that mind of hers was busy. I started to open my mouth, but what was the point? If the topic of conversation wasn't about our picture perfect lives, the Queen of Control was not going to participate.

It was strange riding to school in Mom's car, since Rafa and I usually rode bikes. Before that we tried skateboarding, but everything I did had to be approved by Mom. If we had an actual stamp of approval, it would say, "Appropriate for John Alexander's Public Image." When my skateboard was seized and stamped, "Not Appropriate for John Alexander's Public Image," Mom insisted on driving me to school every day, but I couldn't think of anything worse. We finally met somewhere in the middle when she agreed to let me ride a bike, but Rafa's parents couldn't afford one. That's why I made my parents buy two, otherwise we were riding the skateboards.

When we pulled up to the front of the school, Rafa waited on the corner with the bike my parents had given him. He'd really wanted an orange mountain bike and I'd wanted a yellow one, but even our color choices were deemed inappropriate. Between my red cruiser and Rafa's blue one, we looked like two dorks riding in a Fourth of July parade. I think that was the whole idea.

From the corner, Rafa waved me over like it was urgent, but to Rafa, everything was urgent. I pulled the door handle.

"Pick you up at three o'clock sharp." Mom smiled, which made no sense, except maybe in La-La Land.

Rafa snuggled his baseball cap over my head and scanned the sidewalk. "Keep your face down," he said, but it was too late. Within seconds, a flock of girls surrounded us and I didn't have to look up to know it was the triple Ps.

"Guess you're still too good to be a lowly cheerleader," the loudest voice said. That was Priscilla. A wave of laughter erupted from the other girls as they passed by. I called Priscilla, Presley and Paige the triple Ps because they looked the same—long hair and pretty—and they always traveled in V formation with Priscilla leading the flock. Even though I looked like the triple Ps, on the inside I was different.

"Heartless creatures," Rafa mumbled.

Rewind to last year when the Queen of Control forced me to go to cheerleader camp. With my strong athletic abilities, my half-hearted attempt was way better than most girls' best shots. When the coach announced on the obnoxious speaker that I'd won, I got so upset, I blurted out something about not lowering myself to standing on the sidelines cheering for boys; that I'd rather play on the field and let other people cheer for me. From that point on, Priscilla—who only won by default after I declined—launched a full blown, anti-Abby campaign, but Megan and I just laughed. Together we were indestructible. Nothing could crush us. Nothing. God I needed to find Megan. I cast my eyes beyond the triple Ps to survey the school grounds. Megan was definitely MIA. If she wasn't a prisoner in a jungle, she'd better have a stupendous explanation.

After the triple Ps moved on to humiliate their next victim, I said to Rafa, "I totally don't get it. Priscilla made cheerleader on her own this time. What's her problem now?"

Rafa squinted. "We have a saying in Mexico. Never piss off a crazy person."

When the bell rang, I adjusted the cap, stared at the class schedule, and then looked at the map they'd given us at orientation last week. Ever since the Kat episode on TV, all important facts and information had been deleted from my brain and all that remained were useless things, like feelings.

Rafa squeezed my arms. "Text me if you get in trouble.

I'll be there in a flash." The look in his sweet brown eyes said he meant it. "But don't get caught texting in class." Rafa winked and hurried off.

"That would be the least of my problems," I shouted.

I tried to keep my head down, but I had to look up to find Mrs. Goldstein's U.S. History class. Through the halls, I maintained a steady pace, even when some low scratchy voice said, "Hey Abby. What's news? Ha, ha, ha. Get it? What's news!" I told myself it didn't matter.

Normally I would've taken a front row seat because I loved history, especially since Dad always told fascinating stories about every place we'd ever visited and most of the time, the stories were true. But things had changed. While Mrs. Goldstein passed out papers, I took a seat in the back where I could keep an eye on everyone.

The paper had one sentence at the top:

List 3 things you want to learn in U.S. History this year.

I couldn't think about that now. It must be nice to come in on the first day of school, unburdened by any family drama, and make a list of things that would be interesting to learn. I felt miles away from my classmates, separated by a glass window of public humiliation through which everyone could see every detail of my pathetic life without caring.

Along one side of the room, a boy passed a folded piece of paper to the girl in front of him. She opened the note, giggled, folded it neatly, and passed it to the girl in front of her.

While all that was going on, Mrs. Goldstein collected the papers and thumbed through them. Each time she turned around to write something somebody wanted to learn on the board, the folded-up note got passed to another kid, who snickered and passed it on. When the note almost reached me, the kid passed it sideways to another girl and that's when I knew for sure the note was about me. I sank in my chair.

All heads turned toward the door when one of the assistant principals from orientation came in with a new student. After Mrs. Goldstein stepped out with the assistant principal, Jake jumped from his seat and grabbed the marker. I groaned. Jake may have been hilarious in middle school when he strategically passed out six neon orange posters in the football bleachers that when lifted spelled, "WE SUCK," but what he did next wasn't funny. At the bottom of Mrs. Goldstein's list, Jake wrote:

What senator couldn't keep his pants up?

The roar of laughter was loud enough for the whole school to hear, but Jake was already in his seat when Mrs. Goldstein came rushing back in the classroom. Rather than sit through the humiliation of listening to Mrs. Goldstein lecture the class on why that was wrong, I got up and walked out the door and to my surprise, nobody stopped me, not even the assistant principal who was still standing in the doorway.

I headed out the nearest exit and wandered toward a

giant oak tree. With my back to its trunk, I slid down and pulled my knees up toward my chest. Even though the assistant principal followed me out and slowly made her way toward me, there was still time to send a text to Rafa.

Abby: just kill me now

Rafa: where are you???

I started to text Megan again, but I was beginning to feel like a stalker, so I slipped the phone in my pocket while the assistant principal, whatever her name was, towered overhead. There were too many assistant principals to keep track of and they all acted like plain clothes cops, there to protect the principal from all the rowdy kids.

"Abby?" she said. "Would you like to talk to the counselor?"

I twisted my face. "Um, don't you think it's the other kids who need a counselor? I mean, they're the ones who have a problem with it."

"Abby, honey," she said in a softer voice. "Do you want me to call your mother?"

Okay, first of all, if I wanted to call my mother, I'd do it myself. Second of all, no. "I'll just wait here 'til second period, if that's okay with you." I sounded totally sarcastic, but the assistant principal was obviously cutting me a lot of slack because she gave me a sympathetic smile, which made me feel even worse, and walked away.

I pulled out the phone.

Rafa: where are you???

Rafa: where are you?????

I half smiled.

Abby: im ok c u next period
Rafa: k

Dad once cared like that, but lies had the power to turn someone you love into a total stranger. They don't teach that in school, but it was a lesson I'd never forget, not for the rest of my life.

Before this whole Kat scandal, Dad used to tell me exactly how to handle any situation at school. Even though I kind of hated him now, I needed him to tell me what to do.

What would the old Dad have said? I could hear his deep, Texas voice say, "Baby doll, what other people think of you is none of your business. Don't let them rent space in your head."

Maybe I was overly sensitive, but the bell sounded more obnoxious than ever. I couldn't figure out why they even called it a bell. It sounded like one of those canned horns fans set off at Houston Pistols basketball games, except a lot louder, like someone was holding the can inches from my ear.

My heart sank. Would Dad still take me to Pistols games? Or would he take that Kat creature instead? Mom hated basketball, which worked for me because going to games without her was way more fun. Dad and I laughed and cheered and hugged when the Pistols made three-pointers, but when Mom came along, there was tension. Maybe if I'd had a better attitude about Mom going with us to basketball games, Dad wouldn't have gone off and found a girlfriend who was more fun. And guessing from Dad's banana-sized grin on TV, the Kat creature was way more fun than Mom—maybe even more fun than me.

When the blast of the bell finally stopped pounding my head, I brushed the dirt off my jeans and wandered back toward the building. "What other people think of me is none of my business," I mumbled five or six times on the way to class. I couldn't hear Dad's voice anymore, but at least I knew what he would say.

When I arrived at Mr. Oliver's English class, Rafa waited at the door with a super serious look on his face. First period had been a total disaster. If second period didn't get better, I was so out of there.

— 3 —

"In the back," I said to Rafa, pointing at two empty desks.

His eyebrows scrunched together. "We never sit in the back. The probability of getting called on is highest in the back and lowest in the front."

That's the logic I normally used to get Rafa to sit in front with me. I'd made it up in sixth grade math when we first started learning about probability and it had worked ever since. How could I argue with my own rationale?

Since I wasn't willing to admit I'd made it up just yet, I shot him a weird look and he shuffled to a desk in the far back row. That's when I realized I was turning out like Mom, master of "the look." Or was it Dad? He always used math percentages to get people to support his causes. Maybe I had a little of both in me, which was scary because I'd just decided I didn't want to be like either one. If those were my choices, a cold ruler or a lying cheat, I really wasn't going to like myself when I grew up.

Mr. Oliver stood at the front of the room with his arms crossed, studying students as they wandered in. It freaked me out that he was abnormally tall and as wiry as the oval glasses sliding down his oily nose.

"Um, do people still wear bow ties?" I whispered to Rafa.

"I heard he's good," Rafa whispered back. "He just looks funny."

With a long, pointy finger, Mr. Oliver slid the glasses up his nose and waited for that obnoxious bell to stop blasting.

"Good morning, writers," he said with an English accent. His wicked smile revealed a mouthful of brown stained teeth. Everyone stared in silence, waiting to hear what the odd teacher who looked like a character from a Charles Dickens novel would say next. "You came into this class as students and in nine months, you will leave as writers. To achieve this extraordinary endeavor, you will write in your journals every day."

Okay, first of all, that's not going to happen. Obviously Mr. Oliver and I needed to have a serious conversation about my writing genre. I do not journal. That's for people who aren't creative enough to write a real story. When Rafa asked for a pencil, I gave him one and whispered, "Journaling is puking your feelings over and over."

"Yes, you will write in your journals every day," Mr.

Oliver continued. "No exceptions."

Um, like no. I'm already a writer. I have a genre. My genre is fantasy. I don't do feelings.

Scanning the rows of desks, I spotted the triple Ps doing synchronized gum chewing along the side of the room. I rolled my eyes. "Lovely." I accidently said that in my out loud voice and—whoa—double take! Sitting right behind them, also doing synchronized gum chewing was ohmygod, Megan.

Okay, stop. Breathe. "Megan," I whispered as loud as I could, but she obviously didn't hear me.

"First, I will need samples of your writing." Mr. Oliver took long strides toward the back of the room and reached way down to pick up a small trash can in the corner. With two fingers, he held the plastic can as far away from his body as possible, as if it contained fatally toxic germs. "You may write a piece about anything—any genre, any style, any point of view, as long as it is *not* poetry." Mr. Oliver looked down at the first triple P and nudged her arm with the trash can. "We will write poetry later in the year."

With her pinky sticking out, Priscilla extracted the gum from her mouth and flicked it into the can.

"What you choose to write is entirely up to you." He held the can by Presley now. Mr. Oliver didn't even have to make eye contact to get Presley to put her gum in the trash. "I simply need to understand your various levels of writing."

With her pinky out exactly like the other two, Paige did the same.

Megan had already swallowed her gum because she was way smarter than the triple Ps. I ripped out the first page of my class journal and wrote:

Where have you been? Did u see the news??? OMG Help!!

The first rule of note writing is never put your name, or the name of the intended receiver, on the note. Chances of interception by the teacher: fifty-fifty. Megan and I had created this rule back in third grade when we first discovered the art of carrying on a conversation all through class. Unfortunately, we'd figured out the odds of getting caught the hard way. I folded the note exactly eight times.

After returning the trashcan to the corner, Mr. Oliver bounced a teabag in his cup, which explained the brown stained teeth. "You may take five minutes to discuss your idea for a writing piece with a partner."

Rafa slid his desk toward mine. "I need to be partners with Megan," I said. "We haven't talked…"

Mr. Oliver called on Megan who had her arm stretched high in the air.

"Can we write about something on the news?" Megan peeled her eyes toward me and suppressed a smile.

That one drew snickers, but this time I didn't bolt. With my eyes wide open, Megan had punched me in the heart. I wanted to run, but my legs wouldn't move.

In true British style, Mr. Oliver cocked his head and spoke directly to Megan with an even sharper accent, "If you must write about the sex life of parents, write about your own."

Right. Her family was perfect. Mr. Applegate, the perfect doctor; Mrs. Applegate, the perfect community member; Megan, the perfect everything; all living in a perfect house together. With my whole body shaking, I stuffed the note in my pocket.

Megan sat up straight. "That's why God invented *friendworld.*"

I turned to Rafa for some explanation, but he shook his head in disbelief.

"Huh?" a boy across the room said.

A girl leaned back. "Check *friendworld* tonight."

My face got hot and I felt the thump, thump, thump of my pulse.

"Easy girl," Rafa whispered.

Okay, I'm not sure what I said next. Something about how this town needed a good hurricane to wipe it off the map.

The next thing I knew, Mr. Oliver stood tapping the paper on my desk. "Write about it," he said.

I gagged at mothball fumes rising from his tweed jacket and wrote at the top of the paper:

Hurricane Abby

Born a mere summer breeze, Abby danced upon the waves, delighting in life, until a cruel whisper knocked her unconscious and then went on its merry way. When Abby awoke, her sweetness was gone and all that remained was a bitter anger that stirred deep inside.

The stirring began slowly. Pain fueled the circular motion, until the power of her rage exploded into a life of its own. Suddenly, Abby realized she wielded great powers that before, she'd never dreamed possible. Not wanting to waste her mighty powers, she chose a mark and set her course. It was a small island in the Gulf of Mexico, a beautiful island, but the island's beauty was wasted on its inhabitants, for they were cruel.

Abby was not a murderer. She didn't want to kill anyone; she just wanted to destroy the evil virus that contaminated the island. Even the best scientists at the Centers for Disease Control were baffled by this virus, for it could only be transmitted through words—hateful words—meant to destroy the lives of innocent people. The scientists named the virus: Destructive Island Gossip and decided to call it, DIG.

Abby knew she had the power to destroy the evil virus and relished the thought of using her rage for a good cause. She would become a superhero by doing what the greatest minds at the CDC could not: wipe out the spread of DIG.

Slowly, she entered the warm waters of the Gulf of Mexico, giving the inhabitants time to scatter across the mainland. This strategy not only spread the virus so thin that it quickly died, it also gave Abby plenty of time to build up her powers to become a category five hurricane, the most destructive hurricane possible.

The sight of the gossipy inhabitants fleeing the island amused Abby. It amused her so much, she sent a hearty laugh into the first gust of wind. Her mighty winds blew down enormous trees that crushed houses and flattened cars left behind by the inhabitants. And for the houses not surrounded by trees, she delighted in tearing off their roofs. She was the conductor of a symphony, orchestrating the darkest piece of music ever heard and it was beautiful, in a loud *and angry way.*

For the finale, Abby sucked up the water in the Gulf and created a twenty foot surge that swept the island clean. And when it was over, she looked back upon her work and smiled. The island was nothing more than a sandbar with every trace of human existence gone.

Now at peace, Abby returned to the ocean as a summer breeze and danced upon the waves, delighting in the sweetness of life once again.

Since the whole class was still writing, I had time to jot a quick note on the last page.

Dear Mr. Oliver,

As you can see, I'm already a writer. I would like to have permission to write a fantasy novel instead of writing in a journal. I am a member of the TFW (Teen Fantasy Writers) and they are having a novel writing contest this year. My goal is to win. Every week, I will turn in a new chapter for you to grade in place of a journal entry. Please let me know if this is ok.

Sincerely,

Abby

There. No way would he say no to that.

"In five minutes, I will collect your papers," Mr. Oliver announced.

"What did you write about?" Rafa asked as I was making a few minor punctuation edits to my story.

"A hurricane destroying Galveston."

Rafa blinked slowly. "Nice."

"Uh huh, Mr. I-don't-have-any-problems. What did you write?"

"A new twist on Cinderella," he said with a proud smile.

"Please tell me you're kidding."

"No, this prince, he finds a glass slipper, right?"

I rolled my eyes.

"Okay, so then he searches the country far and wide, but he's not searching for the girl who can wear the slipper." His grin turned sly. "Here's the twist. The prince is searching for the other slipper because he loves the shoes!"

All I could do was gaze at his soft, brown eyes and his sweet, dimpled smile. That story was so gay. My eyes welled up. I just hoped Rafa could wait until they were finished bullying me to come out of the closet, because when that day came, he was definitely gonna need protection and I wasn't sure I had enough fight in me for both of us.

Mr. Oliver collected the papers and dismissed the class. I took a deep breath. Writing had made the forty-five minutes pass quickly.

"No cafeteria today," I said to Rafa. "I need a break from these creeps."

"We'll eat outside." Rafa pulled a brown paper bag from his backpack.

"I didn't bring a lunch, but I'm not hungry anyway."

"There's plenty in here." Rafa dug around in the bag. "If you like chicken and bread and, uh, we can split this orange.

Naturally, every bench was taken and we ended up on the grass. All I could stomach was a bite of bread and a slice of orange.

"I hate Megan more than I hate the Kat creature, if that's humanly possible."

Rafa stared at the ground and mumbled something in Spanish.

"I mean God, does Mr. Oliver really expect me to write in a journal that everyone I've ever known is a traitor and that my life is ruined forever?"

Rafa was quiet for a moment and then he started rambling about something, but depression had already covered me like a heavy blanket. Not a warm, comforting blanket; more like a blanket that cast darkness. I didn't care about anything anymore, not even Rafa, who sat right in front of me explaining which relatives were coming to visit next week. I listened, but his voice sounded far away.

That afternoon, I was on my own. Rafa wasn't in any of my classes, but it was okay because by then, I was completely shut down. The numbness had returned, which worked out fine because math and science weren't exactly emotional subjects. I tuned out the other kids and focused on things that meant nothing to me, like numeric equations and the botanical names for plants.

After school, I ran to the corner where Mom waited in the white Mercedes. I wouldn't have even noticed the news van behind Mom's car if the man hanging out the window hadn't pointed a camera directly at me. I slid in and slammed the door harder than I meant.

"Get me out of here," I said harshly.

Mom didn't say anything. The tension in the air was so thick I could hardly breathe. Her silence felt cold, but at least it felt familiar. I never thought I'd be happy to get home.

Finally, I made it to my room and pulled the note I'd written to Megan out of my pocket. Without opening it, I hurled it across the room. It ricocheted off the wall and landed in front of a framed photo of Megan and me at the beach when we were ten. I dumped the note and the whole framed photo in the trash.

Math equations ran through my brain like the scrolling news feed at the bottom of the TV screen. I opened my math book, but I wasn't sure why. I hated math. Yet I sat on the floor and worked every math problem in the book from beginning to end like some kind of weird alien had taken over my body and was doing whatever it wanted. By the time I finished, the sky had turned black and according to my phone, it was almost midnight. Oh, and I had seven voice messages, not that I cared.

Thank God the ten o'clock news was over. As I flipped through the channels to find some mind numbing sitcom, I heard the word "Galveston" on the weather channel and backed up. Why were they talking about little bitty Galveston Island on a national weather channel?

The image slapped me in the face like a salty wave. A tropical storm near Cuba had just been upgraded to hurricane status with Galveston Island in the center of its projected path. The cone of uncertainty looked huge, spreading from Lake Charles to Victoria, but right in the middle of that cone was a line that connected Hurricane Ike to Galveston Island.

I fell back on the bed, letting my head splash into the pillow. The motionless ceiling fan staring me in the face had a different Chinese symbol on each blade. I had no idea what the symbols meant, but one thing I knew for sure was that today I'd written a story about a hurricane wiping out Galveston Island and now Hurricane Ike was coming.

"Sugar baby," Dad's voice resonated in my mind, "be careful what you wish; you just might get it." The look on his face had said the rest: *and you may not want it.*

I fumbled for the phone. Kat creature or no Kat creature, he was still my dad and I had a right to call. But when his phone went straight to voicemail, my heart landed in my stomach. I listened to the long, computer generated message and waited for the beep.

"Dad?" I said weakly, but couldn't think of what to say next. "This is your daughter." My voice grew stronger. "Remember me?" I might've sounded angry, but I really wanted to cry so I hung up.

Something stirred in the pit of my stomach. I stared at the TV in awe of the weird coincidence. Hurricane Ike was really coming and even though any normal person would've felt panic and fear, I couldn't help but smile just a little.

— 4 —

"Start packing," Mom said as if she commanded an entire nation of fourteen year-olds. For the second morning in a row, the Queen of Control stood in the doorway.

I jerked the red Chinese comforter aside. "Obviously I'm the only one who has to have perfect manners at all times."

"We're evacuating," she said with her chin up. "The movers have arrived." Her face looked hard like a statue, even on the third day of knowing Dad had a girlfriend. Another award-winning performance by the family's best actress.

I scratched my head and tried to wake up enough to think. This wasn't my first evacuation. I knew the drill. First, we pack the car. Then the movers haul the rugs and furniture up to the second floor. Since most of our stuff came from exotic places we had visited around the world, it wasn't easy to replace. The first time we evacuated,

Mom had made this perfectly clear. I mean perfectly. That was four years ago, but the hurricane veered off to the east, which put us on the clean side, so nothing actually happened. It's the dirty side of the hurricane you have to worry about. But right now, I needed to worry about packing.

I grabbed my biggest suitcase, remembering from my last experience I would only get to take one. Mom would have five or six suitcases and boxes full of expensive sculptures and artwork she didn't dare leave behind. "What if the roof gets ripped off the house?" she had said. I thought about the story I had written in Mr. Oliver's English class and how badly we needed a good hurricane. That way, the gossipy island inhabitants would have to focus on their own problems and everyone would forget about mine.

I threw some T-shirts and shorts in the suitcase, but saved most of the room for things I didn't want to lose just in case the roof actually did get ripped off the house. At first I grabbed the basketball I always played with in the driveway, but it was easily replaceable. I needed to focus on things that couldn't be replaced like my other basketball covered with signatures by Houston Pistols that Dad got for me at some fancy fundraiser. He had come home that night in a tuxedo, spinning the ball on the tip of his finger and said, "Sugar dumpling, I brought you a little souvenir from the party." I vaguely remember Mom rolling her eyes and moping upstairs, but I'll never forget the basketball came with two courtside tickets to a playoff game and it was the single most exciting game I'd ever seen in my life. I grabbed the DVD of that game and threw it in the suitcase too. Not only did the Pistols win, the video showed Dad and me sitting right on the court next to the players.

Outside the window, reporters chased the men Mom had hired to move everything upstairs and they scattered like a school of fish when danger approaches. I turned on the T.V. to find out what was happening in the front yard, but all the stations had radar maps and meteorologists reporting on Hurricane Ike. Since the last hurricane turned away just before landfall, the mayor of Galveston said he was waiting to call a mandatory evacuation until Ike got closer. Rarely did I ever agree with Mom, but this was one of those times when she was right. We needed to leave early to beat the rush. Honestly though, that wasn't my real reason. I just wanted to leave.

I flipped through the channels until I found a local station reporting live from my front yard. I guess I could've gone downstairs to find out what was going on, but I might've ended up on the news and that was the last thing I needed today. The reporters had a translator and talked to the men who were now cornered up against the house by a line of TV cameras. Apparently, the movers Mom had hired didn't have any papers to prove they could legally work in the United States. Normally, this wasn't news in Texas since just about every house on the street had undocumented workers, plus Dad always said if all the undocumented workers in Texas were deported, the state's economy would collapse. Still, Mom was in control of Dad's public image and that's why we never hired undocumented workers.

"Ohmygod," I screamed, running down the hallway. "What are you doing?" When I burst through the door to her bedroom, Mom peered through the drapes at the actual scene as it unfolded in the front yard. But that wasn't the weird part. She was smiling. Not an I'm-so-happy-it's-a-sunny-day kind of smile that would've made sense in La-La Land. More like a cold smirk. My head fumed. "Stop getting Dad in more trouble just because you're mad!"

Mom closed the drapes slowly. "Abby, dear." She had that don't-you-understand expression on her face. "I'm simply taking the attention away from your father's affair. By the time they finish reporting on this, the affair will be old news and they won't go back to it."

Queen Doreen was still in control.

I let out a sigh. "We *are* going to Dad's apartment, right?"

"We have no choice," Mom said. "Every hotel in the state was booked the minute they announced the hurricane."

Finally, I'd get to see Dad and actually talk to him, hug him, maybe even start laughing again. It could be a little weird at first, but since Mom was incapable of feeling anything, she would forgive him and our dysfunctional family could go back to normal.

After the undocumented movers finished their job and the media had reported the new scandal on Dad, I stuffed the last bag that could possibly fit into the Mercedes. Mom and I slipped out the back alley and got on the highway that led to Austin. Traffic was thick, but nothing compared to the road jams that would come in the next day or two, even after they opened all the contra lanes. Like I said, this wasn't my first evacuation.

A text bleeped from my phone:

Rafa: At school now. Where r u???

Abby: Evacuating to dad's apt in austin

Rafa: Is he there?

Abby: Bro, we only have two places

Rafa: with the kat woman???

I squinted at Mom. "Dad's at the apartment, right?"

A chilled silence hung in the air and when Mom finally spoke, her voice was low as if someone could possibly overhear our conversation in the car. "Your father's hiding out in Mexico like a common criminal." Her voice dropped lower. "A criminal on the lam." A tinge of anger had seeped out and I was so distracted by her teensy display of emotion that it took a minute for her words to actually sink in.

"Dad's been in Mexico all this time and you didn't even bother to tell me?"

"It was for your own good, dear."

"Ohmygod, knowing the truth would be easier than decoding silence. Am I the only one who gets that?" Since no other words were spoken all the way to Austin, I decoded her silence. Clearly the answer was "yes."

The apartment felt different when we stepped inside. Coming to our "other place" was usually fun, but this time, fun was not the feeling in the room. Everything looked the same—the worn brown leather sofa, the

English barley twist desk, the floor to ceiling bookshelves. Yes, Mom had chosen Harvard Law Library décor, even though Dad had wanted more of a University of Texas Longhorn theme since that was where he actually went to law school. But Queen Doreen had been in charge, at least that's what she thought.

Something crunched under my foot and I bent down to pick it up. The large, silver hoop earring definitely didn't belong to Mom. I don't know about Mom, but I suddenly felt like an intruder and I wanted to leave because this was probably where Dad and Kat spent most of their time. I stared blankly at Mom. "What if this was their home? Not ours—theirs."

Mom had no comment.

Some scribbled words on a page in a book that lay open on the desk caught my eye. It was definitely Dad's handwriting. I picked up the book and read what Dad had written: *What other people think of me is none of my business and what I think of them is none of their business.* The cover said *Alcoholics Anonymous*, which was totally weird because Dad didn't even drink. In fact, he was the most health conscious person I knew. The bizarre book probably belonged to the Kat creature.

"Why does Dad have this?" I held up the book.

"Because your father's a drunk." She said it as if it needed no further explanation.

"But he doesn't drink."

All of a sudden, Mom looked defeated. "I suppose you're old enough to know," she said, collapsing in a chair. "I realized your father was an alcoholic right after you were born and I made him stop drinking. He struggled with it for a few years until he went to AA and then he finally stopped."

All I could do was stare. It wasn't *what* Mom had said, but *how* she had said it. For the first time, she actually sounded like a real person, but then, as if suddenly remembering she wasn't, Mom sat up straight and tucked her skirt under her legs. "I think you were four."

I opened the book to another place where Dad had written something and read it aloud. "Be careful what you wish. You just might get it." I looked at Mom. "He says that all the time."

"I know you think your father's the wisest man in the world, but it's time you learned the truth." Her tone turned bitter. "All the words of wisdom he imparts on you are just things he hears other drunks say in those AA meetings."

"But it's good he stopped drinking, right?"

She waved me off like an annoying fly. "Your father traded one addiction for another. When he gave up drinking, he took up chasing women."

My mind started reeling until something clicked into place. Things were beginning to make sense, like Mom's non-reaction to the news that Dad was cheating on her. She'd been through this before. Maybe she was already over it—way over it.

I took the AA book to my room and flipped through the pages, stopping at a place where Dad had written: *All the world's a stage and all the men and women merely players.*

"No joke," I muttered.

Next to Dad's scribbled Shakespeare quote, he had underlined words that described the typical alcoholic like *self-centered* and *ego-centric*. At the bottom of the page, he wrote, *delusions of grandeur*. I never thought of him that way, but obviously there were a lot of things about Dad I didn't know. Maybe it seemed like he had a big ego when he was trying to be funny, but delusions of grandeur sounded kind of psychotic.

When I heard *The Yellow Rose of Texas* chiming on Mom's phone, I cracked the bedroom door to hear what she was saying.

"I did it for your own good, like I've always done." Mom closed my door, but I could hear her voice rising. "In Texas, illegal workers are a lot less scandalous than infidelity!"

Ohmygod. Our masks and costumes were off. We weren't acting anymore and underneath those masks, it was ugly.

"Tell her yourself," Mom shouted. "I'm tired of doing your dirty work."

Mom opened the door and handed the phone to me. I could hardly breathe.

"Dad?" I said meekly into the phone.

"Hey, sweetie pie." Normally it sounded like he meant it, but this time it sounded forced.

"Where are you?" I already knew, but couldn't think of anything else to say.

"We're in Mexico, baby cakes." Dad giggled and I couldn't figure out what was so funny until he said, "Stop it, baby. I'm talkin' to my little girl."

At that moment, the distance between us wasn't geographical; our hearts were millions of miles apart. At least his was. Somehow, I managed to stay calm and asked, "Where in Mexico?" which was not the question I really wanted to ask.

"A little town called San Miguel. You're gonna love it."

"Well, when are you coming back?"

"When things cool off up there." I had to listen to more giggling before Dad finally said, "We love it here."

My tone turned indignant. "Who is 'we?'"

"Kat," he said happily. "You're gonna love her."

I seriously doubted that.

"Listen, baby." His voice got serious. "Your Mom and I, well, we haven't been happy for a long, long time, but things are gonna get better now." After a dramatic pause, he finally said it. "We're getting a divorce."

His words hung in the air like the clang of a cathedral bell, but when Dad giggled again, everything stopped. Dads weren't supposed to let their kids hear them giggle with a girlfriend, especially one that looked like Kat. It was totally against the rules. For the first time in my life, I hung up on Dad.

My mind went all fuzzy but one thing became clear: Mom and I were no longer in Dad's inner circle. His world revolved around Kat now, whoever she was. Maybe the book was right. Maybe Dad was self-centered. Perhaps Mom had seen it all along, but I was too busy hating Mom to notice.

I never thought I'd say it, but at that point, I wanted to go back to La-La Land. My life had shifted from a well scripted, well rehearsed family movie to the sleaziest reality show ever. Even the multi-colored radar map on TV seemed unimportant because the hurricane about to slam Galveston Island felt less scary than the flood of truth pouring out of my parents.

— 5 —

For the next two days, Mom and I hardly spoke. Mom mostly stayed in Dad's bedroom with the door shut, talking to an attorney about all the things she wanted to get, which was pretty much everything except Dad. While staring at a bottle of vodka Mom had picked up at the store, I wondered why Dad loved alcohol so much. Because I needed an answer, I decided to conduct a scientific experiment.

I set up my lab in the kitchen. Using a glass cylinder, I mixed one part vodka to three parts orange juice packed with vitamin C and calcium, and stirred. The first sip tasted a little weird, like rubbing alcohol, but it wasn't bad. To lower the temperature in the cylinder, I plopped in three cubes of ice and after that, all I tasted was O.J.

I curled up on the sofa and nursed my drink, eyes fixed on the TV, mesmerized by the drama of Hurricane Ike. Slowly, my mind wandered into a world called I Don't

Care and my body melted into the sofa. The results of my experiment were conclusive: Dad's drinking made perfect sense.

Dad cheating on Mom and hiring undocumented workers didn't matter to reporters anymore and I was glad they finally got some perspective on what was important in the world. As Hurricane Ike headed straight for Galveston, thousands of cars crammed onto the freeways, trying to flee Houston all at the same time and even though the contra lanes were open, traffic was at a complete standstill. I picked up the phone and ordered some pad Thai.

The eerie part about being in a state of emotional overload is feeling like nothing is real. I decided to go with that. When I was going through Dad's AA cult stuff, I found a "Serenity Prayer" printed on a little card. I couldn't figure out what the prayer meant, but if serenity meant feeling euphoric, I was completely serene.

By now, most of the gossipy island inhabitants were gone, except for a few die-hard BOIs, a rare breed of people "born on the island" who had a proud tradition of never evacuating for any hurricane whatsoever. Instead, they boarded up their houses and threw hurricane parties that involved lots of drinking and buckets of fried shrimp, but really more drinking than shrimp. And when it was over, the nightmare of surviving a hurricane gave them tall tales to pass down to the next generation of BOIs who were expected to continue this idiotic tradition even though not everyone survives.

But really, who was I to judge? What family traditions

did I have to pass on to my kids? When I was in seventh grade and all the girls had boyfriends, I decided one day Rafa and I would get married and have a big family, but that wasn't looking very promising anymore, especially since he wrote that new twist on the Cinderella story. It didn't matter, though. We'd probably just end up getting a divorce.

The shaky image on TV captured the winds of Hurricane Ike bending palm trees in half along the Gulf of Mexico. The line of arched palms resembled all those people who did yoga exercises in that same spot every morning, bending their bodies into abnormal positions. When a wind gust ripped a big hotel sign right off its pole, I started fidgeting with a sofa pillow. Ike was about to make landfall as a category three hurricane heading straight for our house.

My phone bleeped and my heart catapulted into space. It was Rafa answering a text I'd sent like two days ago, telling him to let me know when he was safe.

Rafa: Hola Chica

Abby: Where r u

Rafa: San Antonio with abuelita

"Who are you texting?" Mom's voice blared from behind as if I were a prisoner communicating with the outside world. She tied her robe and shuffled in like an old person.

"Rafa." I gave Mom a pissy look before glancing down at his next message. "They went to San Antonio. Took them eighteen hours to get there."

Even though anyone else's heart would've gone out to

Rafa and his family for spending eighteen hours in evacuation traffic, Mom waved it off. I hoped I wasn't going to turn out like her, all heartless and cold. Most of my life I wanted to be like Dad, but striving to become an alcoholic with a love addiction didn't sound like such a good plan either.

"What do you want for breakfast, dear?"

"Mom, it's noon." While mom got busy in the kitchen, I sat up to watch Galveston Island get blown off the map. Eventually, Mom came in and sat at the other end of the sofa. I kept my eyes on the TV and said, "Ike's pissed."

"Aren't we all, dear."

Not the reaction I was expecting. Where was Mom's lecture on how my language was inappropriate for a lady? I turned to get a look at this person sitting next to me on the sofa. With her eyes on the TV, she cracked half a smile and in that flick of a moment, we were equals. Even though it wouldn't last forever, I savored that moment like the sweet pad Thai melting in my mouth.

Together we watched Ike's rage make landfall. By the time he reached Galveston Island, the meteorologist had downgraded Ike to a category two hurricane, but his fury still wielded great powers. A TV camera had captured fuzzy images of the storm surge washing through streets like a whitewater river. The images looked as fake as a movie with computer generated special effects, but like the news reports on Dad, the wild images of Hurricane Ike were way too real. I needed more vodka.

"Want some more coffee?" I said getting up.

Without taking her eyes off the hurricane, she held up the cup and said absentmindedly, "Thank you, dear."

I turned on the faucet to drown out any vodka bottle noises and poured twice as much vodka in my glass this time. If a little felt good, a lot would feel better. I topped off the rest of the glass with orange juice and then poured Mom's coffee. Oh God, what did she put in it? I'd never paid attention. While I wracked my brain trying to remember, Mom stood up and said, "I'll get it, dear. You don't know how I like it."

"Ohmygod, just tell me!"

Mom actually obeyed. "Cream and one sugar, dear."

I turned off the faucet and stirred the coffee, but on the way out, I froze. The vodka bottle was a quarter empty. I set everything down, flipped the faucet back on, and filled the vodka bottle back to almost full. There. She'd never know.

By late afternoon, the drama of Hurricane Ike was over. The meteorologist reported that the storm surge had retreated into the Gulf and the damage was done. Water pounded against the window, thanks to Ike's outer bands of rain that had spread all the way to Austin. I'd never felt so relaxed in my life.

That night, I passed out on the sofa and in the morning when I awoke, the mayor was on TV saying we weren't allowed to return to the Island for a week to give them time to fix the electricity. I started to freak. No way could I survive a whole week in Dad's little apartment with Mom.

"If I had it to do over," Mom said from the kitchen,

"I'd become an accountant and adopt children. Men simply aren't necessary."

It was a relief to know she'd keep the children.

Mom took a sip of coffee and said, "Let's go shopping." She raised an eyebrow over the top of the cup.

"Okay," I replied meekly, wondering what she was up to. I hadn't showered in three days and the Queen of Control never said a word. By now I should've heard a lecture on the social implications of a lady's personal hygiene, but even I was getting sick of myself. My oily hair stuck together like wet noodles and I was sure I felt things crawling on my skin. When I took a whiff of my underarm, it smelled like a dead armadillo baking in the sun. "Be right back," I said and trudged to the shower.

Mom waited impatiently by the door when I finally came out. I expected to find her seated on the sofa with her hands folded neatly on her lap. Instead, she waved me over to the door, practically shouting, "Let's go!"

"What's with your hair?" I asked, because she never left the house without a perfectly sculpted hairdo that looked like a snail shell. Yet there she stood, hand on the doorknob with her hair parted in the middle, frizzing out on each side like Albert Einstein.

"I'm cutting it all off," she said, locking the door behind us. "I made appointments for both of us."

Ohmygod. Queen Doreen was having a meltdown.

When rain sprinkled her hair, she didn't even care. She just sashayed to the car as if she loved rain and that's when I knew I was witnessing a full psychotic break. I decided to keep my mouth shut because all my life I'd wanted shorter hair, but Mom wouldn't allow it. This was my chance. I'd have her committed after I got my hair whacked off.

"Let's go to some of those funky clothes shops on Sixth Street, too." Mom grinned the whole time she was talking, which in and of itself was totally bizarre. "I don't have any kicking-around clothes."

My eyes popped. "Any what?"

"You know, clothes to just hang out in."

I tried and tried, but couldn't come up with a visual image of Mom hanging out in clothes she bought on Sixth Street.

"There it is," she said, pulling in front of a sign that read, *Hairy Impulses – Professional Hairdressing.*

Seriously. If it had been anyone other than Mom, I would've cracked up, but this was my mother and I was getting worried.

"Come on, honey," she said, scurrying up to the door. "Let's have fun!"

Honey? That was way too casual for Mom. What happened to, "Come on, dear?" This was definitely more than I could deal with. Correction, the hair salon was more than I could deal with. The lime green vinyl chairs and hot pink walls clashed with the florescent red hair of the girl who came out to greet us.

Mom grinned like a child. "I'm the one who called," she said, taking the young girl's hands as if they'd known each other forever.

The girl's face lit up like the magic wand in the fairy

tattoo that covered her arm. "Who wants to go first?" she asked.

"I do!" Mom shrieked.

I never thought I would say this, but it kind of hurt my feelings that she wasn't treating me like her little girl anymore. She would have definitely wanted me to go first and normally that would've been irritating, but now it was as if I didn't even exist. I wasn't sure which was worse.

"Okay Doreen," the girl said, "tell me what you want."

"Young and sassy," Mom said. "Like yours."

"Um, o—kaaay." I raised my brows and gazed out the window like I shouldn't be watching. The rain had stopped, so I slipped outside and waited on a bench in front of the salon and eyed people passing by, wondering if their lives were going on as planned or if everyone around them had lost their minds, too.

About an hour later, Mom came out with the same red spiked haircut as the girl with the fairy tattoo and said, "Your turn!"

I got up from the bench and acted like her inappropriate-for-an-old-person haircut didn't faze me. I'd have to freak out some other time. First things first. That's what Dad always said.

"You sure you want to cut all this luscious hair?" Fairy Girl asked, unknotting the braid that hung down my back.

"Shorter and sporty," I said. "No color, nothing funky."

"More conservative," she said. "Got it."

Fairy Girl and I didn't speak the whole time she was cutting my hair, mostly because whenever she tried to make conversation, I said yes or no. End of conversation. I had one eye peeled on Mom and didn't want Fairy Girl distracting me. Queen Doreen was out of control.

— 6 —

Dad never called that week, at least he didn't call my phone, and because of Mom's psychotic behavior, I was afraid to ask. Why I waited until she was driving seventy miles an hour on a freeway, I don't know.

"I haven't heard from him," was her reply, as if that were sufficient.

When we finally reached Houston, I said, "How come there's no traffic?"

"Houstonians have already returned. Only those who live on the coast had to wait."

Traffic did slow to a crawl as we approached the bridge to Galveston Island and all the bizarre images I'd seen on TV appeared stranger in real life. Even Mom with her newfound happiness, shook her head in disbelief at yachts laying sideways in the marshlands, like toy boats someone had picked up and tossed aside. Actually, someone had: Ike.

As we approached the bridge, it looked like a war zone. Hundreds of soldiers in camouflaged uniforms lined the streets, gripping semiautomatic weapons.

"Why do they have guns?"

"National Guard," Mom said, digging through her purse. "They want proof we live here."

"Why?" My voice broke.

"For our own protection."

The military man examined Mom's driver's license, then handed it back. With the tip of his rifle, he waved us through. I held my breath.

A few fallen limbs after a rainstorm was about the most damage I'd ever seen in Galveston. This time, it wasn't tree limbs they had bulldozed off the roads. Sticking out of a pile of broken lumber were bed mattresses, a sofa and a little girl's pink bicycle. My breath caught.

Piles of rubble lined both sides of the street. Doors ripped at the hinges, broken chairs and tattered restaurant signs leaned against busted up fishing boats and uprooted oak trees. When Mom turned onto our street, she took my hand and squeezed it gently. I closed my eyes. She stopped in front of our house, but I was afraid to look.

"Come on, honey." Mom's door clicked open. I glanced through the window—our house was still there. Upstairs and down, all the wooden shutters were closed except one. On a kitchen window, a shutter hung by its corner and the glass was broken.

Mom struggled to open the gate in front of the house. A tree had fallen on the wrought iron fence and jammed the gate tight.

"I'll get it," I said, and to my amazement, Mom stepped aside. I lifted the latch and kicked the gate open.

Rather than lecture me on ladylike behavior, Mom said, "Thank you, honey," then hurried through the gate as if what I had done were perfectly normal. At the top of the steps, Mom drew a deep breath as if trying to calm down, but her hand shook like a rattle while trying to get the key in the door.

In the dark foyer, Mom nearly knocked me over when she took a bad slip on the floor. I pulled her up and flipped on the light. It was obvious from the silt line on the wall that the house had been submerged in two feet of water, but something freaked me out even more. I tugged Mom's arm and pointed at the big footprints on the muddy floor that came out of the kitchen and went through the foyer, into the parlor. I had a feeling it wasn't Hurricane Ike who broke the kitchen window.

"He might still be here," Mom whispered. "Let's go."

"Wait," I said. The footprints led straight through the middle of the empty parlor and ended at a bay window that had been opened from the inside. I pulled the window down and locked it tight. "He's gone."

"He must've thought the whole house was empty," Mom said. "Look over here, the footprints don't go upstairs."

"Go see if our stuff's still there." I'd just given Mom a direct order. I didn't even hide my smirk.

"I'm afraid," Mom said. "Come with me."

I looked deep in her eyes and at that moment the

Queen of Control was dead. She must've read my mind that I wanted to give her a hug because she reached over and held me close for a good, long while.

"We have to take care of each other now," Mom said softly.

I wasn't about to let go because tears were streaming down my cheeks and I didn't want Mom to see me cry just yet, especially since she was starting to treat me like a grownup, but mostly because I wanted to make sure she meant it.

"Let's get these shutters open," Mom said.

Mom started at one end of the house and I at the other, until we met somewhere in the middle. Sunlight illuminated the room, and for a moment it seemed ultra bright. Perhaps it was just the sunlight, but something inside me felt a little brighter, too.

Upstairs, everything looked exactly as we had left it, except for a roof leak in my bedroom that had ruined the red Chinese comforter wadded up on my bed. Maybe Mom would let me choose my own stuff now. She was on the phone with one of her real estate friends, asking if an apartment was available for us to rent until the house got fixed.

"All the sheetrock downstairs will have to be replaced," Mom was saying on the phone.

I went from room to room opening shutters to let in more light.

That night we unpacked at the loft apartment Mom's real estate friend had found for us. "There was a waiting list," Mom had said. "She put us ahead of everyone else." Mom was in the closet hanging the new clothes she'd gotten on Sixth Street. "It's the last time I'll use your father's position to get priority. I can take it on my own from here."

Obviously Hurricane Ike had caused no damage to the historic apartment, which wasn't surprising since it looked like a bomb shelter. The walls on the inside had the same worn bricks they used on the outside of the building. I guess they had to drill into the bricks to hang the old oil paintings that hung behind dark antique furniture. Huge hurricane shutters that slid sideways on a track, hung inside the windows. The shutters were open now, but had obviously been closed during the hurricane. I was just glad the place was furnished.

I tried to look miserable. "How long do we have to stay here?"

"A month at the most," Mom said. "I'm meeting the contractor at the house first thing in the morning."

I started to ask about school, but didn't want to put the idea in her head in case she'd forgotten. The last person I needed to see was Megan, the traitor.

The open apartment had a kitchen at one end, two bedrooms at the other, and a living room in the middle. Since there were no walls between any of the rooms, the bedrooms were divided by freestanding partitions, which made it easy to talk from different rooms. This was annoying.

"Marconi High opens on Monday," Mom said from behind the partition.

So much for hoping she'd forget.

"Fortunately, it didn't have nearly as much damage as other schools."

Lucky for her, not for me. I missed that my life used to actually make sense. Like whenever the triple Ps walked by, I always said, "Oh God, it's the Sisters of Perpetual Pandemonium," and Megan always laughed. It didn't matter how many times I said it. She always laughed. Now she was one of them. The traitor.

"Did you hear me?" Mom asked.

"I don't wanna go back."

"Getting back to a normal routine will be good for you, honey." Mom's voice cracked.

Maybe I wasn't the only one hating my life right now. Before climbing into the high, four post bed, I sent Rafa a text asking if he would be at school on Monday, but he didn't answer.

I checked my phone again first thing in the morning. Still no reply. When I crawled out of bed, Mom was sitting at the kitchen table at the other end of the apartment. She looked small and lonely staring out the window with one hand loosely holding a coffee mug.

Even though I'd never tasted coffee, I reached for a mug. For a nanosecond, I considered asking Mom if it was okay for me to have coffee, but she was in outer space, so I pulled the pot from the coffeemaker and poured myself a cup.

"You probably won't like it unless you add cream and sugar."

"Right," I said, amused at myself for having mastered

vodka before coffee.

On my way to the little table, I stirred in the cream and sugar. Mom smiled at me, which I completely ignored because all this sappiness was starting to make me uncomfortable. I mean God, it wasn't normal.

We sat in silence and gazed out the window at the harbor. Mom had a sadness in her face I had never seen before. Her eyes stared out the window, but she wasn't looking at anything. I wondered what she was thinking.

Through the window, broken shrimp boats were piled in the harbor in front of unrecognizable buildings that were once seafood restaurants.

"I'm meeting the contractor in an hour," Mom said. "Do you need anything from the house?"

It was my last day of freedom before I'd have to face the kids at school again and even though it was shocking to see all the damage Hurricane Ike had done, I wanted to go exploring.

After another sip of coffee, I said, "I need my bike."

What I really needed was to see the destruction. Okay, it was twisted, I know, but I felt twisted inside and for the first time ever, my insides matched what was happening on the outside.

Later that morning, I rode to Rafa's house to make sure it wasn't getting looted. Since I hadn't heard from him, I assumed he was still in San Antonio with his family. That's why I was surprised to see him standing in the front yard, grilling all kinds of meats with his dad when I rode up.

"Buenos dias." His dad moved the meats around on the grill and did a double take at my hair.

"Hey, Mr. Espinoza." I put the kickstand down and stood next to Rafa to get a better look at the grill.

"Your hair!" Rafa said. "Where is it?"

"A place called Hairy Impulses."

"You look like a boy."

"You should see Mom's," I said, combing my hair with my fingers. "She's a mid-life crisis in motion."

"I liked it better long."

My eyes welled up and I forced myself to not blink. When your enemies don't like something about you, who cares? But when your last friend on the planet criticizes you, it hurts. "What's with all the food?" I asked, trying to sound stronger than I felt.

"When the electricity went out, all the meat we had in the freezer thawed out," Rafa explained. "We have to cook it before it goes bad."

Sizzling on the grill were beef chunks, chicken quarters and a variety of sausages. Even though I had just finished eating, the rich smell of meat charring on the grill made me hungry. Under a giant oak, Rafa's mother finished smoothing a cloth over a long table she had set up in the front yard and then she came over and gave me a hug. On the porch, Rafa's oldest brother wiped mud off a chair.

"How bad is it?" I asked.

Rafa kicked the dead grass. "Our beds, our sofa, our TV, all ruined."

"Mom said the insurance company covers all that."

Rafa gave me the sometimes-you-are-so-stupid look that he saved for special moments like this. I totally got it. Not everyone could afford insurance. I felt smaller than a hermit crab and immediately, my sick need for wide scale destruction was gone.

With a garden hose, Mrs. Espinoza rinsed silt off a plastic chair and placed it at the table. On her way back in the house, she said something to Rafa in Spanish that I couldn't understand.

Rafa curled his lips like he already knew the answer. "She wants to know if your parents need to come over and eat with us."

"Seriously? She didn't see the news about my dad?"

"She saw it," Rafa said. "You have to understand that in my culture, things are different." He grabbed two chairs. "No matter what happens, you still sit down and eat with your family."

I tried to visualize Mom and Dad sitting down to dinner with me now and said, "Well in my culture, that's not going to happen."

— 7 —

School sucked on the first day back, but the triple Ps plus Megan were nowhere to be found so at least I didn't have to deal with them and neither did Mr. Oliver. Rafa and I sat in our usual spots in the back and since half the kids were still absent because of the hurricane, we weren't exactly well hidden. By the way he paced back and forth and spoke to the ceiling, Mr. Oliver seemed oblivious to the fact that hardly anyone was there.

"Necessitas non habet legem." He read it aloud from a book and placed his finger at his temple as if deep in thought. "What does it mean?"

I could've cared less. I had much bigger things to worry about than trying to translate whatever he'd said and since no one else seemed to have a clue, Mr. Oliver finally decided to just tell us.

"Necessity has no law," he said. "It's a Latin proverb from the Middle Ages."

Rafa poked me with a pencil. "We have to write about the looters?"

If that was the assignment, I didn't have anything to write about because the looter who broke into my house didn't take anything, and if he had gone upstairs and taken something, he probably needed it more than we ever did. A month ago, I wouldn't have felt that way, but a month ago, I came from a family where everyone acted out their roles perfectly. When everyone stops acting and you realize you're the only sane person in the family, material things become less important.

"Taking something without asking is wrong," Rafa whispered, "even if you're homeless."

I disagreed, but didn't feel like debating, even though it was usually my favorite sport. Instead, I wrote a half-hearted essay on a homeless person's right to steal food if they were starving to death. I'm sure it could've been better, but I really wasn't in the mood.

When he was finished, Rafa handed me his paper. Not surprisingly, he wrote about how immoral it was to steal, even if you're the only person left on an island after a hurricane. I guess if you're poor and someone steals your stuff, it's different.

We passed our papers to the front. Rafa's family had solid beliefs in right and wrong. Obviously, my parents didn't believe in anything. I sunk down in my seat and for the rest of class, I could barely look Rafa in the eye.

I'd almost forgotten about the note I'd written to Mr. Oliver requesting to be excused from the sucky journal writing assignment until he handed back my story about

Hurricane Abby. If I was going to win that novel writing contest this year, I needed to get started. I flipped to the last page. Mr. Oliver had given me a ninety-eight on the story, but after my note, he'd scribbled the words: *You may do both.*

That was so unfair. How did he expect me to write a brilliant fantasy novel while constantly puking my sordid life into a journal?

Mr. Oliver peeked over his wire rims at the few kids who dotted the classroom. "Before class is dismissed, I want to leave you with a thought."

Dismissing class was the best thought Mr. Oliver could've left me with at that moment. With slumped shoulders, I waited for his words of wisdom that would probably make me feel worse about myself than I already did.

"I don't want you to answer this question out loud and I don't want you to write about it." He paced up and down the rows of desks. "I just want you to think about it."

I didn't want to be curious about whatever he was going to say next since we weren't even going to be graded on it, but for some reason, I was.

"Most of you are still fourteen, but for a moment, I want you to pretend you know how to drive."

Rafa bolted straight up in his seat. "I know how to drive," he said as if Mr. Oliver had personally insulted him. His jaw was set.

I looked twice. Maybe Rafa wasn't really gay.

"Good." Mr. Oliver smiled. "Then you won't have to

pretend. Now close your eyes and imagine you're driving through the desert. The land is flat and nothing is around for miles and miles."

I never did close my eyes, but Rafa squished his eyes tight and pretended to grip a steering wheel. From the back of the class, I couldn't see the faces of the kids in front of me, but I kept my eyes open.

"Up ahead you see an intersection with a stop sign," Mr. Oliver continued. "Since the land is flat, you can see there are no other cars anywhere in sight. No one would ever know if you made the decision to not stop."

Mr. Oliver raised his black caterpillar brows at me. At first I thought I was busted for not closing my eyes, but then he turned and continued talking.

"The question I am posing to you is this: Would you stop?" He spun around and pressed his paper thin lips. "Just give it some thought. Class dismissed."

"That's a stupid question." Rafa zipped his backpack. "Of course I would stop."

I rolled my eyes.

Under a giant oak, Rafa told stories about his grandmother and cousins in San Antonio and the fun things they did while I was cooped up with Mom in Dad's apartment. I took a bite of a grilled chicken leg from Rafa's lunch sack and said, "Uh-huh," but I was barely listening.

Eventually Rafa ran out of stories and the silence started stressing me out. I tossed the chicken bone on a piece of aluminum foil and said, "Don't you think it's weird that after I wrote about a hurricane, it really happened?"

"I know." Rafa's eyes widened. "I was telling my cousins in San Antonio about that and now they call you la bruja."

I gave him the say-it-in-English look.

"They think you're a witch."

I scrunched my eyes. "So they think Hurricane Ike's my fault?"

"I told them, 'She's not a witch. She's a curandera.'"

"A what?"

"A curandera has magic powers and sometimes they can predict the future."

"But what if I caused all that destruction?" I grabbed Rafa's arm. "Ohmygod, what if I'm evil?"

Rafa laughed. "You're not evil."

"Probably just a coincidence," I said, looking around for a trash can.

"There's only one way to find out…" The bell rang over whatever Rafa was going to say next. He jumped up and slung on the backpack.

"Wait!" I followed Rafa back to the building. "How?"

"You have to write another story and see if it happens," he yelled over his shoulder. "This time, write about something good." Rafa winked and disappeared into the crush of kids in the hallway.

That night, Mom sniffled in bed on the other side of the partition. I started to go see what was wrong, but she had been on the verge of tears all afternoon and it was probably another one of those serious grownup things that would turn my stomach if I knew. I was almost asleep when dishes rattled quietly at the other end of the apartment as if Mom was doing her best to not make any noise. I decided to get up.

"Hey," was all I could think of to say. Mom sat at the kitchen table with her forehead resting on the palm of her hand. In the other hand she twirled the stem of a glass full of wine. When I sat down, she bunched a napkin in her eyes and tried not to sob, but it wasn't working very well. I swear, in my fourteen years on this planet, I'd never seen Mom cry. I didn't know what to do, except sit quietly and wait like Rafa had done for me.

Finally she said, "I spoke to my divorce attorney today."

My stomach squished like a sponge.

"Your father has an enormous amount of debt that I knew nothing about." Mom started to get up. "Would you like some cookies, dear?"

"No. Please. Chill."

"I wish I could." She scooped up the glass, gulped down several swallows of wine, and stared out the window. "We have to sell the house."

I could deal with that. Mom was obviously having a full-blown panic attack, but I was surprisingly calm.

"We'll live here," I said. Wait, we needed bedrooms with doors that shut. "Or we'll get a house. A smaller one."

"We can't buy another house," she said. "There's no money."

I got up and pulled an orange soda from the fridge,

but what I really wanted was a glass of that wine.

"We can't stay here, either," she said. "This apartment is more than your father can afford."

I slid back into the chair. "We're homeless?"

"No honey, it's not that bad."

"Right. And where exactly are we going to live?"

"After the divorce, which your father is pushing through the courts quickly—" Mom took another gulp of wine. "I'll only get a few hundred dollars a month in child support."

"For me?"

"Well, yes. But the money isn't yours. It helps me pay for your food, clothes and everything else you need."

"What about Dad's place in Austin?"

Mom shook her head. "He's selling it. We'll get a cheaper place here in Galveston."

"And Dad's gonna pay for that?"

"No, honey," she said without looking up. "I have to get a job. I applied at a place that sells appliances today."

Silence. I mean pure silence, except for the ticking of a clock at the other end of the apartment. Tick…Tick. The sound grew louder, slower.

"Appliances?" I asked.

When Mom emptied the bottle of wine in the glass, my heart sank. We were definitely going to need more wine.

"I don't have any sperience, Abby."

Oh God, Mom was drunk.

"I married your father right out of high school. He always did like younger women."

She took another gulp.

"Anway, I'll go to college online or somesing, you know, at night." Her head was bobbing.

"Let's get you to bed," I said, trying to gather her up.

At first I led her by the arm while her feet shuffled across the hardwood floors, but after taking a tumble on the living room rug, I grabbed her waist and had to practically pull her to bed. She chattered on and on about something, but most of it didn't make sense. Still, I understood the things she told me after I tucked her in. They weren't things parents were supposed to tell their kids, but I didn't stop her. I couldn't stop listening.

After Mom was fast asleep, I returned to the kitchen. The things she'd blabbed about our family were twisted and wrong on so many levels. I sat at the table, just like Mom had, and polished off her glass of wine. As it went down, a wave of euphoria washed over me and I smiled for no reason. Yes, for one long, slow moment, I was simply happy, which made no sense, except maybe in La-La Land.

— 8 —

A month later, the repairs to our Victorian house were finished and a *For Sale* sign appeared in the yard. Mom rented an apartment on the other side of Broadway. It wasn't the tiny white rooms with low ceilings that made it horrible; it was the bathroom Mom and I had to share. The bathroom itself was disgusting enough and the fact that we had to share it—well, that was like sharing clothes with your mother. Between generations there's an enormous fashion gap, even if your mother does shop on Sixth Street in Austin. What I'm saying is this: her bathroom stuff and mine were never going to mix.

Since we couldn't afford movers, Rafa's brother helped us move what little furniture would fit in the apartment. I ended up with the smaller French furniture in my bedroom.

When we finished moving, Mom tried to give Rafa's brother some cash, but he wouldn't take it. With his arm hanging out of the truck, he said something to Rafa in Spanish.

I waved and shouted, "Thanks!" as he drove off.

Mom stood in front of the apartment door wringing her hands and scanning the weeds that surrounded the building. "Come inside, children," she said to Rafa and me, as if it were not safe to be outside of our new home or apartment or whatever. Normally, I would've had a comment or two about how we weren't children, but Mom was sniffling again, so I decided to leave it alone.

We moved some boxes off the sofa and collapsed in the air conditioning. For the end of October, it was still awfully warm.

"What about the furniture that's still at the house?" I asked.

Mom dabbed her eyes with a tissue. "We'll have an estate sale." She scurried to the bedroom and even through the closed door we heard gut wrenching sobs. I was getting used to it, but Rafa looked stunned.

Noticing a funny odor in the wall-to-wall carpet, I said "She'll be okay."

I wanted to gag. The carpet smelled like a dirty clothes hamper, except a little moldier. At first I thought poverty wasn't a big deal, but when my eyes started burning from the mold, I knew why Mom was crying.

Mom advertised the estate sale in the local newspaper and by the first weekend in November, the weather had finally cooled off. At six forty-five in the morning, all sorts of people lined up and chatted excitedly in front of our big house. The holiday season had begun and it looked like people were in the mood to shop.

Mom folded price cards in half and placed them on pieces of furniture. "I hope everything's gone by noon," she said, taking the rest of the cards upstairs.

I peeked out at the line of people driving up, looking for places to park along the street. Rafa was busy in the kitchen doing something.

"I can't believe your mother is selling her décor de United Nations." Rafa's hands gripped a sterling silver tray full of paper coffee cups with little pop-out handles. The coffee smelled like cinnamon and on the tray stood a tent card that read:

International Coffee $1.00

"What makes it international?" I asked.

"Hey," Rafa raised one eyebrow, "I'm just trying to run a business. You know, furniture from around the world, international coffee. It's a sales gimmick." He moved in close to my face and with cinnamon coffee breath said, "The money's for your mom."

At seven a.m., Mom descended the staircase with her chin up and eyes straight ahead. She was definitely nervous. She sucked in a slow breath and opened the door. It reminded me of all the years our home was on the Historic Houses Tour, only this time, they didn't come to gawk. Like vultures, they were here to scavenge the remains of our lives.

Speaking of scavengers, Mrs. Applegate, mother of

Megan, strolled in at the end of the long line that weaved in and out of every room in the house. Behind Mrs. Applegate were the mothers of Priscilla, Presley and Paige. It didn't surprise me when the mean girl moms didn't say hi to me, but when Megan's mom walked right by my mom without even making eye contact, I clenched my jaw and squinted. I thought Mom and Mrs. Applegate were friends.

After the Triple-P Moms strolled in the parlor, Megan's mom split from the pack and sneaked back into the foyer where Mom sat behind a table with a cashbox. Mrs. Applegate dragged a chair over and carried on a low volume, serious conversation with Mom like they were discussing top-secret information.

The Triple-P Moms circulated through the rooms downstairs looking more bored than three atheists at Mass. When they came back in the foyer, Mrs. Applegate sprang to her feet as if she'd been caught socializing with the enemy. Mom wrinkled her forehead like she did when she was confused.

At that moment Rafa came in, but before I could stop him, he had lifted the tray of coffee to Priscilla's mom. With her arms folded, Priscilla's mom curled her lips and shook her head in disapproval.

Mom rushed over to Rafa. "This is an estate sale, dear. The coffee should be complimentary."

"Is he legal?" Priscilla's mother asked with a smirk.

Mom froze.

"Oh what the heck," Mom finally said. "Charge her for the coffee."

I busted out laughing and had to go out on the porch to keep from peeing my pants.

On their way out, Priscilla's mom said, "I didn't see a thing I would dare put in my house." She had that if-you-know-what-I mean look on her face.

"No point in even going upstairs," said Presley's mom.

Like a double agent, Mrs. Applegate stuck right with them. I was glad she was gone, the traitor.

By early afternoon, the house was practically empty and Mom's metal box was so crammed with cash and checks, she couldn't snap the latch. Even the porch furniture was gone, which meant Rafa and I had to sit on the steps.

"Your mom's doing good today," Rafa said. "She hasn't cried once."

"Uh-huh." I checked my watch. "She's makin' money."

"She'll be rich after she sells this house."

I shook my head and gave Rafa the finger-over-the-lips quiet signal. "You wouldn't believe the things she told me one night when she was drunk," I whispered. "I don't think she even remembers."

Rafa scooched in closer.

"We're not getting any money after she sells the house."

A big truck pulled up in front and two fat men got out.

"I saw how much this house is selling for," Rafa said with a stubborn tone. "It was in the paper."

I waited for the bubbas to go around us and whispered, "My dad's in debt."

Rafa draped his arm over my shoulder and touched his forehead against mine. "So you're poor like me," he said playfully.

If he was trying to make me feel better, it wasn't working. "Dude," I said pulling away, "she told me something else."

Rafa's eyes widened big as bird splat. He looked a little too fascinated, if you know what I mean.

I grabbed him in a headlock. "You've got to swear to keep it secret," I said, squeezing harder.

"I swear it! Stop!"

After I let go, Rafa fussed over his hair. He was so gay.

"You kids gotta git outa the way," one of the bubbas said from the doorway.

We moved to the shady corner of the gingerbread porch and the big-bellied men maneuvered that Chinese throne I had in my bedroom down the steps to the truck.

"Come on, give me the dirt." Rafa struggled to not smile.

"It's not funny!"

"I don't think it's funny," he said. "I think you're cute."

I didn't take that too personally because I wasn't going to be cute anymore once Rafa realized he was gay.

"All right, look," I said, "when Mom was drunk, she told me the truth about why we have furniture from around the world."

Rafa's laser stare seemed to search inside me. "And why is that?"

I moved in closer and whispered, "Every time Mom

caught Dad having an affair, she made him take us to some new foreign country. Dad always so felt guilty, he let her buy all this stuff.

Rafa's face had no expression. He was probably afraid to say anything because he didn't want me to mess up his hair again.

An elderly couple came out the front door carrying an English tea cart that was supposedly used at Buckingham Palace a few centuries ago. Behind them, a man in his thirties carried a German cuckoo clock.

"Wow," Rafa said. "That's a lot of affairs."

"Now you know why Mom's not crying about selling all this stuff," I said. "She really hates it."

Rafa pulled a wad of one dollar bills from his pocket and counted them. "Here's twenty-eight dollars." He stuck the wad in my hand. "For your mom."

"Rafa, you don't have to—." I got choked up.

"Gotta go," he said. "We're going to my cousin's today." With an upward nod on his way down the steps he said, "See you at school."

Oh god, school. As if I didn't have enough going on in my life. When the last truck drove off, I went inside and found Mom counting cash with baggy circles under her eyes. I tossed Rafa's wad of cash on the table.

"From Rafa," I said in my most bored voice.

"This oughta tide us over 'til money starts comin' in from the appliance store."

Um, okay first of all, my mother speaks perfect English. And second, when did she get a Southern twang? This was not the ever-proper Queen Doreen or even the new young-and-sassy Mom who bought her clothes on Sixth Street. No, this was one-stoplight-town, swap meet Mom. I squinted and peered at her from different angles.

"Mom?"

— 9 —

From way down the hall, I spotted graffiti on my locker and dreaded finding out what it said, but in five seconds I'd be reading it in front of everyone and there was nothing I could do about it. The hallway chatter practically stopped, except for a few whispers. Kids stared, watching for my reaction. I couldn't decide whether to have no reaction or some kind of outrageous over-reaction. I mean really, I hated to disappoint my audience. Okay, whatever. I was practically there and I could start making out the words: *Ghetto Girl.*

Taped underneath it was a photo of the run-down apartment complex where Mom and I lived. All I can say is my reaction surprised even me. Even though this was clearly the work of the triple Ps plus Megan, it still hurt. Actually it was the plus Megan part that really hurt.

It's not that I had anything against poor people because unlike Megan, I wasn't a snob—or at least that's what I thought. Now that I was poor, I looked forward to coming to school just to get away from that crappy old apartment. But there was my new ghetto home, staring at me in living color, right on my locker. Truly, I was stunned, which was probably the reaction they wanted.

"Ghetto Girl." Rafa draped his arm over my shoulder. "I like it. Makes you sound like a rock star." He snatched the photo off the locker and wadded it up. The photo was gone, but the black spray paint wasn't coming off.

"It does sound kinda cool," I said with a weak smile.

"Open your locker. The bell is ringing."

I got out my books and Rafa walked with me to American Government even though it was out of his way.

"You don't have to come in," I said when he followed me in the door.

"Just sit."

I slid into my desk, but didn't look up, even when I felt Rafa's hand messing up my hair.

He backed away and pointed with both hands. "See ya, Ghetto Girl." To the rest of the class, he said, "Ghetto Girl rocks!"

That was okay since he was pretending, but when he patted his heart, I turned bright red. It got worse when the other boys oohed and whistled like they believed him. Truly amazing. Not one person laughed at me through the whole class.

I stuffed a book in my backpack and shoved everything else in there too. Next period wasn't going to be that easy. As embarrassing as Rafa's little drama had been, secretly I was glad to see him waiting outside the door, ready to escort me to Mr. Oliver's English class.

"I don't need a babysitter," I said with my most ungrateful tone.

"Hey, I'm doing this for me." He winked. "I don't want to miss a chance to be seen with Ghetto Girl."

"You're such a liar."

"So are you."

It was true. We were both lying.

Rafa shoved me in a corner behind a door and pulled a pocket knife out of his backpack.

"What the—?"

He slit my shirt at the shoulder, grabbed a sleeve and ripped it off.

"Stop!"

"Be still," he said, doing the same to the other sleeve.

"You know that knife is like totally illegal at school."

"That's a stupid rule," he said.

"What about that paper you wrote about always following the law?"

Rafa didn't answer. Instead, he ripped the T-shirt shorter and gave it a slash over my belly.

"What, are you a clothes designer now?"

He messed up my hair again and said, "We're late."

Definitely gay.

Before we got to the room, Rafa tucked the knife away and pulled out some shades.

"I'm not wearing those."

He slid them on my face anyway. By the way his jaw clenched, it was best to not argue.

The triple Ps plus Megan, a.k.a. the locker vandals, sat

on top of their desks when Rafa and I drifted in, acting like we didn't notice them. Mr. Oliver was busy writing something on the board.

In the back of the room I put one hand on my hip and the other on Rafa's shoulder. We did this weird mumbo-jumbo-pretend-talking thing. I tried to keep a straight face when Rafa let out the lamest fake laugh I'd ever heard. Whatever we were doing, I just hoped it wasn't going to backfire.

Right after the tardy bell rang, a kid from my first period class stopped by to high-five me on the way to his desk. "Wassup Ghetto Girl," was all he said.

I didn't move my head, just my eyes, and behind those dark shades, the triple-Ps didn't know where I was looking. But I was looking at them and they were looking at me.

A girl I barely knew squirmed around in her seat and smiled. I didn't know what to do, so I smiled back. When she waved meekly, I kept my hand on my hip and nodded.

"That's Ghetto Girl," someone whispered. Two kids gazed at me in awe. The triple Ps looked disgusted, but Megan had no reaction. She was way cooler than them.

Mr. Oliver cleared his throat, obviously not amused by any of this. "Today we will discuss grammar."

I cringed when Mr. Oliver headed straight toward me and I actually considered removing the shades, but decided to finish playing out my leading role as Ghetto Girl. While sliding down in my seat, I spread my legs and slung an elbow over the back of the chair. If Mr. Oliver wanted the shades, he'd have to come and get them.

"If you don't use proper grammar, you're not writing." Mr. Oliver towered over my desk but never looked down. Instead, he snapped his long, skinny fingers in front of my face and held out his hand. "Writing is like learning to drive an automobile. First, you must learn the myriad of laws pertaining to traffic."

By now, most of the class had turned to see what Ghetto Girl would do. I didn't know what the freaking heck to do. I wasn't as cool as Ghetto Girl.

Rafa grinned at my dilemma.

I ended up being my usual nerdy self. I sat up straight, pulled off the shades and placed them in his hand. "Thank you Mr. Oliver," were the words that came out of my mouth. That came from years of growing up under the reign of Queen Doreen.

Eyes widened. Did I just blow it? The triple Ps smirked and I'm thinking, yeah, I blew it. This whole thing was a stupid idea anyway.

Rafa low-fived me under the desk. Whatever.

"In the world of English grammar, some things actually make sense." Mr. Oliver chuckled in a self-amused way. "For example, let's examine this rule. Shall we?" He pointed to one of the rules he had written on the board:

Two negatives make a positive.

"Ah, a pencil." Mr. Oliver waved a pencil in the air in a desperate attempt to wake up the class. "If I were to say,

'I don't have no clue what this pencil is made of,' what does that mean?"

Presley fluttered her fingers way up high and made "oooh, oooh" noises like she was having a seizure.

Mr. Oliver had a rare look of astonishment, probably because one of the triple Ps might have actually been listening. "Yes, Presley," he said with a hint of excitement.

"It means, um," she twirled a long, blond lock of hair, "that you're absolutely sure you don't know what the pencil is made of."

The room was silent.

"No wait," she said. "That's not right." Presley stared hard at the pencil on her desk. "It means you don't know the things the pencil is not made of, like it's not made of plastic. That you know for sure. No, wait. That's one of the things you don't know."

By now, the class was laughing.

Mr. Oliver looked pleased. "Thank you, Presley, for illustrating to the class the confusion created by double negatives. Actually, one negative cancels out the other, so the person is saying they do know, even though that probably wasn't their intent."

Nothing was duller than talking about grammar—probably because I didn't have to think about it anymore. Grammar had become instinctive, thanks to the old Queen Doreen. Maybe in the world of English grammar, two negatives made a positive, but in life, it didn't work that way. Like when the whole school teased me about Dad's affair (this was the first negative), I reacted by wishing for a hurricane (this was the second negative). But the mean girls didn't get wiped out and now they're meaner than before, which meant in life, a double negative makes a bigger negative.

"Abby?" I heard Mr. Oliver say. "Abby!"

The whole class stared at me, waiting.

"Would you repeat the question, please?" I sounded like a contestant on a game show.

Mr. Oliver pursed his lips, but quickly gathered his British composure and said, "In the original example given for a double negative, what was the other grammatical issue?"

"It ended with a preposition," I replied.

Mr. Oliver's face lit up. "Well done. Yes indeed, well done."

The lesson moved on and Mr. Oliver pretty much left me alone. After class, it was kind of freaky the way kids gazed at me on their way out the door.

"Ghetto Girl has it going on in the cranium," one boy said.

"Totally cerebral," said a girl who looked star struck.

The triple Ps plus Megan filed out the door like a little army of ants.

Rafa winked at me and smiled. "A babe and a brainiac."

It's weird because I used to hate that the old Queen Doreen had been a task master of proper grammar and etiquette. Now these things were part of me. Maybe they were the good part.

"This whole Ghetto Girl thing is truly psychotic," I

said to Rafa on the way to lunch.

"Chill," he said. "Have fun with it."

When Rafa held his arm out to protect me from a group of kids who wanted to know where I sat in the cafeteria, I did feel like a rock star.

"Ghetto Girl does not eat in the cafeteria," he said. "She likes to be in nature."

The truth? We were totally anti-social and would rather eat on the dirty ground than sit with them in the cafeteria. That's why for the rest of the day, I decided to keep my mouth shut and let Rafa be the spokesperson for Ghetto Girl.

— 10 —

It was an odd feeling to walk out and not see Mom's car waiting to pick me up after school. That was definitely a first. Riding my bike was too dangerous she'd said, the day we moved into the ghetto.

"Guess we're walking." Rafa pushed his bike up the sidewalk.

"You go on," I said.

"And miss a chance to be seen walking home with Ghetto Girl?"

"That was insane," I said, poking him. "Still can't believe it worked."

"Hey, I'm a freakin' genius."

I pulled out my phone.

"Any messages from your dad?" Rafa asked.

"It's not like his phone doesn't work in Mexico. He calls Mom."

Instead of turning right toward my old house, we went left into a neighborhood with small, run-down houses.

"You don't have to walk me all the way home."

"I want to say 'hi' to your mom," he said. The liar.

"She's probably working."

Houses with taped up windows and makeshift garages lined both sides of the street. Except for grass growing in the gutters, nothing green grew and fast food trash was everywhere.

"Did Hurricane Ike do all this?"

Rafa made a funny face. "It looked like this before."

A woman screamed from a white house as we passed by, and then a man yelled about how she had taken all of something. I couldn't make out exactly what he was saying. After a loud bang, probably the screen door slamming, the woman stumbled into the yard and locked her eyes on mine, which totally creeped me out.

"Walk faster," Rafa said.

"Definitely on drugs," I whispered.

Rafa glanced over his shoulder. "Crack."

When we finally got to the apartment complex, Mom's Mercedes sat in the parking lot, but when I knocked on the door, no answer.

"Do you have a key?" Rafa asked.

"Somewhere in here." I dug through the pockets in my backpack.

Rafa knocked again. Still no answer.

"Here it is," I said.

The key didn't go in smoothly like the key at my old house; it kept getting stuck in the rust speckled doorknob. When the door finally unlocked, the apartment was pitch black.

I flipped on the light and heard groaning. Stretched out on the sofa laid Mom with a washcloth folded neatly over her eyes.

My heart skipped a beat. "What happened?"

"Turn off the light," she snapped.

Rafa hit the switch.

"Migraine," she said in a muffled voice. "Go away."

By now, my eyes had adjusted to the dark. Rafa and I looked at each other, but said nothing. "You'd better go," I finally whispered.

Rafa slipped out the door quietly. "Put the chain on," he said softly, pointing up at the latch.

I locked the door as instructed by my self-appointed protector and then dumped my backpack in my room. Why did boys think girls needed protection? I totally didn't get that.

In the bathroom I ran a fresh washcloth under cool water. After wringing it out, I folded it neatly and took it to Mom, who lay still as a corpse.

"Mom," I barely whispered.

She didn't move.

"Here's another washcloth," I said a little louder.

Still, nothing.

Finally, I lifted the cloth off her eyes and gently replaced it with the new one.

"I need silence," she said sharply.

My stomach growled so long, it sounded like a weed eater. I grabbed my belly to quiet it for Mom, but some noises I didn't have any control over. On the way to my room, I picked up a box of dry cereal, Mom's bottle of vodka, and an orange soda.

Mom had never been sick, before. In fact, she'd always bragged, "I'm hale and hearty," to which I'd always said, "That's redundant." Anyway, considering it was a headache, she'd probably feel better in the morning and our dismal lives could go back to normal. I took a gulp of orange soda and then poured some vodka in the can.

I rummaged through shirts, looking for something Ghetto Girl would wear, keeping in mind this might just be a fad. If it wasn't going to last, I didn't want to rip all my clothes, so I picked out two shirts I wouldn't mind trashing, but was only willing to sacrifice one pair of jeans. This time, the vodka tasted less like rubbing alcohol and more normal.

I had no homework since I'd already done every math problem in the book and there was nothing Mr. Oliver could teach me about grammar that I didn't already know. I stretched out across the bed with my computer and went to my *friendworld* page. My twenty-three friends that I barely knew had been busy writing stuff on my page. It was all from today. I added more vodka and took another swallow.

A guy whose parents were friends with my parents wrote: "Go Ghetto Girl! Style has nothing to do with MONEY!!! Intelligence and good manners, that's what I'm about!"

A girl from last year's track team wrote: "Clothes aren't important. The only thing that matters is what's inside. YOU ROCK!!"

I started to scroll down to read more when the "new

friends" icon caught my eye. After I clicked it, two hundred and seventy eight people wanted to add me as their friend. If I accepted them, I'd have more than three hundred friends, twice as many as Megan. Just to piss her off, I accepted them all.

I must have had a lot of vodka because in the morning, someone was pounding my head with a hammer, or at least that's how it felt. I wondered why I was even playing this stupid game. Was I really Ghetto Girl?

In the living room, all that remained on the sofa were a pillow and a wadded up blanket. If Mom had noticed the missing vodka bottle, she would have burst into my room screaming, but her door was closed and I didn't dare open it. Instead, I sent Rafa a text.

Abby: Riding bike…c u at ur house.

God my head hurt. My bike took up most of the space in our skinny patio. It wasn't easy maneuvering the bike through the maze of living room furniture without making any sounds that might disturb Mom. When I finally twisted the handlebars through the front door, Rafa was there, waiting.

"You stalking me, dude?"

"Uh-huh."

Just as I was about to throw my leg over the bike, Rafa said, "No, no, no. Let me see the clothes."

I pulled open my jacket and Rafa examined the shirt I'd torn.

"The jeans look ghetto, but the suede jacket, too rich."

"I have a hoodie."

"Get it," Rafa said.

I tip toed through the apartment, snatched my hoodie, and tip toed back out.

Rafa held up the shiny blade on that pocketknife he'd attacked me with in the hallway yesterday.

"Not my hoodie!"

"Be still," he said, slicing the sweatshirt here and there until I looked like a victim in a slasher movie.

Our bikes hummed through the streets and even the crack house was quiet as a graveyard at seven o'clock in the morning. Six blocks later, we rounded the corner and whizzed past a long line of cars that inched their way to the place where parents dropped off kids.

I locked my bike and thought about how stupid I looked with ripped clothes when Rafa knocked my arm and pointed to the crowds of students heading toward the school. The way their clothes were shredded, they looked like escapees from a jungle prison camp.

"Ohmygod," I said, "the whole school's gone ghetto."

"They love you," Rafa beamed.

I must've stood there with my mouth open for a long time because the next thing I knew, Rafa gripped my arms and said, "Smile big."

The custodian still hadn't gotten the spray paint off my locker, but today *Ghetto Girl* had a whole new meaning. As far as I was concerned, the longer it stayed up there, the better. Kids in ripped up clothes nodded at me and said things like "salty" and "academic." One girl confessed to another, "I skipped a grade," as if she didn't have to be ashamed of it anymore. That was my favorite until a cute guy with a slashed gray T-shirt flashed an enormous smile and said, "'Sup." I had to pinch myself.

Rafa threw an arm over me and giggled like a girl. "You walk by yourself today. It's safe."

I felt safe, finally. But just as I was starting to enjoy being the coolest girl ever, the principal showed up in my American Government class and told Mrs. Goldstein he needed to see me. The last time I saw Mr. Bald, I mean Mr. Baldwin, was sometime last year when Mom had a dinner party for some people who had contributed to Dad's campaign. Mr. Bald—all the kids called him that for one obvious reason—talked to Dad through the entire dinner about the importance of supporting public education. I followed Mr. Bald to his office and wondered how much trouble I was in for getting everyone in the school to rip their clothes.

After he shut the door, Mr. Bald rubbed his head and waited for me to sit in one of the chairs in front of his messy desk. When he finally got settled in a big leather seat, he said, "It must be really tough on you, what with the TV coverage about your family and all."

Ya think? It took every bit of restraint I had to not roll my eyes. Instead I shrugged and focused intently on a crack in the glass at the bottom of a window.

"How you holding up?" he asked.

My day was absolutely fantastic until Mr. Bald made me come in his office and I saw no point in letting him ruin my absolutely fantastic day. I smiled, looked him square in the eye and said, "Fabulously."

"Look," he leaned forward, "I saw what some kids wrote on your locker and I want you to know we have a strict 'no bullying' policy at this school."

"Do you?" I said in amazement because that was about the funniest thing I had heard all day.

"I assure you we have zero tolerance for this kind of behavior."

"And exactly how many bullying incidents have you had so far this year?" I asked, while counting in my head all the occurrences I had seen.

"This is the first," he said, "and as far as I'm concerned, it's one too many. My goal was zero."

"Sorry to disappoint you, Mr. Bald. Win. Mr. Baldwin, sir."

"No, no, it's not your fault," he said frantically. "I want your parents to know I'm doing everything I can to discipline whoever's responsible for this."

"I'll be sure to pass that on to my Dad when I talk to him tonight." I was such a liar.

"Please do, please do."

I couldn't figure out why Mr. Bald was anxious. Was I in trouble or not? Finally I asked, "Why am I here?"

"Well," he said, "Since it was your locker that was vandalized, I thought you might know who did it." Mr. Bald's voice was still shaky.

"Is that the only reason?" I asked.

"Well, yes. I need you to help me so I can help you."

The man was truly clueless—oblivious to the whole Ghetto Girl craze happening right before his eyes. Vandalizing my locker was the best thing Megan could've done and that's why I said, "I don't know who did it."

"I was afraid of that." Mr. Bald shook his head. "In

nine cases out of ten the victims know the bullies. Guess I'll have to start questioning other kids."

"That's it?" I asked.

"Abigail," he said. "I want you to know I'll do everything in my power to discipline the person responsible for this."

I didn't say anything. When he stood up, I stood up and got out of there as fast as I could.

Kids in American Government class looked awfully busy texting under the desks when I slipped into the room. Mrs. Goldstein fiddled with the Smart Board while explaining how the justice system worked and didn't seem to notice no one was paying attention. When the bell rang, I headed straight for Mr. Oliver's class to tell Rafa about my chat with Mr. Bald.

Down the crowded hall, Rafa's head popped up and down in front of Mr. Oliver's door like a fishing bobber. We made eye contact on the third pop.

"What happened?" Rafa asked, shoving the phone in his pocket. "It's all over school you went to the principal's office. Did you rat out Megan?"

"You know me better than that!"

Rafa grinned and pulled out his phone.

Even with my head perched over his shoulder, I couldn't read the text. "What does it say?"

"Ghetto Girl is not a rat. I promised to let everyone know."

With my arm dangling over his shoulder, I pulled him in the door. "You're such a good manager."

"Too bad you're not rich anymore." Rafa winked. "I

wouldn't mind getting paid."

Ouch.

The triple Ps plus Megan filed in, arms crossed, and simultaneously slid in their seats. It was a pouty party for four and no one wanted to go. Instead, everyone crowded around me—and if I'd been wearing a mood ring, the black would have instantly turned all lavenderish.

Of my ten years in school, this was the best day of my life. Never had so many kids been that happy to see me. Everywhere I went, I was high-fived, low-fived and bumped. People smiled and nodded or winked. I could live with that. Unfortunately at three o'clock, the school day came to an end and it was time to return to the dismal dungeon of darkness.

On the ride home, Rafa said, "Someone wanted to know why you ride your bike to school."

"And?"

"I told her, 'Ghetto Girl believes in going green.'"

Rafa definitely had a future in this kind of work. He could sell a bible to an atheist and the fact that he was cute certainly helped. When we got to the street where he lived, Rafa announced, "Tonight you eat with my family."

"I can't. I really need to check on Mom."

With his most serious tone, Rafa said, "I understand," and instead of turning off, he kept riding with me. I had to smile at his chivalry, riding me home.

In the dark apartment, Mom wasn't lying on the sofa, but since her bedroom door was closed, I assumed she was home.

"Did you see her car outside?" Rafa asked.

"Yup, she's sleeping."

The fruit bowl was empty—no bananas, or apples, or anything. Nothing in the cereal cabinet either. "Check the fridge," I said to Rafa.

"Uh, mustard, mayo and some—," he pulled out a bottle, "salad dressing."

I swung open all the cabinets hoping to find cookies, crackers, peanut butter, anything, but the only crumbs of food were on the dishes in the sink.

"We're going to the store," I said.

"And carry bags on our bikes?" Rafa shook his head. "You can eat at my house."

"We need money," I said like I didn't hear him.

I squeezed the door knob to Mom's bedroom and twisted it slowly, placing a finger over my lips to signal Rafa to keep his yaky mouth shut. The pitch black darkness in her room made the living room look lit. With the tiny bit of light that crept in from the hallway, I spotted her purse on a chair in the corner and lifted it carefully, then tiptoed out and slowly shut the door.

"You would make a good thief," Rafa said.

I didn't think that was funny, mainly because my stomach needed food and when that happens, nothing is funny. Inside Mom's wallet, we found forty-four dollars and some change. I stuffed a twenty in my pocket and stared at the keys.

"No, no," he said wagging his finger in my face. "We're not doing that."

"You know how to drive." I set my jaw. "You already admitted it."

"It's breaking the law," he said matter-of-factly. "I am a law abiding citizen."

"Oh, but it's legal to bring a knife to school."

"Look, it's a little pocket knife," he said, holding it up. "Something you need every day, like a toothbrush."

"Shhh." I gently extracted the keys from Mom's purse. "You don't have to drive. Just show me how."

"Ay caray," Rafa said, rolling the r.

"What exactly does that mean?"

Rafa touched his hands to his cheeks like he was imitating a girl and said, "Oh. My. God."

— 11 —

We locked the apartment and headed to Mom's Mercedes out in the parking lot, tightly sandwiched between an enormous pickup truck and a carpet cleaning van. I fumbled through the keys and picked the black plastic thing with the Mercedes symbol, but when we got to the car, I wasn't sure how to unlock the doors. Of the button choices on the pad, I pushed the one that looked like an opened padlock. We were in.

From the passenger side, Rafa grabbed the keys. "Which one is it?"

"Mom sticks this round thing in here."

Rafa looked perplexed when I stuck the end of the key pad into a little place just to the right of the steering wheel. I pushed a button. I remembered watching Mom do it a million times and like always, the car started instantly.

"Wow." Rafa stared at the key in total amazement.

"Now what?" I asked.

Rafa swallowed hard. "You have to back up."

"Obviously!" I said more sarcastically than I meant. "How exactly do I do that?"

"See this thing?" Rafa pointed to the joy stick by my knee. "Move it to R. The R is for reverse."

It took everything I had to not say "Duh!" But there was a limit to Rafa's patience and if I didn't want him to leave, I had to start being nice. I drew in a deep breath, moved the joystick to R, and somehow managed to keep my mouth shut. Without any kind of warning, the car glided backwards.

"Stop!" Rafa yelled. "Stop!"

"I don't know how!" I screamed.

"The brake! Push the brake!"

"Where is it?" The car kept moving backwards, all the way out of the parking space and into the lot.

"The floor," he pointed. "Push it!"

I looked at the floor and pushed my foot on the pedal, but the car went faster.

Rafa shrieked, "The other one!" and crossed himself.

I moved my foot to the other pedal, but not before the car hit a hard bump. When I finally got it to stop, the back end of the car was higher than the front. Rafa shoved the joystick to P, got out and slammed the door.

Even though my legs shook like they were having seizures all by themselves, I needed to get out of the car to see what I had done. I stepped out with my heart fluttering way too fast, but my legs started working, so at least I could walk. The back wheels of Mom's car had driven over a curb and were sitting in dead grass. Fortunately, the front wheels were still in the parking lot.

Even though it was cool outside, Rafa wiped sweat from his forehead. "Why can't you just come to my house to eat," he said.

I wanted to cry, but clenched my teeth instead.

He marched over to my side of the car. "I will drive to the store."

"I need to learn! In case you're not around."

"I will teach you, but not here."

After I shut the door on the passenger side, Rafa moved his trembling hand to the joystick. While turning the steering wheel, he stretched to search through the windows. "A dog is growling. Where is it?"

"Um, it's my stomach." I held my belly.

Rafa sank back and pulled the joystick to the D. The car crawled forward and made a scraping sound when the back wheels rolled off the curb. I don't think I was breathing.

Rafa steered the car through the parking lot and turned onto the street. I started breathing again when I saw he really could drive and even though he drove super slow, at least he knew what he was doing. We zigzagged out of the neighborhood and got on the main street that went straight to the grocery store. Cars passed us, one after another, but I didn't say a word about how slow he was driving. I tried to gaze nonchalantly at the Gulf of Mexico on the other side of the street.

When we finally reached the grocery store, Rafa turned into the huge parking lot and stopped the car far away from where all the other cars were parked.

"Why don't you park closer?" I asked.

"I'm parking here." He moved the joystick to the P.

I forgot I was trying to be nice and quickly added, "You're a fantastic driver."

He didn't say a word.

A cold wind blew during our hike through the parking lot and the second we stepped in the store, my teeth started chattering. "It's a freezer in here."

"What do you want to buy?" Rafa asked, narrowing his eyes.

"Everything. Cereal, milk, eggs, macaroni and cheese, peanut butter, chips, pizza, ice cream—."

Rafa pointed and said, "There's the cereal." His finger was shaking.

I pushed the cart toward the aisle that had endless boxes of cereal and grabbed my favorite chocolaty kind that Mom refused to buy. Rafa was definitely anxious, like I'd pushed his law-abiding-citizen personal policy over the limit. I decided to start rambling on about something. That always calmed him down.

"My Mom believes everything she reads about food," I said, trying to sound relaxed. "All my life we ate wheat bread because white bread was bad for you. Then all of sudden, wheat was bad because it had gluten. Same with tofu. I had to eat that nasty tasting crap forever. I mean seriously, it tastes like Play Dough, that stuff kids play with that comes in different colors. It comes in little cans." Rafa didn't say anything. "Anyway, a study found tofu wasn't so great after all. Turns out all this time I could have been eating pork."

Rafa followed me around like a child as I went from aisle to aisle, complaining about sales gimmicks, tossing things in the cart, and entering the price in the calculator on my phone. When the running total reached twenty dollars, I didn't have enough for ice cream or pizza, which was pretty disappointing, but I could live with that. I pushed the cart to the front of the store and found an open lane.

While I paid the cashier, Rafa put all the stuff in plastic bags.

"Mom keeps those green shopping bags in the trunk of the car," I said. "I hope no one from school sees us using plastic bags since you told everyone Ghetto Girl believes in going green. Seriously, I have a public image to maintain."

Not even a crack of a smile from Rafa, but at least he'd stopped shaking.

Twenty dollars only got us two bags of groceries and during our long trek to the other end of the parking lot, a few teensy water drops sprinkled my face. Out over the Gulf, dark clouds hovered. I pulled out a big bag of potato chips, ripped it open and stuffed a few in my mouth.

"Ohmygod, have some!" I tilted the bag toward Rafa. "My taste buds are having a party to celebrate the end of my potato chip deprivation. Mom never let me eat junk food, but I'm in charge of the grocery shopping now and I'm sure a study somewhere found that potato chips make you live longer."

Rafa pushed the bag away.

"Fine," I said. "More for me." I got in the driver's seat and rummaged through the bag that held the peanut butter and crackers. My hunger level bordered on critical. The crackers kept breaking in the peanut butter, but that didn't stop me from scooping as much as possible. In the corner of my eye, I could see Rafa judging me, like I was gross. He should've been grateful I was eating because without food in my stomach, I wasn't going to be nice.

When a few larger drops splattered the windshield, I screwed the lid on the peanut butter and handed everything to Rafa.

"What are you doing?" he asked while I fished for the keys in my pocket.

I inserted the round plastic thing back in the slot and started the car. "You're going to teach me to drive."

"Not in the rain." Rafa grabbed the door handle as if he needed to escape.

I gave Rafa the look.

Rafa didn't argue, probably because I was on a mission and he knew it.

"Okay," he blew a quick breath and wiped his palms. "On the floor you have two pedals. The one on the right is the gas and the one on the left is the brake."

"I think we established that last time."

Rafa gave me the, you-really-need-to-shut-up look. "Put your foot on the brake," he commanded.

I did exactly what he said.

"Now move the stick to D."

"Check."

"Okay, look around for other cars. If you don't see any, slowly take your foot off the brake."

Since we were in the no-man's-land section of the parking lot, I took my foot off the brake and the car rolled forward. I gripped the steering wheel tight.

"Good," Rafa said in a calm voice, even though his eyes were about to pop out of his head. "See that big light pole down there? Drive to it and stop."

Unlike last time, I eased my foot on the gas pedal and the car gradually sped up. As coordinated as I was in sports, I was surprised at how difficult it was to think about steering and pressing the gas at the same time. Since I gently pressed the brake, my stop was smooth, except for the very end when I gave the brake one final push and jerked the car. My heart pounded. I had done it.

Rain fell harder on the glass. Since I had no idea how Mom turned on the windshield wipers, I played with the gadgets until I found the one that worked.

"I will drive," Rafa said.

My eyes welled up and I sat still.

After a long pause, Rafa said, "I will show you how to turn."

I drove all over the vacant end of the parking lot until my stops and turns were nearly perfect. Through the whole driving lesson, Rafa was kind, even when the rain came down hard, but his patience vanished when I insisted on driving home.

"Loca de la cabeza!" he shouted. "You're crazy in the head!"

"I can do it."

Rafa crossed his arms. "Excuse me but I am not in the mood to risk my life today."

"You're pouting."

"I will walk home in the rain." He reached for the handle.

"DQ alert." I moved the joystick to D and turned toward the street.

"What is that?" he asked. "DQ."

"Drama Queen."

I was too busy concentrating to watch him roll his eyes, but I knew he had. A stop sign at the street had my attention and I lifted the left turn signal the way Rafa had shown me in the parking lot. Next I had to figure out how to make the windshield wiper go faster when the rain really started coming down. After several cars passed, an opening appeared in the traffic and I took it. When my leg started seizing again, it was hard to control the amount of pressure I put on the gas pedal, but no way would I tell Rafa I was nervous.

I crept down the main road with the Gulf of Mexico on one side and Sharky's Seafood Grill on the other. Up ahead, a red light turned green, which meant I had plenty of time to make it through. Even though all the other cars were going faster, I maintained my same slow speed and leaned forward to get a better view through the blurry window. I had no idea what was going on with DQ and I couldn't take my eyes off the road to glance over, not even for a millisecond.

From riding with Mom, I remembered the traffic lights were synchronized and sped up a little to make it through as many as possible. Applying the brake wasn't something I wanted to do, mainly because I didn't know what my nervous leg would do if I moved it. Rafa must've been in a state of shock or praying or something because I had to wipe the fog off the inside of the windshield by myself. There was a button for that somewhere, but I didn't have time to search the dashboard. I made it through at least five lights when my luck ran out and the next one turned red.

Gripping the steering wheel tighter, I waited 'til I got closer to the light to start slowing down, and then lifted my foot off the gas pedal and pushed gently on the brake. The car slowed, but I must have misjudged the distance because I was about to go through the red light.

Without thinking, I shoved my foot hard on the brake. Rafa gasped. Instead of slowing down, the car actually sped up and turned sideways, sliding toward the Gulf. I turned the steering wheel to go straight again, but it was like the steering wheel didn't work anymore. After a three-sixty spin, Mom's Mercedes slowed to a stop on the edge of the Seawall just before falling into the Gulf of Mexico. My heart hammered through my chest and the sound of a siren grew louder.

Rafa totally freaked. With wide eyes, sunken cheeks and a dropped jaw, he looked like the skeleton his mom always set up on their porch for Day of the Dead. I turned around and through the downpour, watched a blue flashing light pull up behind us.

"Um," I said, "this is serious." I moved the joystick to P. "Not like we're grounded serious; more like we're going to jail serious."

Rafa's face bunched up and tears streamed down his cheeks.

Should've kept my mouth shut.

— 12 —

I wanted to bolt, but Rafa was in no condition to run, plus the rain pounded harder. When a policeman stepped up to the car in a bright yellow rain jacket, I pushed the button on the door that opened the window and within seconds, my hoodie was drenched.

The policeman bent down and got a puzzled look on his face. "I need to see your driver's license."

A million answers streamed through my mind, like: I forgot it. I lost it. I'm practicing for the test. I'm a fourteen-year-old driving prodigy. But the truth actually made more sense and would probably be easier in the long run, especially if they checked the computer and found out I'd lied. So I pointed to the groceries in the back seat and said, "My mom's sick and I'm bringing her something to eat." He probably thought I made it up because I sounded like Little Red Riding Hood, but it was the truth.

"Do you have a driver's license, Ma'am?"

"No, Sir," I replied.

He peered in at Rafa. I couldn't see what Rafa was doing and I really didn't want to look. I just wanted to go home.

The policeman cocked his head. "How old are you?"

"Fifteen," I said, "both of us."

He asked more questions and when I explained the car was Mom's, he said, "All right kids, I'm gonna have to take you in."

Should have followed my first instinct and bolted.

The policeman waved someone over and another policeman went to Rafa's door.

"Please step out of the car," my policeman said. "Both of you."

Rafa and I got out at the same time and I wasn't sure if I was supposed to put my hands in the air like I was being arrested, or behind my back to make it easier to put on handcuffs, or what. It turned out I didn't have to do anything except walk over to the police car and get in the back seat. By the time I got there, every inch of me was drenched.

"I need the key," my policeman said.

"Why?" I asked, shivering.

At first he seemed annoyed, but then he got a nicer look on his face and started explaining it to me like I was six. He said they had to impound the car, which meant tow it to a city parking lot.

"And how's my mom supposed to drive to the city lot without a car?" I asked.

The officer said nothing, so I handed him the keys.

"I don't need all the keys," he said, handing them back, "just the car key."

I peeled the Mercedes control off the keychain and realized Mom wouldn't be able to lock the apartment door when she came to get me out of jail because I had all the keys. I was in way more trouble than I thought. At the other end of the back seat, Rafa rested his elbow on the door and peered out even though there was nothing to see except rain splattering the window.

"Excuse me, Sir," I said to the policeman before I realized he was talking to someone on a radio. Finally, he turned around.

"Can't you just take us home?" I asked, which seemed like a perfectly reasonable request.

A voice blared on the radio. "It's registered to Doreen Alexander. Isn't that the Senator's wife?"

The two policemen in front gave each other looks and the one who arrested me said into the radio, "We're bringin' 'em in."

I scooted over next to Rafa who was squeezing his eyes so no more tears could come out and wrapped my arms around him.

"Mamá will not understand," he said, fighting sobs.

"I'm sorry," I said, rubbing his arm through a soaking wet denim jacket. A sick feeling hit me in the gut. I was truly sorry—sorry I had dragged him into the mess my life had become. I was used to things going from bad to worse, but Rafa wasn't. He didn't deserve this.

"Put on your seatbelts," Rafa's policeman said.

I went back to my side of the seat and did exactly what I was told. "My friend can walk home from here." I clicked the belt. "He didn't do anything."

They ignored me and the police car moved out into the street toward the police station. For Rafa's sake, I hoped this wasn't going to be on TV.

All the way to the police station, rain fell hard and the windshield wipers sliced through it. The car stank like vinyl, BO, and aftershave, but not the good smelling kind like Dad's, and when the heater kicked in, the odors got worse. I couldn't stop worrying about Mom because she had no food at home and I had her keys and the city parking lot had her car.

When we got to the police station, the policemen escorted us inside where there were no TV cameras anywhere. They made us sit in metal folding chairs in front of a desk, where a female officer with orange hair, red lipstick and pink fingernails smirked. I wanted to tell Rafa that if the fashion police were here, she'd be the one who'd have to answer some questions. He would've at least cracked a smile, but clearly Rafa was not in the mood, so I didn't.

The orangey haired lady leaned in. "Officer Topple," she said in a super-loud voice. "And who are you?"

I had to look away because some of the red lipstick stuck to her teeth and it was grossing me out. Eventually Rafa cleared his throat to get my attention and I said, "Abigail Alexander."

Officer Topple nodded in slow motion. Never taking her eyes off me, she said, "And your parents are?"

"John and Doreen Alexander."

"As in Senator Alexander?"

"Yes, ma'am."

"I'm going to need your parents' phone number." Each word had been stretched out while she lifted the receiver.

At first I wanted to give her Dad's number because he could handle this way better than Mom. A magazine article once said Dad could charm the gun off a bank robber and since Officer Topple had a gun, I was pretty sure she was easier to charm than a robber. But Dad was in Mexico and Mom was here, which meant I had to give the officer Mom's number even though she couldn't come get us.

Rafa looked relieved that Officer Topple forgot to get his name. I just wanted to get out of my wet clothes.

"Is this Mrs. Alexander?" she asked. "This is Officer Topple. I have Abigail at the police station and we need you to come down here." She bounced a pencil on its eraser. "Operating a motor vehicle without a license. Yes, Ma'am, she's okay. They were lucky, though. The officers who picked them up said the car hydroplaned and nearly fishtailed in the Gulf."

God only knows what Mom was saying.

"Okay," Officer Topple said. "Thank you."

Probability that Mom was freaking? One hundred percent.

Officer Topple fixed her gaze on Rafa. "Son, what's your name?"

"He wasn't driving," I burst in. "It's my fault."

She never took her eyes off Rafa.

After a long silence, Rafa crossed his arms and muttered, "Rafael Espinoza."

Office Topple was still scribbling his name when my policeman came over and said, "Don't put anything in the computer 'til we talk to the Senator's wife."

"You mean ex-wife," said the other cop and they both snickered.

Seriously? Kids at school did that all the time, but I thought grownups weren't supposed to act like that.

"We can't ask you any questions without a parent present," Officer Topple said, "but you can tell us what happened on your own if you want."

The two cops who arrested us stood behind Officer Topple and all six eyes were on me. Even though I didn't have a good feeling about this, I figured if they knew the truth, they would finally get it that we weren't criminals.

"Okay, so my mom's been in bed with a migraine for a week," I explained. "I was trying to help out by doing the grocery shopping."

My policeman started acting all fidgety like he wanted to ask a question, but remembered it wasn't allowed.

"We were out of food and I was hungry!"

Officer Topple's eyes widened. "Is that lady from CPS still here?"

"What's CPS?" I asked.

"Child Protective Services," said Officer Topple, but I still didn't know what it meant.

"Whoa," said my policeman. "You don't want to be on the news for putting John Alexander's little girl in a foster home."

"I was helping my mom!"

"You should stop talking," said Rafa.

"And that's the other thing," I continued. "Rafa had nothing to do with it."

The cops went into a huddle and I couldn't hear anything they were saying, but I heard some commotion at the door where two younger cops escorted a man in handcuffs and forced him to sit at another desk. He looked kind of scary and I hoped they weren't planning on putting us in a jail cell with him.

I glared back at the cops in the huddle. What could they possibly be talking about? I'd explained it to them like they were six. Hello! What part of "hungry" did they not understand?

Our cops were still chatting to each other when Mom stormed in collapsing a wet umbrella. With a green scarf and no makeup, she could've had the flu, which helped my case since I'd said she was sick.

"Don't say a word," Mom said, rushing over. "I'll handle this."

"Mrs. Alexander!" Officer Topple's eyes grew big. "I didn't recognize you, but your daughter said you haven't been feelin' too good, so I reckon that's why."

Mom glared at me.

"I'll take these children home," Mom said. "Where's my car." It was more of a demand than question.

"We had to impound it, ma'am," said Officer Topple. "Don't worry, we'll get it for you right away." She snapped at Rafa's cop to go get the car.

Rafa and I peered at each other and grinned. "I think your mom is better now," Rafa whispered.

When the policeman returned with Mom's car key, he said, "Better keep this in a safe place. You know how kids are."

Mom ignored him and led us out the door. Rafa was inches behind Mom, like he couldn't get out of there fast enough.

"Tell your dad we wish him lots of luck," Officer Topple said. Before I even got out the door, I heard another cop say, "He already got lucky. Did you see his hot girlfriend?"

I don't know what all Mom heard, but in the parking lot she muttered, "This town would still love that man if he outlawed barbequed crabs."

Rafa got in the back seat. After I fastened my seatbelt in front, my hands got all sweaty. Obviously the hydroplaning, fishtailing experience had affected me more than I realized because now I had a fear of riding in the car. Mom gave us the silent treatment, which was fine since I needed to focus on breathing.

We pulled up in front of Rafa's house and the silent treatment ended two seconds after he got out of the car.

"Are you crazy?" Her teeth were clenched. "Stealing my car?"

Since it was our family car, I never thought of it as stealing. "Mom, I just—"

"Don't you say a word." She gripped the wheel and screamed, "Can't you see what you're doing to me? You're killing me!"

I wanted to shrink into a little ball and disappear. Mom had no idea how much I cared about her. Nothing was said the rest of the way home, but her last three words kept echoing in my mind. I felt a million miles away.

— 13 —

When we got to the apartment, I gathered groceries in the back seat and carried them to the kitchen where Mom waited, shaking her head like we were going to talk.

I went to my room and shut the door. I expected Mom to come in, but then I overheard her talking to Dad on the phone, so I cracked the door a bit.

"She's a teenager now," Mom yelled. "I had to pick her up at the police station!"

I wish I knew what Dad was saying.

"They went for a joy ride in my car and nearly drove into the Gulf!"

Okay, I needed equal time.

"Look, John. You better start spending less on your little floozy and more on your daughter. I can't support her on the pocket change you call child support. You ought to be ashamed!"

My stomach tightened.

"I don't have a job," she said.

I don't know what Dad talked about after that, but it must've been bad because Mom shrieked and turned off the phone.

I squeezed the door shut, stretched out on the bed and closed my eyes. Just as I tried with all my might to erase everything from my mind, Mom came in. I shot up, wild-eyed.

"How 'bout burgers and fries tonight?" She looked defeated. "Watch TV?"

"Sounds good," I said with a weak smile.

While Mom went to get burgers, I sat on the sofa and texted Rafa. My elbow knocked something off the end table, but I was too busy texting to see what it was.

Abby: u ok?

Rafa: yes ok

Rafa: u?

Abby: fabulous

I reached down and picked up an orange bottle filled with some prescription Mom probably had for her migraines. Take one every four hours for pain. Oh. My. God. Painkillers. They ought to prescribe these to kids whose parents are crazy. I popped one in my mouth and downed it with some watered down vodka. I deserved it after nearly going to jail. I mean God, those police officers have traumatized me for life. I closed my eyes and waited for the vodka to swim through my soul.

A burger, some fries and two sitcoms later, I had to ask. Even though the risk of Mom blowing up again was huge, I didn't care. The painkiller brought a smile to my face and put a fluffy cloud around me. Nothing Mom might possibly say could penetrate my feel-good cloud. I peered sideways. "So, ahem, Mom, what happened to that job you had at the appliance store?"

"Oh honey," she picked up the burger wrappers and took them to the kitchen. "I disagreed with the store manager on the first day. Apparently, you're not supposed to do that."

I don't remember anything after that.

I woke up in my bed with Mom standing over me, saying something about taking me to school.

I sent Rafa a text:

Abby: c u at school. Mom's taking me.

Rafa: ok c u

I loved Rafa, but painkillers were my new best friend. Mom seemed okay on the drive to school, but I was cautious.

"Why'd you rip up those jeans?" Mom asked.

I wasn't about to tell her my nickname was Ghetto Girl and that I had started this fashion trend. Instead I said, "It's the latest thing," which wasn't a lie.

When she pulled up to the school, a group of kids walked by with their clothes all torn up and Mom said, "I see."

Rafa waved me over at the steps of the school. "Everything good?" he asked.

"Lovely. Did you get in trouble?"

"No one in my family can know about the police thing," Rafa said. "You can't tell anyone at school or my parents could find out."

"No prob, shish kabob." That sounded lame and I'm

not sure why I said it. I think it was something Dad used to say when I was little. When I got to my locker, the custodian had painted over the black spray paint and the vandal had used red paint this time to write, *Ghetto Girl Germ* with an arrow pointing to a dot that had been circled.

Rafa and I stared at each other and shrugged. Most kids passing by gripped yellow pieces of paper and they seemed to walk as far away from me as possible. While reading a new message on his phone, Rafa got a funny look on his face.

"What?" I asked.

"You have mono?"

I grabbed his phone and read the message:

Extreme Mono Alert!!! Ghetto Girl Contagious!!!

A yellow flier lying in the hallway with a big sneaker footprint said the same thing.

I glared at the yellow sheet. "Megan," I said softly. Ouch.

Rafa dropped his head. "I can't fix this for you."

"Oh, I'm sure Mr. Bald is all over it." I didn't let Rafa see me rolling my eyes.

Everyone stayed away from me, which wasn't necessarily a bad thing, but it wasn't making me feel good about myself either. By the time I got to English class, I was used to it.

The second I walked in, the room went silent like someone had flipped a switch that cut the sound. The triple Ps plus Megan sat along the wall, hands clasped on desks, looking straight ahead, smiling. I wanted to smack them. Instead, I turned to Rafa and said, "Never hate people who are jealous of you. Respect their jealousy because they think you're better." Again the aliens had taken over my body. I had no idea where that came from. Wait, actually I did.

"Well said!" Mr. Oliver wrote it on the board. "To whom do I credit this quote?"

"John Alexander," I said. "My dad."

"Perfect." Mr. Oliver wrote Dad's name on the board.

A few kids sneered. I chalked it up to jealousy and gave it the respect it deserved.

"Today you will write a story about jealousy." Mr. Oliver bounced a tea bag in a cup. "You may begin."

At first I wanted to write about how the Organization of Mean Girls, better known as OMG, invented Ghetto Girl to glorify their meanness. But when OMG got jealous of their own creation, they destroyed her. I didn't write about that, but it made me realize Ghetto girl was only fiction, which meant the attacks on Ghetto Girl were fictitious, too. Forget Ghetto Girl. It was time to be Abby again.

I wrote my name at the top of the page. Hopefully it was true I possessed some kind of freaky magic powers and whatever I decided to write about would actually come true. I touched my pen to the paper and began writing:

Once upon a time, there lived a Princess named Abigail who spent much of her time playing with fairies in the family castle. The fairies had magic wands and made all of Abigail's wishes come true. When she wished for a basketball, the wish was granted. When she wished for a yellow mountain bike, one appeared out of nowhere. Princess Abigail loved the fairies and they loved her.

One day, the King came home and announced to the Queen he had fallen in love with a different Queen and he left the castle forever. The old Queen was jealous and the Princess was sad because they both loved the King and couldn't understand why he didn't want to live with them any longer. "I don't love you anymore," said the King. "I am in love with a more beautiful Queen."

After the King left, the old Queen didn't have enough money to buy food for herself and the Princess. She sold her most valued possessions, including her throne, but soon that money was gone, too. One day she called the King and asked for some gold coins and the King said, "No" because the prettier Queen had already spent all of his coins. Now the old Queen was mad.

Finally, the old Queen had to sell the castle. On a cold and rainy day, the old Queen and the Princess moved into a hut in a nearby village. The old Queen was so sad, she could barely get out of bed. Princess Abigail wished for a big pot of gold so she and the Queen could move back into the castle and their lives could go back to normal. But there was a problem. The fairies who granted the wishes lived in the castle.

One night, Princess Abigail sneaked out of the hut, borrowed the old Queen's horse, and rode to the castle. She found a fairy who waved her magic wand and said the wish had been granted. When Abigail returned to the hut, gold coins overflowed from the huge kettle in the fireplace. The old Queen and the Princess moved back into the castle and when the flowers bloomed in Spring, the King came home, too. He told the old Queen and the Princess he loved them very much and they all lived happily ever after.

Just before the bell rang, Mr. Oliver told us to pass our papers to the front.

"Well?" I said to Rafa.

"Well what?" Rafa handed his paper to the girl sitting in front him.

"What did you write about?"

"None of your business."

I really didn't care because he probably wrote about how the prince was jealous of some girl's dress at the ball.

"I hope you made a good wish this time," he said. "Maybe you are a curandera."

I smiled half-heartedly. My writing had sucked. A princess in a castle—I mean seriously, could that story be any more unoriginal? I could forget about winning the Teen Fantasy Writers' novel contest this year. It was official. I'd been reduced to a shallow, self-obsessed girl who constantly writes about herself in a journal because she's completely devoid of talent.

After school, I was surprised to see Mom's Mercedes parked out front. Her pills must have worn off for a few minutes.

Rafa looked up while unlocking his bike. "Tell me your wish."

"I wished for money, lots of it."

"Then you better buy a lotto ticket," he said.

Mom gave me the silent treatment all the way home and I had no idea why, but it didn't matter. If she wanted to hate me, she was going to have to get in line.

Finally, when we stepped in the apartment, Mom said, "Why did Mr. Baldwin call to ask if you had mononucleosis? You better not be having sex."

My mouth dropped but no words came out.

"Go to your room," she said.

"It was a prank!"

"You think that's funny?"

"The kids at school pulled a prank on me. They were being mean."

Mom studied my eyes like she was trying to figure out if I was lying. "I better not find out you're having sex," she said and turned away.

I went straight to my room, shut the door and curled up in a little ball. The only thing standing between me and the vodka and painkillers was Mom. At some point, she would have to pee. I waited patiently, like a lioness waiting for her prey.

Later that night, I arrived in the pain-free zone. While I was deleting my membership on *friendworld*, Mom opened the door, but didn't come in.

From the hallway she said, "I just spoke with your father."

I was surprised at how unexcited I was about that.

"You're going to Mexico for Thanksgiving."

That got my attention.

"You leave Sunday," she said, "for the whole week."

Nothing came out of my mouth, even though I had a

million questions. Mom waited a few more seconds for me to speak, then closed the door.

I picked up the phone and called Rafa.

"I get to see my dad," I said the second he answered.

"Ah, that is good. When?"

"Sunday. For a whole week."

"Don't forget to buy a lotto ticket," he said. "You will win. I know this."

"I have to get a dollar first—I'll get some quarters out of Mom's car."

"My brother says you cannot buy the ticket because you are not eighteen."

"Did you ask if he'll buy it for me?"

"Yes," Rafa replied. "He will do it."

I turned off the light and got under the covers. Tomorrow was Friday. I'd give Rafa four quarters for the lottery ticket, win millions of dollars on Saturday, and on Sunday, I'd finally be with Dad. Just like the hurricane story, the new story I wrote in Mr. Oliver's class would come true. I squeezed my eyes and made the wish.

— 14 —

The earth below moved farther away as the plane climbed toward the clouds and that was fine with me considering I hadn't won the lottery. Finding out my magic powers weren't real was a huge let down, but in two hours I'd get to see Dad and I'd be his baby girl again.

A stewardess served sodas to the people in the seats up ahead and then asked the nun sitting next to me if she wanted anything to drink.

"Orange juice?" the nun replied, but made it sound like a question.

"And you?" asked the stewardess, looking at me.

"Same."

She looked young for a nun. The nuns in Galveston were old and wore regular clothes, but the one sitting next to me wore a black habit and wasn't much older than a teenager. Maybe nuns went to Galveston to retire and that's why they were old and didn't wear habits.

The nun took a sip of orange juice and asked, "Who do you see in Mexico?"

By her accent, I guessed she was more fluent in Spanish. "My dad." I gulped down some juice. "You visiting someone?"

"Family." She was beaming, probably because her parents were still married, if nuns had parents. "I am with the Sisters of Perpetual Adoration."

I guess she thought I was being friendly when a huge grin widened my face, but I was really thinking about how Megan and I used to call the triple Ps the Sisters of Perpetual Pandemonium. I clenched the glass of juice on the wobbly fold-down tray. Megan, the traitor.

"What is your name?" she asked slowly.

"Abby," I replied without looking up.

"I am Sister Angélica Constantina." She waited a moment and then asked, "Where is your mother?"

"Back in Galveston." I sighed. "They're divorced."

Sister Angélica Constantina crossed herself and then closed her eyes for a long time. I didn't know if she was praying or going to sleep, but the conversation was definitely over, which was perfectly fine with me. I turned back toward the window to stare at white puffy clouds below and wondered if that's where people lived after they died. If so, they were all invisible, except probably not to each other. Maybe divorced families got back together in heaven. Maybe that's why Sister Angélica Constantina was praying. I missed going to Mass with Mom and Dad.

Two hours later, the plane landed on a runway. The

airport was so tiny, we had to climb down steps to the ground and walk all the way over to a building. The dry air smelled fresh and the sun warmed my face. Dad was somewhere in the building and I tried to find him through the windows, but couldn't see him just yet.

From behind, one of the stewardesses called my name and told me to wait. I completely forgot they were supposed to escort me to my other parent, which was annoying since I wanted to hurry and see Dad. I guess it was for the best though, in case he wasn't at the airport yet, but Dad wouldn't be late, not for me.

When the stewardess caught up, I showed the guard my passport and we went to the baggage carousel where everyone had to wait. My green bag came in the first group and the stewardess led me to the place where they x-rayed everything, but I still didn't see Dad.

I had to show my passport again and the stewardess gave the man a piece of paper Mom had filled out at the airport in Houston. In all the other airports around the world, I didn't remember going through all this. Maybe I wasn't paying attention because back then I was a child and my parents took care of everything.

With my bag in tow, I rounded a corner where I saw a crowd of people gathered at the end of a walkway. I scanned the crowd for Dad and when we got closer, I heard his big Texas voice say, "There's my sugar dumpling!"

Dad looked thinner and more tanned and at first I wasn't sure it was him until he scooped me up in a big hug and said, "God I missed you, baby."

I could've stayed right there the whole week.

"I need some identification, Sir," the stewardess said.

"Yes ma'am." Dad put me down and reached for his wallet.

After studying Dad's driver's license the stewardess said, "You're that senator."

Dad pressed a finger over his lips and winked at the stewardess. "We'll keep this our little secret."

Mom had said Dad was hiding in Mexico like a criminal on the lam and that's probably why he didn't want the stewardess to tell anyone. The stewardess giggled and that's when I spotted the Kat woman.

Like Sister Angélica Constantina on the plane, the Kat woman was young, but no one would ever mistake her for a nun. Her tight leather jacket with six-inch fringe that she wore like a shirt may have been black as a habit, but I was pretty sure nuns wore undergarments. A denim miniskirt rode low on her hips, wrapped with a wide silver belt that had a huge brass imprint of the Virgin of Guadalupe on the front. Through two circles of heavy eyeliner, fierce green eyes zeroed in on mine like lasers. I jumped when she came at me.

"I'm Kat." The hug felt awkward and she smelled like cigarettes.

I smiled weakly at Dad, who picked up my bag and grinned as if things had never been more perfect.

The three of us walked to a parking lot where I immediately spotted Dad's black SUV. Dad wore blue jeans and a gauzy white shirt with sandals, a straw hat and brown sunglasses, which seemed a lot more normal for an

American tourist than what Kat wore. I looked plain in blue jeans and sneakers, but Mom would've definitely stamped Kat's costume: Not appropriate for John Alexander's public image. Seriously, black leather shoe laces snaked all the way up to the top of her legs.

We got on a road in the middle of nowhere and I wanted to ask Dad where we were going, but he was busy playing with Kat in the front seat. Kat wanted a CD that Dad had in his hand and he wouldn't give it to her, but eventually she tickled him and he handed it over. Staring intently at the back of his head, I wondered if he even knew I was there because it seemed like he didn't want to do the Dad thing anymore. I settled down in the seat and watched rocks and tumbleweeds go by. He had to let me visit because I was his daughter, but I didn't get the feeling he really wanted me.

Nearly an hour later Dad said, "Look up ahead, baby. There it is." I assumed he was talking to me since he had raised his voice, but I wasn't sure until he turned his head to see if I was looking. I leaned in toward Dad and the most radiant city I'd ever seen appeared.

"That's San Miguel, baby girl."

Nestled between green treetops were orange and pink square buildings of various shapes and sizes that spread for miles over rolling hills. In the center of town, a cluster of enormous cathedrals rose high in the air, as if by their majesty couldn't be real. If fairies had their own city, it was San Miguel because it looked like something a fairy would create with the wave of a magic wand. We made our way down a winding road toward the cluster of cathedrals until we reached the inner city with its narrow cobblestone roads that made the car vibrate.

"You holding up back there?" Dad asked.

"Feels like that massage chair from your apartment." I smiled, wanting Kat to know Dad and I went way back, like almost fifteen years.

But what Kat did next was totally disgusting. She practically climbed in his lap, ran her finger over his ear and said, "We had some great nights in that chair, didn't we, honey?"

I nearly gagged.

Dad grinned and said, "Baby, you better let me drive or we're not gonna make it home."

I wanted Dad to turn around and take me back to the plane. When Mom first told me about our apology vacations, I didn't totally get it, maybe because I remembered our vacations as happy times. But this was Mom's reality—the R-rated movie now playing in the front seat—and today it was my reality too. Even if this whole Kat thing blew over and Dad wanted to take us on another apology vacation, things would never be the same.

We climbed to the top of a hill where a wrought iron gate opened in front of a magnificent stucco hotel with a huge fountain in front. We drove all the way around and parked in back near a tiny guest house that was probably Dad and Kat's apartment. It looked smaller than our apartment in Galveston and I wasn't sure I could take sharing that small of a place with the Kat woman for an entire week. As long as I had my own room with a door that shut, I'd probably be okay. But when Dad carried my bag to the back entrance of the hotel, I had to say something.

"We're not all sharing one room are we?"

"No, baby cakes," Dad flashed a big smile. "You get your own room."

When Kat hurried by me to catch up with Dad, I shivered. In real life, she was creepier than on TV. We entered through a kitchen with blue and green tiles and copper pots hanging above. Two women washing tomatoes in the sink turned and smiled. The older one said, "Ah, bueno, señor." She had to be the teenager's mother because they looked exactly alike.

"Buenos tardes, Berta," Dad said with his Texas accent. "Esta es mi hija, Abigail."

"Abby," I said, letting her hug me. A little dog sprang in the air and licked my hand.

Berta kept grinning. "Mi hija, Gabriela."

"Gabby," the daughter said and kissed both my cheeks. "I speak English."

"Good." I sounded totally relieved.

"Abby and Gabby. How 'bout that," Dad said, grinning. He reached down and rubbed the dog's ears. "And this is Fandango."

Kat moved straight through the kitchen without saying hi to anyone and waited in the next room. Fandango squealed and hid behind Berta. Dad followed Kat and I followed Dad.

"Nice meeting you," I said to Gabby on the way out.

"You too," she said.

The next room wasn't really a room; it was more like an open area with a grand spiraling staircase in the middle. In a dramatic movement, Kat spread her arms and in a super fake voice said, "Welcome Abby. Mi casa es su casa."

I turned to Dad and said, "I'm really tired. Can I just have my room key?"

Dad cocked his head as if I had spoken a language he didn't understand. "This isn't a hotel, baby. This is my house."

Kat huffed at him.

Pulling Kat close, Dad said proudly, "Our house."

"Mom said you were broke."

"Well," Dad said slowly like he was trying to think of what to say next, and then his face lit up. "This is Mexico. You can live like a king on practically nothing."

I'm sure I looked perplexed because I truly was. Finally, I said, "You should tell Mom. She might want to move here."

Kat's mouth dropped.

Dad marched up the steps with my suitcase. "Let's get you settled and I'll give you the grand tour."

I trailed behind Dad, hoping Kat wasn't coming too. When I turned around to check, she was still downstairs lighting a cigarette. I picked up my pace.

At the end of a long hallway, Dad pushed open a door and said, "Hope you like it."

The minute I stepped in, the warmth of the orangey washed walls and hand carved wooden furniture melted my tension. Dad plopped my bag on the lime green colored bedspread that matched all the pillows around the room. It was the kind of room that could cheer up the most depressed person in the world, even Mom.

Dad pulled an empty drawer from the chest. "For you."

I had a million questions, but couldn't put one together.

Next to the bed, Dad opened a window surrounded by vines of yellow flowers. "If you need anything, tell Berta," he said and squeezed me tight. "I missed my little girl."

"Thanks, Dad."

"Dinner's at seven." He winked on the way out.

In the distance, a light pink bell tower glowed in the sun against the clear blue sky. Below, Gabby came out of the guest house with a heavy bucket and handed it to a man, who tossed the whole bucket of sudsy water on Dad's SUV and got busy scrubbing it down while Fandango, who looked part Chihuahua, bounced around, doing spins in the air. I wondered what Mom was doing today. If she knew we could live like a king on practically nothing, or really a queen and a princess, she would want to come.

It was weird having to wait until seven o'clock to go downstairs, like I had to have an appointment to hang out with Dad at home. Since Mom turned the data off on my phone, I called to let her know I'd made it, that the plane didn't blow up or anything, but there was no answer.

I pulled out my laptop and sent her a quick email. I told her about Dad's mansion and that we should think about moving here, too. I even shot a few photos of my room and the view outside, and then downloaded them to the computer so Mom could see what I was talking about.

Finally, I sent Rafa an instant message:

Abby: Dad's insanely rich, but the kat woman's a freak.

Rafa: pics! send pics!!!

Abby: hang on

I emailed the same photos of my room that I'd sent to Mom and waited.

Rafa: not the house! the kat!!!

Abby: OK!!! OMG dad has maids!!

Rafa: all gringos have maids. I want to see the freak.

Abby: you're the freak

Rafa: you wish

Wandering through the maze of rooms, I heard dishes clinking and found Gabby placing colorful plates on a long wooden table with a black wrought iron chandelier above.

"Need some help?"

"No," Gabby said. "Please, have a seat."

Gabby set five places at one end of the table. I pointed at two and said, "Let's sit here."

She looked puzzled. "This is not for me."

"Um, okay then. Who?"

Gabby shrugged and left the room. When I heard Kat giggling, I figured Dad was somewhere nearby.

"I love our afternoon naps," Kat said, clinging to Dad like a monkey.

I wanted to point out I was standing right there and could hear them, but I think they already knew that. From another room, a bell chimed and Dad said, "They're here."

Kat hurried to get the door.

"Kat invited some friends over for supper." Dad flashed what Mom used to call his photogenic smile.

The man and lady were older than Kat, but younger than Dad. Berta and Gabby appeared with four glasses of wine and passed them out to the grownups, who stood around laughing until Dad finally remembered I was there.

"This is my daughter, Abigail." With his hand on my back, he guided me into their circle. The couple nodded at me and then Dad raised his glass and told everyone to have a seat.

Dad went to the head of the table and Kat slid in a chair next to him. The couple sat on the other side and I had to take the only seat left, which was next to Kat. I wanted to ask Kat if I could sit next to Dad since I hadn't seen him in three months, but she turned her back to me so it didn't feel like a good time to ask. That's when Gabby came in and placed a plate of bacon wrapped shrimp in the middle of the table. I gave Dad a look of surprise and he winked at me while Berta put smaller plates on top of everyone's bigger plates.

"Shrimp Brochette," I said to Dad with a huge grin.

"I knew it was your favorite, baby."

Kat snapped her napkin open and said, "Broch-ay, not brochette," then turned to me and in a you're-so-stupid voice said, "It's French."

Dad picked up a shrimp by its toothpick and said,

"Abby said it right." He peered at me and added, "I had to teach Berta how to make these."

"It's broch-ay," Kat insisted. "You don't pronounce the t."

"Yes you do, babe," Dad argued in his usual sweet way.

The man across the table had already eaten one and said, "Whatever it is, it's delicious." He drank some wine and asked, "What's in these things?"

While Dad explained how to stuff the shrimp with cream cheese and jalapeno, "then wrap 'em in bacon and fry 'em up," the lady next to him was doing something on her phone. "It's a Texas tradition," Dad said proudly.

"According to all the dictionaries," the lady reading her phone said, "you do pronounce the ts."

Kat tensed up. If she had been a real cat, I'm pretty sure she would've swiped a claw at someone. I felt bad for having started the whole argument, so to change the subject I asked Dad, "How come you're drinking wine? Mom said you were in AA"

Dad's face turned red and he whispered to the couple, "messy divorce," as if that explained everything.

"AA's nothing to be ashamed of," said the lady.

The man cleared his throat as if he didn't know what to add.

"John doesn't have a drinking problem anymore," Kat said. "I got bored drinking wine all by myself, night after night. I mean, how romantic is that?" She placed her hand on Dad's. "I taught him the art of moderation."

"Moderation with drinking." Dad raised his glass.

"Not anything else."

Everyone laughed but I didn't get it. I decided it was probably a good idea to keep my mouth shut through the rest of dinner. Even when Berta and Gabby brought out the chicken with rice and Kat made a big deal out of how Dad had requested it just for her, I didn't say a word. I just wanted the night to be over.

I Skyped Rafa to give him a rundown of my rapidly deteriorating dinner conversation. He loved the part about the shrimp brochettes but was frustrated that I hadn't taken any photos.

"It's not like I could eat dinner with my phone up in the air."

"Tomorrow," he said. "I need to see her."

"Okay! Goodnight!"

"Sleep with the angels, chica."

— 15 —

I don't know if it was the fresh air or what, but when I woke up, it felt like I had come out of a coma. I couldn't remember ever sleeping that hard and at breakfast, Dad said it was the altitude. Kat must have still been asleep because Dad and I sat alone at the kitchen table in our pajamas and it felt like home.

When Berta came over and refilled Dad's coffee cup, I said, "I'll have some," and then remembered Berta didn't speak English.

Dad gazed at me. "When did you grow up?"

"Like, a long time ago?" I rolled my eyes.

In Spanish, Dad went on and on to Berta about something and then said, "Berta's makin' us some mango and papaya crepes. You're gonna love it."

Across the kitchen, Berta pulled down a copper skillet and beamed until Kat paraded in and the smile on Berta's face dropped.

"Mornin' sugar," Dad said. "We're just fixin' to eat."

Kat was already dressed—at least parts of her were covered—in all black, heavy eyeliner and red lipstick.

"Why aren't you dressed?" she asked Dad.

I must've been invisible because she didn't even look at me.

"Berta," Kat yelled as if Berta were deaf. "Stop! No breakfast!" Kat turned back to Dad and planted her hands on her hips. "You said we were eating out."

Dad stood up. "Well, uh, lunch. But we can eat out for breakfast too."

As much as I wanted those papaya and mango crepes, I got up and headed to my room and on the way up the long, spiraling staircase, I wondered how Kat became the boss of us.

At the restaurant, Dad said to the waiter, "Tres café por favor," and I beamed because without asking, he had ordered coffee for me too. I scanned the part of the menu written in English for those crepes.

While Dad and the Kat creature ordered scrambled eggs, I found crepes on the menu, but they were filled with cream, not fruit. Dad saw my finger underneath the word crepes and said something in Spanish to the waiter. The waiter smiled, took our menus and left.

Dad leaned toward me. "Mango and papaya crepes weren't on the menu, baby doll. They're making 'em special just for you."

A woman sashayed in front of our table wearing a gauzy dress and Dad stretched his neck to finish watching her go by. I swore she was a model in a magazine I'd seen somewhere before. The Kat wrapped her hands around Dad's face and moved it to hers. "Aren't you glad I'm not high maintenance when it comes to ordering breakfast?" She kissed him lightly on the lips.

Dad nodded, looking all dazed.

My stomach churned. I tried to remember if I had said something to make her mad. It started at dinner last night when she didn't know how to pronounce brochette, but it was other people who disagreed with her, not me. The waiter set three glasses of orange juice on the white linen table cloth. Dad raised his glass and waited for us to do the same.

"Here's to my two favorite ladies in the world," he said.

The Kat's shoulders sank and she put the glass down without taking a sip, which only left Dad's and my glasses to clink. The Yellow Rose of Texas started playing and Dad reached for his phone.

"Mom has that ringtone!" I said.

Dad started talking to someone and got up from the table. The whole time he was gone, the Kat fidgeted in her chair and I was afraid to say anything. It was a good thing I still had the orange juice in my hand because drinking it gave me something to do; only I wasn't expecting it to taste that yummy—I'm talking mouth watering sweetness. This was some serious orange juice. I emptied the glass and the second it hit the table, the waiter appeared and took it away.

"We need to change that ringtone," the Kat said when

Dad got back to the table.

"Baby, it's my signature song."

The Kat gave Dad a cold stare. "It makes you old."

Fortunately the waiter brought our food before Dad handed the phone over to the ringtone police and next to my plate, another full glass of that awesome orange juice appeared. I was so absorbed in the sweetness of the fully ripened papayas and mangos that I tuned out the Kat because feeling good and listening to the Kat were two things that didn't go together. When I took the last bite, Dad said, "Wait 'til you try Berta's."

I couldn't imagine anything tasting better.

The Kat spent ten minutes in the bathroom after Dad paid the check, but she didn't look any better when she came out. Heading downhill, we walked in a single file line on a skinny sidewalk with Dad leading the way. I was last. When we arrived in the town square, the cathedral I first saw from far away stood in front of me and I gasped. Pink spires reached through the sky as if they dwelled in heaven.

"Let's go to Mass," I said, really just wanting to see the artwork inside.

The Kat rolled her eyes.

Dad pasted on a strained smile and said, "Not today, honey."

I peered at the Kat. Dad sure liked 'em bossy.

We weaved our way through the mango and papaya colored shops draped with pink bougainvillea from the flat rooftops above. The Kat bought everything she liked and Dad paid for it with pesos. When Dad's hands were full of shopping bags, I became the second bag carrier.

In one shop, the Kat bought a replica of an old Spanish sword. I told Dad it reminded me of the one we bought in Spain when I was little and Dad explained that the Spanish swords had made their way here when Spain ruled Mexico. "You still have it?" Dad asked.

I made a sympathetic face. "Mom sold it."

"You should've never let your ex-wife sell all your good stuff," the Kat said to Dad. "Why'd you let her take advantage of you like that?"

Dad shrugged and smiled like a little boy. I wanted to scream. First of all, our family stuff was none of Kat's business. And second, it was Mom's stuff anyway because Dad had to make up for cheating on her. And third of all, if the Kat creature wasn't blowing all Dad's money, Mom and I wouldn't have had to sell everything in the first place. I didn't know who was pissing me off more, Dad or the Kat, but I had to physically clamp my hand on my mouth to not scream.

I was still angry when Dad wanted me to pick out a T-shirt and that's why I picked one with a man who had bullets strapped across his chest like a big X.

"Ah, Pancho Villa," Dad said chuckling while the Kat shook her head in total disapproval. "A revolutionary who fought for the poor about a hundred years ago," he added.

"Perfect," I said, since Mom and I were poor.

"He was a bandit," the Kat said with a look of disgust.

"But he stole from the rich to give to the poor," Dad argued. "A Mexican Robin Hood."

The fact that Kat hated the shirt made me like it more. I wore it to the dinner table that night, hoping the Kat would have more of her friends over to see it, but it was just the three of us at that long table in the dark dining room.

"Hey baby," Dad said, holding a glass of wine. I had to remember that ninety nine percent of the time when he said "baby," he was talking to the Kat. It was hard to adjust because when he used to say "baby," he was talking to me one hundred percent of the time. I checked to see where he was looking and this time he was talking to me. "Since you like Mexican history, I'm gonna take you to the place where it all began."

"Where's that?" The Kat sounded annoyed.

Dad finished off the wine and his cheeks turned all rosy. "Delores Hidalgo, birthplace of Mexican Independence."

"Fine," said the Kat. "I need more Talavera anyway."

"What's Talavera?" I asked.

The Kat didn't answer. Finally, Dad explained it was the colorful plates and bowls we were using. "We just bought this whole set," Dad told the Kat.

"I need more." She squinted and held up a bread plate. "I'm tired of this pattern."

Dad smiled. "Looks like we're goin' to Delores."

I was ready to go home.

— 16 —

When we got to Delores the next morning, it didn't look anything like San Miguel. Delores was plain; I mean it had some cool old buildings and stuff, but the dull colors and flat concrete streets were boring, or maybe it was just me not wanting to be anywhere with the Kat. I wore my Pancho Villa T-shirt again just to annoy her.

The Kat insisted we go to the Talavera factory first, since she was obviously the most important person in the car. Okay, she didn't actually say that, but did she need to? In the factory, poor Dad had to translate the Kat's rude remarks to the lady who was showing us the dishes. I'm pretty sure he changed everything she said because Dad could never treat anyone that way. But then again, I never thought he'd treat me like I came second to some floozy, as Mom had called her.

Anyway, two thousand pesos later, the men at the factory loaded the Kat's new dinner set for twelve in the back of the SUV. Dad said it sounded like a lot, but two thousand pesos was really only two hundred dollars. I didn't say it out loud, but Mom and I could've bought groceries for a whole month with that much money.

With the Kat creature climbing all over him, Dad drove to the Delores Hidalgo town square and found a parking place next to a huge church.

"Come on, baby," Dad said nudging her away. "I'm tryin' to park."

The Kat giggled and gathered her purse.

My stomach felt weird and I may have said in my out-loud voice, "Could you be any tackier?"

We climbed some steps to an open area as big as four basketball courts, except it was made of flat stones. At one end, an orangey, ancient-looking cathedral had two square bell towers that stretched three stories above the clock tower in the middle.

"It all started here." Dad stretched his arms wide.

I felt myself grinning because Dad was getting ready to launch into one of his good stories.

"More than two hundred years ago, from the pulpit in that church, Father Hidalgo told the people of Mexico to revolt against the Spanish and take back their country. Within minutes, six hundred men gathered on this open square with machetes. That's how the Mexican War of Independence got started."

"Did they win?" I asked.

"They sure did," said Dad. "Every year on September sixteenth, people come here to celebrate Mexican Independence Day."

"Like our Fourth of July?"

"Yup, exactly like ours."

"So Pancho Villa was here?" I stretched out my T-shirt even though I was looking at Pancho Villa upside down.

"No, baby. He led another revolution about a hundred years later. That was against a corrupt president."

I thought about the Spanish sword the Kat bought and how insulted Rafa had felt when Mom said Mexico was represented under Spain in our décor de United Nations. I looked up at Dad and said, "I want a machete."

"Oh God," the Kat moaned. "I need a margarita."

"Well baby girl," Dad said to me, "I'd buy you one, but I don't think they'd let you take it back on the plane." He put one arm around the Kat, the other arm around me, and started walking. "How 'bout an ice cream cone instead."

For once, I agreed with the Kat. I needed a drink.

On the way to the park, we walked past a giant statue of Father Hidalgo raising a banner of the Virgin of Guadalupe and calling the people to revolt. It seemed right that he would carry that banner, but when the Kat wore that belt with the Virgin of Guadalupe at the airport, she looked like a weirdo. When we got to the ice cream cart, Dad ordered helado con besos de ángel, meaning ice cream with angel kisses and I had helado de pétalos de rosa, or ice cream with rose petals. The Kat ordered tequila ice cream.

"Does it really have tequila?" I asked, realizing I'd made the wrong decision. It was the first time I'd spoken to the Kat directly, but she didn't answer.

Finally Dad said, "It probably does, sugar. This is Mexico."

I could trip on a crack in the sidewalk and drop my ice cream cone, but I seriously doubted Dad was going to let me buy the one with tequila, so I just kept walking.

We sat on a bench under a tree licking our ice cream cones and watching children play with toys their fathers were selling along the sidewalk. I felt like Dad's kid again, listening to him tell stories about the history of Mexico. He always made every place we visited more fascinating and I missed that—I missed him. I identified with the story he told today because Mom and I were like the poor people and Kat was the foreign ruler who had made us poor. Dad was definitely on the wrong side—he needed to get some guts and overthrow the nasty ruler.

That night, Dad and the Kat went out to meet some friends after dinner and I Skyped Rafa, even though I knew he would be upset I still didn't have a photo of the Kat.

"It's not like we're a big happy family smiling for the camera," I said.

"Try to sneak one when she' not looking," he urged.

"Okay, okay."

When I woke up in the morning, Dad's SUV was still gone. I didn't know if they had come home already and gone back out or if something bad had happened, like they got drunk and had a wreck. I asked Berta while she was cooking migas, but she couldn't understand me.

I waited at the breakfast table for about an hour with Fandango at my feet and then went back to my room to shower. I figured by the time I finished with that, Dad would be home. After towel-drying my hair, I ran to the window and the empty driveway gave me a sinking feeling. I wondered if Dad even wanted me here.

I nearly cried and decided the best way to avoid that was to get some fresh air in the garden. When I scurried downstairs and through the kitchen, Berta and the man who had washed Dad's car were drinking coffee and talking about something in Spanish. Rather than interrupt, I went on outside where sunshine warmed the top of my head and a hummingbird darted in and out of an orangey flowering vine.

On a chair at the corner of the patio, I sat and wondered if it was my fault Dad didn't want to come home. Fandango jumped on my lap and I nuzzled him close. It was pretty obvious the Kat and I didn't like each other. Maybe Dad thought I was cold and irritable like Mom. That made sense because he left Mom and never came back, but can you divorce your kid too? I waited in the chair for a long time and let Fandango lick tears off my face as quickly as each one appeared.

When I got tired of that, which didn't take long, I went upstairs and called Mom to make sure she was okay. Mainly, I needed to know she was still there, but again, no answer. Not even a reply to the email I sent on the first day. Maybe she didn't want me anymore either.

Speaking of Mom, I'd stashed a couple of her painkillers in the pocket of a pair of jeans. I flung off the covers and dug through a drawer, checking all the pockets until I felt the pebble-like pills deep in the front pocket of my favorite jeans. I swallowed one. With the afternoon sun streaming in, Fandango and I burrowed under the lime green covers and drifted away. La-La Land wasn't such a bad place after all.

— 17 —

Hours later, I sat at the kitchen table staring out the window when a small pickup truck pulled in the driveway. Gabby got out and the man who worked outside got out too.

"Heard you need a translator," Gabby said.

"That your dad?" I asked.

Gabby nodded.

"Do your parents know where my par—." Something caught in my throat and the coughing attack that followed was clearly over the repulsion of almost calling the Kat my parent. "I mean my dad, do they know where my dad is?"

Gabby and her mom spoke in Spanish for a minute and finally Gabby said, "They didn't come home last night and she doesn't know where they went."

"I hope nothing bad happened," I said softly.

Berta said something in Spanish. "She says they do this

all the time. Sometimes they disappear for days and don't tell her."

Dad wouldn't do that when I only had three days left. Besides, tomorrow's Thanksgiving.

Gabby tossed her backpack on a chair. "Hey, let's go into town."

I crossed my arms. "I don't need a babysitter."

"I know." She slung her arm over my shoulder. "But you do need a Spanish speaking friend."

We headed into town on foot, hiking through narrow cobblestone streets, and I tried not to think about what the Kat creature had said about driving on cobblestones. It's funny how when you try not to think about something, it's all you can think about, and the thought of Dad having weird sex with the Kat in a massage chair was truly disgusting. Mom didn't need to worry about me having sex and getting mono because after being around Dad and the Kat, anything sexual made me queasy.

"Hungry?" Gabby asked.

"Not really."

"Mamá said you didn't eat today, only breakfast. Tía, my aunt, has a restaurant around the corner. We can eat for free."

Why was Gabby being so nice to me? Guess I wasn't used to it.

The small, dark restaurant had only six wooden tables and five were empty. "I always sit over there," Gabby said, pointing to a table in the corner.

A woman who clearly looked like Berta's sister came out and patted Gabby's cheeks. They spoke in Spanish and when they got to the part where Gabby introduced me, I tried to muster up some of the manners Queen Doreen had drilled in my head, but a weak smile was all I could manage.

"She's making something special for us." Gabby put napkins and silverware on the table and lit a candle. "Tell me about your high school in America."

"Not much to tell." I said it like the thought of school left a bad taste in my mouth. It was rude, I know, but I couldn't exactly say, I love my school. Everyone calls me Ghetto Girl and thinks I have mono.

Gabby looked perplexed.

"I've only been there three months," I said.

"You're fourteen?" She asked.

I nodded. "You?"

"Sixteen."

"What's your school like?" If I didn't hear from Mom soon, it was entirely possible I could get shipped to Mexico and I needed to know.

"It's a dual language school so everything's taught in Spanish and English."

"No wonder your English is so good."

Gabby leaned back. "Thanks!" Her aunt brought two big bowls of stew and placed them on the table, and then wrung her hands and grinned at Gabby. "She wants us to taste it," Gabby said.

With a big spoon, I scooped up bits of tomato, corn and cabbage, and nudged on a piece of beef. I chewed and nodded in praise, but it wasn't until the second spoonful when I tasted the broth by itself that I realized how good it was. That broth had some zing.

"This is what real Mexicans eat." Gabby winked.

"Speaking of real Mexicans," I said. "Do you know any curanderas?"

Gabby's face lit up. "You know about curanderas?"

"My best friend back home thinks I am one. I figured the only person who could tell me is another curandera."

"Why does she think you're a curandera?" Gabby asked.

"My best friend's a boy," I said. "Rafa,"

"Oh," Gabby grinned. "You have a boyfriend."

"Um, like no. He's probably gay."

"Okay," Gabby said slowly. "Why does Rafa think you're a curandera?"

"I wrote a story about a hurricane destroying our Island and a few weeks later it happened."

"But hurricanes happen all the time," Gabby said.

"Not in Galveston."

With narrowed brows, Gabby slurped a big spoonful of soup, then another. Finally, she said, "I know a curandera."

My smile widened until I remembered I had no money. "How much does she charge?"

"Twenty pesos," Gabby replied. "Do you have it?"

I shook my head and calculated that twenty pesos was only two dollars. "I can pay you back when my dad gets home."

Gabby winked. "I need to say goodbye to my aunt." And she disappeared in the kitchen.

My feet wobbled on the cobblestones because I was

thinking so hard about what to ask the curandera that I wasn't paying attention to my step. The orangey sun set aglow colorful buildings with rich, warm hues that filled me with wonder and a new hope that something good was about to happen.

When we got to the bottom of a hill away from the center of town, the scenery totally changed: fancy tourist filled restaurants and art galleries became Mexican mom and pop shops with skinny dogs panting in the doorways and produce stands out front. Though they were poor, everyone seemed happy selling goods to one another.

The sky darkened as we climbed a hill past makeshift houses wrapped in sagging laundry lines with white sheets billowing in the breeze. Everything seemed gray and white except one thin line of red in the sky. We picked up our pace even though the moms and dads with small children passing by were in no hurry to get anywhere.

"Turn here." Gabby pointed down a narrow street with no people, but the sound of barking dogs filled the sky. Above us, dogs lined rooftops on both sides of the street and they woofed and howled as we passed by. We walked until the street led to a dead end and in the dim light, we faced a big, black door. Gabby drew in a deep breath and knocked, which made the chorus of barking come to a halt and the only sound was my heart beating like a Native American drum.

A clicking sound came from inside the door just before it opened a crack. Glowing candlelight shone through, which seemed perfectly normal considering she was a curandera, but I didn't expect to hear the loud, shrill whistle that came from somewhere inside. It sounded like a man whistling at a woman on the street! I peeled my eyes to Gabby, who swallowed hard.

The door opened a bit more and a wrinkly old woman with long hair and three teeth appeared. Gabby said something in Spanish and handed the woman two gold coins. The woman waved us in. Just inside the door, that same shrill whistle freaked me out and that's when I saw the parrot perched on the woman's shoulder.

"Upstairs," Gabby whispered.

Through glowing candlelight and smoky incense, my thoughts slowed to a relaxing pace. I followed the curandera up brown tiled stairs with Gabby close behind. The curandera led us to a small red room with dozens of candles illuminating walls covered with angels and saints, except for one bare red wall that held a flaming sacred heart on a single wooden cross. Gabby and I peered at each other and waited for the curandera to tell us what to do.

In the middle of the room sat an old wooden table with a purple cloth and four wooden chairs. Three chairs were plain and one, light blue. With a crooked finger, the curandera lifted the parrot off her shoulder and moved it to the back of one of the plain wooden chairs. She pulled out the blue chair and signaled me to sit, and then sat across from me and folded my hands in hers. Gabby took a seat across from the parrot while the curandera closed her eyes and spoke in little whispers.

"She's praying," Gabby said softly.

I didn't say anything because talking could interrupt

her prayer and I didn't want to take any risks. Finally, the curandera said something.

"She wants to know why your heart is broken," Gabby said.

I had to think about it. I mean, this was complicated. "Tell her my parents hate each other and they don't exactly care about me anymore."

Gabby's eyes welled up. She turned to the curandera and repeated it quietly in Spanish. The curandera squished her eyes together and prayed harder. I started having doubts about this whole thing.

"Ask her if I have magical powers," I said. "Tell her about the hurricane."

Gabby talked in Spanish for a long time and I wasn't sure what all she said. Pretty soon they were having a two-way conversation. "She wants to know if this ever happened before," Gabby said.

I shook my head. "After the hurricane, I wished for lots of money for my Mom, but it didn't come true."

After Gabby translated, the curandera went to the wall and brought back a candle that said St. Chamuel.

"Who's St. Chamuel?" I asked.

"The archangel of love and tolerance," Gabby replied. "She's asking St. Chamuel to watch over you."

"Isn't there a saint for money?" I asked.

Gabby spoke back and forth with the curandera and finally said, "The money will be there when you return, but she is worried about your heart."

"So I'm a curandera?"

"She says you have powers, but they are worth nothing

without your heart."

I had no idea what they were talking about with the heart thing. My heart was fine. "Will we win the lottery?" I asked.

"She says the money will come from someplace unexpected."

"What about Mom and Dad. Are they getting back together?"

After all the translating, Gabby said, "No."

In the center of my palm, the curandera pushed a hand carved wooden heart no bigger than a pebble. On the way downstairs, I stuffed it in my pocket and giggled when the parrot shrieked a street whistle again.

With her eyes on me, the curandera unlatched the door. The worried look on her face didn't freak me out because old people always seemed worried about something. Besides, I was ecstatic knowing money was coming, hopefully enough to move out of the ghetto.

Gabby and I stepped out on the street and the moment the curandera shut the door, the barking roof dogs picked up right where they left off. It was freaky how the dogs stopped barking whenever she held the door open, but dogs had a sixth sense. They knew she was a curandera.

A full moon cast just enough light to see; otherwise everything would have been pure black because there were no streetlights anywhere. Gabby kept a quick pace and soon the chorus of barking roof dogs faded in the background.

Gabby marched so fast, I had to hurry to keep up.

"She was awesome," I said, "the curandera."

Gabby grinned, turning left out of the little neighborhood and up the sidewalk where all the mom and pop shops had closed. "They say she is the best curandera in San Miguel de Allende."

When we got back to the touristy part of town, the noise level rose and streetlights shone on bars with drunk Americans stumbling through the streets.

"This way," Gabby said. We turned onto a street that looked familiar and a few stores down we passed the shop where I got the Pancho Villa T-shirt. After that was a crowded bar and when Dad's big Texas voice boomed from inside, I froze.

"To Wednesday!" he said, holding a shot glass in the air. Perched on his lap like a burlesque dancer, Kat tossed her head back laughing. Everyone in the bar raised shot glasses and said, "To Wednesday!"

Gabby pulled my arm.

"Wait," I said, trying to break away. "That's my dad."

Gabby pulled harder. "Don't go in."

I broke away and stared through the window at Dad. Never before had I seen him so happy, not even on TV. I mean he literally glowed with radiance. All the exciting times we'd had were nothing compared to the fun he was having without us.

Gabby pulled me up the street and I must have had one of those moments where I went into safe mode because even though I didn't remember walking the rest of the way home, I did remember lying in bed and wanting to cry. But crying was always a bad idea, so I got up and wandered through the big empty house until I found an open bottle of wine in the kitchen with about an inch left in the bottom.

Out of the kitchen window, the lights were off in the guest house, which meant Gabby and her parents were asleep. I pulled out the cork and tilted the bottle up against my lips. The first sip tasted tart and as soon as it started tasting good, the bottle was empty. I pulled another bottle out of a wine rack and rummaged around for a corkscrew. Dad had made it look easy, but it wasn't. I finally got the bloody cork out and took the bottle upstairs.

Most kids my age would find it liberating that neither of their parents wanted them. Something was wrong with me. I ransacked the jeans drawer and located another one of Mom's pills. I wanted to vanish. I placed the painkiller on my tongue and washed it down with a good swig of wine. With a pillow propped behind my head, I sat up in bed and let a river of wine wash through me. I let out a long sigh. I loved wine. Tilting the bottle up, I took another swig. In fact, I realized I loved everything… and everyone. Yes… every living thing on the planet, especially Fandango.

When I awoke, it was Thanksgiving morning and my head pounded so hard I could barely focus on Berta, who was mopping puke off the floor next to my bed.

— 18 —

I sat at the kitchen table with my head propped in my hands, waiting for the pounding to stop. The coffee made it worse. Berta used hand signals to ask if I wanted scrambled eggs, but the thought of food made me nauseous. She was filling my cup with more coffee when Dad and the Kat pulled in the driveway.

"Hey sugar dumpling!" Dad said in the doorway.

"Where've you been?" I asked in my most disapproving voice.

Dad came over and squeezed me while the Kat walked straight through the kitchen and disappeared. "I had some business to take care of," he said.

"All night?" I cringed at my own words. I'd always hated when Mom interrogated Dad that way.

"We were outta town, baby."

"Don't lie to me!" A waterfall of tears drenched my cheeks. If I had been physically able to run, I would have, but I was still sick from the wine, and so all I could do was hobble to the stairs, sobbing uncontrollably. God it was pathetic.

On the way up, Dad tried to comfort me, but I elbowed him away and just before shutting the door said, "Oh, and Happy Thanksgiving!"

It was official: I had become Mom.

Someone might as well have been pounding my head with a rock while I cried. After I was all cried out, the hot shower helped clear my sinuses a little and I was glad it was over because I had survived my first real cry.

Out the window, the green rolling hills seemed farther away and then a soft knocking on the door interrupted my empty thoughts.

"Baby, can I come in?" Dad entered timidly and sat on the corner of the bed. "I know everyone's a little over-emotional today, so I have an idea I think will please both of you."

I went back to staring out the window. Like I cared about Kat's feelings. What did she have to be upset about? That I was visiting my own dad?

"There's a little spa just down the road a piece—Aguas de Dios—it means God's natural springs or somethin' like that. We'll relax in some nice warm mineral baths, have lunch in the jardin, you know, chill."

"But—"

"What's that word you used to say all the time?" Dad rubbed his chin. "Chillaxin!"

"Dad, please. Nobody says that anymore." My forehead wrinkled. "What about Thanksgiving?"

Dad chuckled like he was laughing at me. "This is

Mexico. We don't have Thanksgiving."

I felt stupid. Seemed like we could've still had turkey with dressing, like we'd done for the past fourteen years of my life.

"I told your Mom to be sure and pack your swimsuit," he said. "You have it?"

I nodded that I did.

He gave me a quick hug and on the way out said, "We're leavin' in half an hour."

Mom always told me to think of something I was grateful for on Thanksgiving Day. I closed my eyes. I was sort of grateful Dad had come home, even though he probably would have rather been someplace else.

Dad was alone in the car listening to a message on the phone when I climbed in back. I wished he would drive off and leave the Kat behind so we could spend a day by ourselves. It was okay if the Kat wanted to be alone with him for a whole day, but apparently it wasn't okay for me to spend a day with my own dad. She had him every day, but I was only staying for five days. It pissed me off that she took away one of my days, and just when I was really getting stirred up about it, the back door opened. With a cigarette in her mouth, the Kat shoved a big beach bag on the seat next to me without even acknowledging my presence.

I held up my phone like I was trying to read something and snagged a photo. She wasn't dressed any differently today, but that cigarette hanging out of her mouth pushed hooker chic down to a whole new level and I knew Rafa would scream over that shot. When the Kat climbed in front, I studied the photo. Dad traded this for Mom? I totally didn't get it.

Good thing it only took ten minutes to get to God's Natural Springs because in that short time, the Kat had insulted enough Mexican people to trigger a new revolution. Even Dad agreed the Kat was out of line when she got mad at an old man pulling a donkey with two big milk cans strapped on its back. The Kat had leaned over to Dad's side and honked the horn because she thought the milkman was taking too long to cross the street.

"Baby," Dad said pushing the Kat back to her side of the car. "Remember we're guests in his country. Have some respect." It was the first time Dad showed any sign of irritation toward the Kat and it gave me hope this whole thing could blow over and Dad might still come home.

After Dad parked and we carried all our stuff through the gate with a sign that read, *Auga de Dios*, Dad had to go into a locker room for men, which meant I had to be alone with the Kat. Inside the women's room, people changed into bathing suits and stuffed their clothes in lockers. The Kat basically ignored me while she took off what few clothes she had on and wiggled into a hot pink bikini. All I had to do was pull off my T-shirt and shorts because I was already wearing my favorite blue and white striped one-piece swimsuit underneath.

The Kat eyed me up and down. "You wore your bathing suit under your clothes?" It was more of a putdown than a question. "You're not riding home on our leather seats in a wet bathing suit."

The hangover was making me overly sensitive and I wanted to explode. I put my sneakers in the locker and placed my clothes on top.

"First of all," I said to Kat, "when did our family car become your car?"

The Kat looked stunned.

"Second, if you wanted me to do something a certain way, all you had to do was say it." My voice shook. "My mom would've told me before we even left the house to wear my underwear and change into my bathing suit later."

I wasn't normally claustrophobic, but I sure felt that way all of a sudden, or maybe the Kat and I were like two magnets repelling each other. I rushed outside to look for Dad.

He stood under a shady tree talking to someone on the phone. By the time I got there, the Kat was running up behind me, holding out a towel. Dad got off the phone just as the Kat was saying to me, "Here's your towel, honey." Clearly this was an act. I snatched the towel and headed toward the rock pools.

While I swished my foot around to check out the water, about a dozen people relaxed in the warm pool with their eyes closed like they were praying or meditating. I was in no mood for either.

Dad must not have noticed their eyes were closed because he shouted across the pool for me to come over. When I got there, he was beaming. "Kat found this nice shady spot for us."

"Great," I said with less enthusiasm than a broken guitar string and spread my towel on the grass.

"I'm here with two good lookin' women," Dad said with a huge grin. "How lucky can a guy get?"

Ewww. Putting me in the same category as a hooker totally creeped me out. The Kat thrust her chest and arched her back until she looked like one of those women on the mud flap of a semi truck. I nearly heaved until the Kat slid her eyes to my flat chest and gave me a look of pity. My shoulders hunched and I wanted to crawl under a rock.

"What are we waitin' for, ladies?" Dad pulled the Kat up with one hand and when he reached out his other, I turned away. Again, the creepy factor.

The second we got in the water, the Kat wrapped her arms and legs around Dad and he carried her, bobbing up and down. I moved as far away as I could.

At the other end of the pool, a plump Mexican woman waded through a maze of rocks toward a huge stone dome that must have been hundreds of years old. I followed her through the maze until we reached a tunnel.

The woman waded in the tunnel, also made of stones, and even though it was dark, I followed her through waist-high warm water for at least a hundred feet. At the end of the tunnel, I entered the ancient dome.

Tiny streams of sunlight let in just enough light to see the peaceful faces of the people inside. Water dripped from the rocks above and the dome was so tranquil, I heard each drop with perfect clarity. This place was sacred. I closed my eyes and savored the moment. I didn't want to be out in the rock pools with Dad and the Kat crawling all over each other like wild animals on some nature show. I didn't want to be in the stinky ghetto apartment with Mom acting like I'm not even there. I didn't want to be at school with kids spreading rumors that I had mono. I just wanted to listen to the drips of water echo inside the dome.

In the warm water, I heard my breathing—in, out, in, out, a soft drip, in, out. But the stillness shattered when a familiar voice giggled.

"You're so bad."

I didn't have to open my eyes to know it was the Kat. Of course I did open my eyes and when I saw what they were doing, I wanted to get out of the dome fast. Apparently, I wasn't the only person who felt that way because all the other people had lined up at the only escape route: the tunnel.

Porno stuff was weird enough, but when it's one of your parents, it's beyond gross. When the last person waded out through the tunnel, I turned to Dad and screamed three words I never in a zillion years thought I would say to my favorite person on the planet.

"I hate you!"

Those three words hung in the hollow dome longer than I'd wanted. The Kat climbed off Dad and gazed at me like I was crazy. All the words I wanted to say filled my head—so many words I couldn't say any of them. Until right there in God's natural springs, all the words flew out of my mouth before I could stop them.

First I glared at the Kat. "What gives you the freakin' right to wiggle your butt around in the middle of my family like we're nothing more than a pumpkin pie you can slice up and take the biggest piece!" I had no idea if that even made sense. "And you Dad—you just stand around and let her. What's wrong with you?"

Dad started to say something, but I cut him off when my laser eyes zeroed back in on the Kat. "My mom never drank around my dad and if you cared anything about him, you wouldn't either!"

By the look in her eyes, the Kat was ready to kill, but that didn't stop me. "And my mom never makes me feel bad about being flat chested. That's so freaking weird. I'm not your competition—I'm his kid!"

That's when the Kat went into victim mode, looking all hurt and everything, and Dad obviously bought her act because he started comforting her. I trudged through the water toward the escape tunnel. If Dad was gonna take her side, I was so outta there.

Needless to say, we packed up and left.

— 19 —

Rafa wasn't on Skype or IM or anything because on Thanksgiving Day he was doing what everyone in the United States of America was doing—sitting down to dinner with his family. That's what you do on Thanksgiving Day, no matter what. How did I get stuck with the only family that didn't understand that concept?

A car ignition started in the driveway and I watched Dad back out the SUV, but I didn't see the Kat. Even if Rafa was busy eating, it was a sure bet he had his phone. I emailed the photo of Kat with the cigarette hanging out of her mouth and it only took five seconds for him to call.

"That's what she looks like in person?" he said.

"Freaking lovely, huh?"

"Looks like a prostitute."

"You wouldn't believe how much money Dad gives her."

"Dang, that's—. Hey, you okay?"

"Not really," I said.

"So what did you do today?"

"Well," I said slowly, "we went to a spa and I told Dad and Kat I hate them. That's what my family did for Thanksgiving. How 'bout yours?"

After a long pause, Rafa slowly listed all the relatives at his house, like he didn't know what to say. I was only half listening when someone knocked on the door. "Hang on," I said to Rafa. "And don't hang up—it could be the Kat."

Fortunately it was just Gabby. "Come in," I said. "Rafa, gotta go."

"That was your non-boyfriend?" Gabby asked.

"Exactly. Emphasis on non."

"Uh-huh." Gabby crossed her arms. "Mamá wants you to eat with us. Your dad had to leave unexpectedly."

"Did the Kat creature go with him?"

Gabby busted out laughing. "Is that what you call her? They're both gone. Come help us make tamales."

Considering the fact that Berta had to clean up my puke the last time I was left alone too long, I decided it was the least I could do.

"Sounds like fun," I said with a weak smile. I really wanted to say, "Why the hell not? My own parents don't want me." But after making Rafa squirm on the phone, I had to remember what's normal in my family was probably way too bizarre to share with other people, so I kept my mouth shut.

We went downstairs and I expected to see Berta

making tamales, but the kitchen was empty. "This way," Gabby said, leading me out the back door. At the little guest house, Gabby's dad stood at the top of a ladder and pushed a new terra cotta roof tile into place. We ducked under the ladder to get in the door and even though it was bad luck to walk under a ladder, I didn't hesitate because I wasn't exactly on a lucky streak.

In the little house, a big room with a huge wooden table in the middle held buckets of what looked like wet cornmeal and I knew from watching Rafa's mom it was masa. Next to the buckets were two neat stacks of corn husks. I breathed in the hearty aroma of whatever Berta had cooking on the stove—probably the stuff that goes inside the tamales.

The house felt warm, not temperature warm, the kind of warm you feel inside. It wasn't just the rose colored walls or the handmade wooden furniture. It was the smiles for no particular reason, like being at home was reason enough to smile. I don't think I'd ever felt like that.

Take our Tuscany styled kitchen in our old house, for example. Mom had paid a lot of money to make it appear warm and cozy, but it didn't feel all warm and cozy, not like this. When Gabby and her mom looked at each other, their eyes sparkled and they didn't have to speak. They were sending signals of happiness to each other, happiness that came from just being together. I had never experienced that with Mom, but I was sure it was the best feeling in the world. I remembered when it felt that way with Dad, but those days were definitely over. Gabby was lucky. She probably didn't even know how lucky she was.

With elbows out and Fandango at her feet, Berta lifted a pot from the stove and set it on the table next to the buckets of masa. Gabby had slipped a tile under the pot just before it touched the table. Berta said something to Gabby in Spanish that involved me, but I wasn't sure how, until Gabby's eyes lit up at mine. "She wants us to start rolling tamales."

More than anything, I wished I could return the eye sparkling thing, but it was like something inside me had died and I wondered if I would ever get it back. I turned my attention to the pot Berta had placed on the table.

"What's this?" I asked, staring down in the pot.

"Pork, onions, garlic and hot peppers," Gabby said. "Have you ever made tamales?"

"No," I said, "but I've seen it done."

"At your non-boyfriend's house?"

"Right." I half smiled that Gabby wouldn't let go of the boyfriend thing. If only she knew what a girl he could be sometimes.

The three of us must have rolled at least fifty tamales, which drove Fandango crazy. I slipped him a bite of pork and said, "I love your dog. He has so much personality."

Gabby looked at me quizzically. "He is your dog."

"Huh? Why is he always here?"

"He is afraid of—" and then Gabby stopped.

"Poor puppy," I said, pulling Fandango up on my lap. "Are you afraid of the mean, ugly Kat?"

Gabby giggled and placed the last tamale in the pot. When Berta put them on the stove to steam, Gabby said,

"Now for the sweet tamales."

Gabby mixed sugar and raisins in the other bucket of masa. Berta wiped her forehead and sat at the table to rest.

"You only need a little cinnamon," Gabby said.

I sat next to Berta and said, "Tomorrow's my last day here."

"Oh! What will you do tomorrow?" Gabby asked.

"Don't know," I said in a monotone. "Not even sure Dad'll be home."

Berta wanted Gabby to translate what I'd said and after Gabby finished, Berta shook her head sadly.

Gabby stirred the sweet masa. "You should talk to your dad, tell him how you feel."

"I already did," I said, rolling my eyes. "You can see how well that went. I'm here with you on Thanksgiving night." As soon as I said it, I heard how bad it sounded. I was getting really clear on why nobody liked me. I didn't even like myself anymore.

Berta said something and then Gabby relayed the message, "She thinks you need to have a heart-to-heart talk with your dad." Gabby scooped some sweet masa into a corn husk. "She wants to know what you would say."

"I've already said more than enough."

"She says if you love someone in your heart, you should tell them because it is a message from God."

I kept my head down and rolled tamales because I really didn't want to talk about it anymore. Dad was once my number-one human being on the planet. But now when I looked at him, "I love you, Dad" were not the words that wanted to spew forth from my mouth.

Later that night, we sat around the table, Gabby, her parents, Fandango and I. The moon glowed through an open window and a gentle breeze drifted in while we ate tamales and washed them down with fizzy limeade. Gabby and I spoke a little. Mostly we listened to her parents talk softly to each other in Spanish, their voices gentle like music that calmed me. I stayed well into the night and in my mind, created my first poem.

— 20 —

Mom never responded to my email or the five phone messages I left begging her to let me come home. Obviously Dad didn't want me either and that's why I was shocked to find his SUV in the driveway the next morning. When I went to the kitchen, he was leaning on the counter, watching Berta assemble mango and papaya crepes.

"There's my girl." Dad opened his arms to give me a hug and even though my heart wasn't in it, I hugged him back. "Sorry 'bout yesterday," he said.

At first I thought he meant the disastrous day at the spa, but then he said, "We met some friends for a quick drink, then business got in the way—you know how it is."

I knew exactly how it was. "Dad," I said. "We need to talk."

"We're headin' out to a ranch for some good ol' fashioned Texas barbeque. We can visit all day long."

"Is Kat coming?"

"Well of course she is, baby. Why wouldn't she?"

"Then we won't have all day long to visit. We won't have any time to talk." I turned around to leave. "I may as well not even go."

"Y'all are just jealous of each other," Dad said with a sly grin.

Again, the creepy factor. "Dad, you're not in high school and we're not two girls fighting over you." My face felt hot. "I'm your child!"

"Now listen here," he said. "If my little girl wants to spend her last vacation day with her Daddy, then that's what we're gonna do."

"Okay, what does that mean exactly?"

"Kat's been itchin' to go shoppin' in Mexico City and today's a good day for her to go." He strode out of the room like he meant business. I slowly shook my head. Dad had a lot of guts, but not when it came to the Kat.

Berta made a sympathetic face, which made me feel more pathetic, if that was even possible. I forced a weak smile because I knew her heart was in the right place and sat down with a plate of crepes. They were way better than the mango and papaya crepes at the restaurant, mostly because the fruit tasted sweeter. Just as I was shoveling another bite in my mouth, Fandango bolted out the kitchen door and I heard the clickity-clack of the Kat's high heels coming toward the kitchen.

Having my back to her was never a good idea, so I dropped my fork and spun around in the chair. Sure enough, those cat eyes were set on me and she came at me like a leopard closing in on its prey. I turned on the video camera and stood my phone on the table.

The Kat stuck her finger in my face and said, "You ruin this for me and I'll git you a apple and a roadmap quick as a hiccup."

She sounded like swap meet Mom, only Mom wasn't mean. I tried not to laugh, but totally failed. "Looks like Dad just gave you one."

I was glad I waited to turn off the video camera until after Kat slammed the door. It was a fabulous finale for our little morning drama. Dad came in just as I was naming the video *welcome to my life* to send to Rafa later. Believe it or not, I actually missed the Perfect Family Show produced and directed by Mom, which got cancelled when the lead actor stopped showing up.

Dad and I drove out of town on a winding road past twenty-foot cacti surrounded by lone mesquite trees. We turned on a dirt road and drove a good while before entering a gate with a sign overhead that read, *Rancho de los Tejanos*. I was still in shock that Dad had gotten rid of the Kat creature for a whole day.

"These are good folks," Dad said. "Fine Texans."

A crowd of people stood around swigging bottles of beer outside a house made of stone that blended in with the hills. Dad introduced me to the Tanners first, who owned the ranch. Mr. and Mrs. Tanner were nice enough and the brisket they served was awesome. I devoured it way too fast, probably because I hadn't had any melt-in-your-mouth brisket since Dad left home.

"There's plenty here," Mrs. Tanner said, placing her

hand on my shoulder. "Hep yourself."

Dad winked at me and then proceeded to do the outdoor version of what Mom called "working the room." He shook hands with every person there, stopping to talk with each one as if they were the most important person at the barbeque. I wasn't sure if Dad was even a senator anymore, but he was still a politician. I filled another plate with brisket and found a table where no one was sitting. Eventually, Dad showed up with a bottle of beer.

"You're not eating?" I asked.

"I ate with some folks over there. You know how it is."

I was totally getting Mom's side of the story. "Dad," I finally said, "Kat's not very nice to me."

"Abby."

"You don't know how she treats me when you're not around."

Dad scanned the other tables to see if anyone was listening. "Let's go for a walk."

We didn't have to walk far to get to the edge of a cliff with a panoramic view of the rolling hills. Dad sat on the ground with his legs crossed near the edge of the cliff and stared out into the distance. I sat right next to him.

"Look Abby, I need you to try and get along with Kat."

I froze. "Did you hear what I said about the way she treats me when you're not around?"

"Think about how Kat feels," he said. "When you keep talkin' 'bout your mom or your mom and me like we're still married, it hurts her feelings."

He was kidding, right?

"Try to be more sensitive," he added.

"My sensitivity's been on overload for so long that any minute now, I could implode."

"Huh?" Dad said, furrowing his brows.

"Parents should have to go through sensitivity training for their kids the minute they decide to get a divorce." I couldn't stop my voice from getting louder. "That should be the law. You're a lawmaker. Make it a law!"

"Are you sayin' I've been insensitive?"

"Dad, please. You're living in a castle with your new princess and servants, while Mom and I can barely buy food. Mom can't afford to take care of me anymore, but your princess can go on a major shopping spree in Mexico City?"

"Look," he said in a tone I had never heard before, "your Mom got all the furniture and then sold it. I can't help it if she's too lazy to get a job."

"She's not lazy; she's depressed because you dumped us."

"Honey, your mother's been takin' anti-depressants and a bunch of other pills for ten years. I didn't cause it."

Okay, this was news I needed to process. Finally I said, "Dad, I want to come live with you. It's bad at home. Really bad."

By the long silence that followed, I knew the answer. The old Dad would have been stoked about having me, but the new Dad just sat there and shook his head. "Your Mama wanted custody, so I gave it to her. I can't change the court ruling."

"Mom doesn't act like she wants me."

"She's a hard woman to figure out, Abby. I know we kept a lot from you, but it was for your own protection. Your Mama's always been mentally ill."

"Then why'd you let her have custody? Why didn't you fight for me?"

"Because Kat likes kids, but she wants her own."

"Ouch."

Dad shrugged. "What am I supposed to do?"

"Nothing. I totally get it. Kids are like sneakers. Out with the old, in with the new."

"Hey," Dad said. "You're comin' right back here for Christmas."

The seemingly endless panoramic view fueled my spinning thoughts. Mom wasn't the only mental case in the family—they were both nuts. I stopped to make sure I wasn't speaking in my out-loud voice because I had definitely lost my mind when I asked if I could live with Dad and the Kat creature. Craziness was probably genetic.

After our lovely heart-to-heart talk, I couldn't stomach socializing, so I stayed at the cliff's edge while Dad went to the house for another beer. He never did come back, which was not surprising. I was fine with that because I needed a beer, too. I kept my distance from Dad and none of the strangers around me said anything when I picked up a beer and took a swig.

About a six-pack later, Dad called my name and we drove back to his mucho grande casa as if nothing had happened and it was just another sunny day in Mexico.

That night, I finally got an email from Mom saying she couldn't wait to see me at the airport tomorrow, which was a huge relief because I was beginning to wonder if I would ever see her again.

The next morning, I packed my clothes and went to the guest house to say goodbye to Gabby and her normal parents. Fandango sprang into my arms and licked my face while I squeezed him tight. Maybe walking under that ladder had given me a little luck since I never saw the Kat again for the rest of the visit. Dad drove me to the airport and we hardly spoke, which definitely meant I had over-stayed my welcome. I knew how it was.

"See you at Christmas," was all he had said.

On the flight home, there was no nun to talk to, just an old Mexican cowboy who didn't speak English, which was fine with me. After the stewardess escorted me off the plane and through customs, Mom stood waiting with a big grin and I wasn't sure what that was about, but it felt good to be back in La-La Land.

"How was Thanksgiving?" Mom asked.

I didn't even know where to begin and the thought of reliving it made me totally nauseous, so I just said, "Fine." She seemed okay with my answer, which probably meant she didn't really want to know.

"What about you?" I asked. "Why didn't you call me back?"

"I'm sorry, honey." Her hand rested on my shoulder. "I took a little vacation. No phone, no internet service."

"Where?"

"No place interesting."

"Fine," I said. "Don't tell me anything. I'm used to it."

"Abby."

I waited for her to say more, but that was it. "Okay, so did anything happen while I was gone?" *Like did we get a huge pile of money from someplace unexpected?*

Mom fished in her purse for her keys. "You were only gone a week."

Ohmygod, it seemed like a year. I just hoped the curandera was for real and something good was about to happen.

— 21 —

Monday morning, I trudged through my classes like a zombie. Dealing with Dad and the Kat had obliterated whatever teensy bit of parental trust I had left. I expected Rafa to be wildly entertained by the photo and especially the video of the Kat creature, but he kept giving me this weird look that I'd never seen before. At lunch, I found out why.

He opened a sack of tamales and handed one to me.

"I actually made tamales in Mexico," I said, opening the corn husk.

"The Kat woman cooks?"

"God no." I shot him a look. "Berta and Gabby, I told you about them in my emails."

Rafa handed me another cornhusk with a string tied around it that looked more like a present. I pulled the string and unwrapped the cornhusk. The ring inside reminded me of the zillions of silver rings I'd seen in nearly every shop in San Miguel, only this one looked a lot like a wedding band.

"In Mexico, we have a saying," he said, sounding all serious. "If you feel love in your heart for someone, you should tell them because it is a message from God."

"Berta told me that in Mexico!" I was so caught up in the coincidence, it took a moment to grasp what Rafa was actually saying.

Placing both hands on his chest he said, "I feel love for you, in my heart."

I may as well have been shot with a stun gun.

"I want you to wear my ring." He leaned over and kissed me, and I don't mean on the cheek. The kiss only lasted a second, well maybe three, or five, ohmygod. At first his lips pressed softly against mine, and then he sucked my lower lip into his warm mouth, gently tugging with his teeth. When I thought it was over, he raised up from the ground, his body tensing, and came at me whole mouth. My breath caught. His hand gripped the back of my neck and his tongue reached in, massaging mine, warm and wet, and then forceful, his grip tightening, and then soft again, reaching in, tugging my lip, until my body tingled and I wanted him to devour me. I'm not sure how long that part went on, but when it was over, we both breathed heavily and everything about Rafa seemed different. His face softened and his eyes looked as if a fairy had waved a magic wand and put him in a trance. Or maybe I was enchanted. Before I knew it, I had taken the silver band from the cornhusk and slipped it on my finger.

"You accept?" he asked, looking totally surprised.

I giggled like a girl, which I had never, ever done in my entire life. I always thought it was lame when girls acted that way around boys, but I didn't seem to be in control of myself anymore.

When Mom picked me up after school, I pulled the ring off and squeezed it in my hand until we got back to the apartment. Having a conversation about the ring was the last thing I wanted, especially since Mom had already accused me of having sex. Today I'd had my first kiss and I didn't want Mom to ruin it.

When we got home, Mom went to the bathroom and I went straight to the kitchen. I poured vodka in a glass and put a little water back in the bottle. The toilet flushed. No time to add juice. I took the glass of vodka to my room and closed the door because I really just wanted to put the ring back on and stare at it.

The vodka still tasted like rubbing alcohol, but it made me feel good inside. By now the whole love spell thing had eased up and I was thinking more practically. What had happened with Rafa was still hard to believe because I knew him too well, but this was a part of him I had never seen, a part that didn't make sense. For years he'd been my friend, which was completely different from the whole boyfriend–girlfriend thing. I guess when you get older things have to change whether you want them to or not. Considering all the major changes that were already going on with my parents, I wasn't sure I wanted anything else to change.

Still, most of the girls in high school had boyfriends and if I had to have one, I wouldn't want it to be anyone other than Rafa. I did love him, so maybe this was all perfectly normal. Really though, I wouldn't know normal if it bit me on the butt. All I knew was that I needed my friend, so if he wanted to be my boyfriend too, that was okay.

I twisted the ring on my finger and stared at the white ceiling that looked like it had been splattered with cottage cheese. Our old home had smooth ceilings and layers of carved molding. I closed my eyes and remembered Rafa's lips touching mine, but when my mind went deeper into the kiss, I had visions of Dad and the Kat all over each other.

The door swung open and there stood Mom with a grin the size of Texas. This I had never seen. The only grin I'd known was her perfect-family-photo grin, which did not exactly ooze happiness. Like a cheerleader waving a pom-pom, Mom shook a piece of paper and made little squealing noises that were so not her.

"Everything's going to be fine! Our lives can go back to normal."

"Okay, first of all, no." I pulled the ring off fast. "Nothing on that piece of paper can fix what's wrong with our family."

She came over and sat on the bed. "Honey, there's something I need to tell you, now that you're old enough to know."

Now see, that's the part Mom and Dad don't get: I'm not old enough to know. I braced myself for whatever was coming next.

She shoved the paper in my face, which was actually a check with a three and lots of zeroes. When I read the part that spelled out the amount, I nearly choked. *Three million dollars and zero cents.* The old Mexican curandera was for real.

"This may be a dumb question," I said sarcastically, "but why is Price Pharmaceuticals giving you three million dollars?"

Mom gazed at the wall, her mind busy formulating an answer. "Four years ago, I filed a lawsuit and apparently, I won. Actually they settled, according to the letter."

I cocked my head. "Let me rephrase the question," I said in my most sarcastic voice. "Why did you sue them?"

"Well, I'm not proud of this, honey." Mom said softly, folding the check. "For years I took medication to get my emotions under control. A painkiller. It was really for migraines, but I took them whenever anything upset me and somehow I got addicted."

"An anti-depressant?"

"Well, I was taking that too, but this was an addictive narcotic drug."

"My mom, the druggie. Nice."

"When they recalled the painkiller for causing heart disease, I got checked and found out my heart had suffered damage." Mom batted her eyes. "I found the whole thing ironic since I started taking the medication because your father was breaking my heart."

"So, like, are you okay?"

"I can't get too stressed out anymore. The heart

doesn't heal."

Okay, so the curandera had obviously confused Mom's heart with mine. At least nothing was wrong with my heart and the money had come, which was the important thing because I was so over being Ghetto Girl.

At school, Rafa had a new strut—like a rooster—as if having a girlfriend was the same as winning a hunting trophy. I rolled my eyes.

Even though I'd been back for nearly a week, the reality of what had happened with Dad in San Miguel hit me while walking through a crowded hallway with Rafa strutting by my side. When you're little, parents are just another body part, always there, like an extension of you. But that's not exactly true. Obviously, a parent can love you for a long time and then stop whenever they want. My mind was busy with all that when Megan bumped me and said, "Check *friendworld* lately?"

"Um, like no," I replied.

With a smirk, her eyes swept up and down Rafa's cocky stance. "You should," she said and winked at Rafa before sashaying off.

"What's she talking about?" I asked Rafa.

He shrugged and kissed me on the cheek before turning the corner to his last class. Rafa knew. My own boyfriend was hiding something.

After school I didn't feel like talking to Rafa, even though he rode all the way to the apartment with me. I wasn't sure why, but I still hadn't mentioned that Mom and I were rich again and that we'd be moving out of the ghetto soon. Maybe it seemed too good to be true. Maybe I didn't trust him.

When Rafa said, "See you," I didn't even look at him. As far as I was concerned, the jury was still out on whether he was lying.

Mom wasn't home and that was a huge relief because I had one thing on my mind. I grabbed a can of orange soda and the vodka bottle Mom seemed to have completely forgotten about, and headed to my room to read Megan's *friendworld* page. On the bed, I powered up the laptop, took a big gulp, and clicked. The first sentence sent orange vodka spewing from my nose and I couldn't stop coughing long enough to wipe the laptop with my T-shirt.

Does Your House Have Unfaithful Furniture? Abby's ex-furniture gives a whole new meaning to foreign affairs. When Abby and her mom had that international estate sale, who knew it was unfaithful furniture? Uh-huh, every time Senator A got caught cheating on his wife, he tried to make up by taking Mrs. A and Ghetto Girl on fabulous shopping sprees around the world. Now that unfaithful furniture is all over town. Do you have a piece in your house?

Hunkified: I have the CHEATING COUCH!!!
Sweets: we got the two timing table!

The comments went on, but I shut the laptop. Only one person knew the truth about the furniture and that was Rafa. I should've known when Megan winked at him, he'd betrayed me. Rafa could've socked me in the gut and it would've felt the same. I took another gulp of orange vodka. New rule: Trust no one.

The front door closed. After stashing the vodka bottle under my bed, I fell back like a dead animal shot in the wild. Mom knocked on my door. Why even knock when she immediately opens the door afterward?

"I bought a house," she said, without noticing I could be dead.

I opened my eyes and stared at the cottage cheese ceiling.

"We're moving over the holidays."

I blinked slowly. "I'm visiting Dad those two weeks."

"Oh honey, I forgot to tell you." She sat on the edge of the bed. "Your father cancelled your visit. He's going on a cruise with the floozy. They're getting married."

I sat up.

"She's pregnant," Mom said. "Twins."

"Oh. My. God."

Mom patted my knee. "I'll show you the new house. That'll cheer you up."

I collapsed on the bed. "In a minute," I said in a distant monotone.

After Mom left, I picked up the phone and called Dad. While the phone rang, I tried to think of what I wanted to say if I had to leave a message, but then I heard, "Hey Babe."

"Hey Dad."

"How's my girl?"

"Totally weird question, considering." Long pause. "Is it true?"

"I was lookin' forward to seein' my little girl over Christmas, but then this thing came up."

"Define thing."

"Well, babies." He sounded kind of proud. "We're havin' two." Another long pause. "I've asked Kat to marry me and she said yes."

"Big surprise there," I said.

"She wants to get married on a cruise ship."

"What Kat wants, Kat gets."

"Try to see it my way," Dad said.

"I am. You're not inviting your own daughter to your wedding."

"Look baby, it's not me. Kat doesn't want you to come." Silence. "You two didn't exactly hit it off and she wants this to be a happy occasion."

I nearly choked. "So it's my fault?"

"No baby, the wedding is supposed to be about Kat. You know how it is."

"I know exactly how it is," I said. "Oh, and have a great life." I clicked off the phone and rolled Rafa's ring in my fingers. Just like Dad had lied to Mom about the Kat creature, Rafa was lying to me about Megan. That's exactly how it was.

I blazed through the living room and slammed the door with Mom saying, "Wait, where—."

Pushing the handlebars, I jumped on and pedaled past the crack house to Rafa's street. Veering in the driveway, I skidded to a stop and made a long black tire mark that snaked all the way up to the house. Even though I flipped the kickstand, the bike fell over, but that was the least of my problems. I knocked hard and waited.

Rafa opened the door, which was a good thing because I wasn't in the mood to be polite. At first he grinned, but his eyes grew big as baseballs when I took a pitcher's stance and threw the ring at him.

"Traitor!" I shouted. The ring missed his shoulder and landed somewhere in the house.

"You're breaking up with me?"

From deep in my gut came the words, "Like you don't know what you did."

"What did I do?"

I yanked the bike and pedaled home with adrenaline rushing through my veins. Finally, I'd taken control of my life and from now on, this was how it would be. Mom stood in the same spot when I got home, like she was still in mid-sentence. I looked her in the eye and said, "Let's go see that house."

— 22 —

Rafa pretty much stayed away from me at school, which made my life a lot easier. Whenever I saw him, he looked like a puppy who'd been spanked for the first time by the person he loved most. I knew exactly how he felt because that's how I felt around Dad, but my feelings toward Rafa hadn't changed. I had zero tolerance for traitors.

Mom and I spent all our time packing boxes, getting ready for the move. Our new house was half the size of the old house, but Mom said it was perfect, plus it was right around the corner from where we used to live. I liked that it had three bedrooms instead of five and only one living room. With no dad and no more friends, I had lots of empty space inside me and didn't need more all around.

Still, the fact that we had three million dollars fascinated me. "If we're rich again," I said to Mom, "how come we're packing our own boxes?"

"We're not exactly rich," Mom said from the kitchen. "This three million is all I'm getting for the rest of my life. I have to make it last." She pulled a stack of dishes out of the cabinet and wrapped one in paper. "I paid cash for the house. Half a million's already gone."

"I know we'd save money," I said, "but Rafa's brother can't help us move."

"Oh, I've hired movers," she said, wrapping a glass with paper. "We just need to do our own packing."

I wanted to tell Mom about the endless teasing and what Megan had written on *friendworld*, but I didn't dare since the jokes were mainly about her.

"Wish we'd never sold the furniture," was all I said.

"Glad it's gone." Mom raised her hand, shooing it away. "Nothing but bad memories for me."

Good for her, bad for me. I stacked some CDs in a box and tried to ask in my most casual tone, "Are you still friends with Megan's mom?"

"I think so." Mom paused. "I called when we didn't receive our usual invitation to the holiday party and she explained she simply didn't have our new address, but of course we were invited. She sounded kind of funny, though."

I stretched packing tape across the box and squished it down. "So we're going?" My voice sounded panicked, which meant I needed to put myself on mute immediately if I didn't want to have to explain anything.

"I don't care about the prestige of going," Mom said. "I just want to see my friends." She gave me the look. "And I'm not going alone."

Obviously this was non-negotiable. "God, that's so not fair!" But Queen Doreen had disappeared and as usual, my words hung in the air and died. Nothing could be worse than going to a holiday party at Megan's—I was definitely going to need access to alcohol. Fortunately, at this party, I did not foresee that as a problem.

I missed Rafa. Even though he looked sad in Mr. Oliver's class on the last day before winter break, I still couldn't get over the fact that he'd told Megan the real story behind our furniture. And was he seriously flirting with Megan behind my back? It was like watching a bad remake of the way Dad treated Mom. Still, I missed talking to Rafa about important things, like the Kat's pregnancy. He would have cracked up and said, "She's having kittens!" Even though Rafa's jokes made reality more bearable, I couldn't forgive him for betraying me.

When class was over, I left without saying goodbye. I gave Rafa the royal silent treatment; it seemed like the only thing to do. With the Three Ps plus Megan still snickering at me on one side of the room and certain other kids snickering back, I was over it—way over it. Winter break hadn't come soon enough.

I pulled another track and field trophy out of a box and put it on a shelf in my new room. I didn't even know who that person was anymore, the fastest hurdler in the Houston-Galveston region. My life was complicated now and I didn't have time for trivial sports. Trying to get all the knives out of my back consumed all my time.

When Mom passed by my door, it hit me—her migraine headaches were gone. No more lying in dark rooms in complete silence with cool cloths on her forehead. No more open bottles of painkillers lying around. Doctors in those drug commercials on TV should tell people three million dollars will cure migraines better than any prescription drug.

"Mom," I shouted, hoping she was still in earshot.

She backed up holding a lamp.

"When's that party at Megan's?"

"Saturday night," she replied, unwinding the lamp cord from around the base.

"I'm not going," I said firmly.

Mom's face dropped. "I need you to go, for me," she said quietly. "It's my first social event without your father."

"Okay, God!" Megan was not exactly on the list of people I wanted to impress. I didn't even have a list. The only person I ever cared about impressing was Dad, and it was safe to say, he was no longer impressed.

It didn't occur to me until we arrived at the party that Megan might have invited Rafa. Wearing a red skirt and jacket, Mom tapped the knocker on the door of Megan's nineteenth century mansion. Earlier, when Mom insisted I wear the same red dress I wore last year, I'd cringed. Fortunately, the dress didn't fit anymore and so for the first time ever, I got to pick what I wore. I chose all black: black shirt, black pants, black shoes. Clearly, I was in mourning over all holiday festivities.

A caterer in a white coat swung the door open, which was a huge relief, considering Megan could have opened the door. Chatter rose above piano music—that song about chestnuts in the fireplace, or something like that. Last year, and all the years before, Mom had orchestrated the timing of our arrival at this party. For Dad to make the most noticeable entrance in a room filled with his constituents, we had to arrive late, but not too late. Apparently, there was an exact science to figuring out what time a politician should arrive at a party. This year, we were just plain late.

The caterer took our coats and led us through the narrow hallway with wooden floors and ridiculously high ceilings to the grand room designed with contemporary furniture, thanks to Mom the rebel. We couldn't exactly see the furniture because the room was crammed with women in red dresses and men in suits, but I remembered that room from when Megan and I were friends.

Mom's lips trembled when she put on her best fake smile and I figured she was nervous. To me, it used to matter what other people thought, but not anymore. Nobody liked me anyway and that somehow made my life easier. When a caterer held out a tray of champagne glasses, Mom turned away. I lied to the waiter and said I was taking a glass for Mom, but I downed it before she turned back around and stashed the glass under a napkin on an end table.

While I was busy suppressing a burp from the sparkly champagne, my eyes met the not-so-sparkly eyes of the triple Ps, standing in V formation with Megan in the center glaring at me. Megan wore a short red dress, Priscilla a shiny gold dress, Presley a polka dot dress, and Paige looked like a red and white striped candy cane. I rolled my eyes and turned to Mom, who was staring at the grownup version of the triple Ps—the mothers of Priscilla, Presley and Paige—who were standing on the other side of the room in the same V formation with Megan's mom in the middle. Seriously. I'm not making this up. In unison they glanced at Mom, whispered to one another, and gazed back at Mom with the most fake looking smiles.

"What are we even doing here?" I asked Mom.

With raised brows, Mom replied, "Spending time with friends."

"Whatever." I went off to the bathroom, figuring that would kill some time.

In the hallway, a dozen women waited in a line that snaked all the way to the kitchen. I squeezed through the hall to the end of the bathroom line. All the women were Mom's age or older, but they whispered and sneered like girls in the hallways at Marconi High School. When the line moved up enough for me to hear the gossip...let's just say it took a minute for what I heard to even register.

"I found out last week," said one in a red-beaded dress.

"I heard it over a month ago," another stated firmly.

"She's young enough to be his daughter," the one in front of me whispered.

At first I thought they were talking about Dad, but everyone found out about him four months ago when it was all over the news.

"Don't believe everything you hear," another lady said. "You know how this island is."

"Do you see him here?" the red-beaded dress lady asked.

Silence. Some strained their necks to see and others squinted as if trying to remember what they had seen over the course of the evening, while Paige's mom squeezed past me to the end of the line.

Finally one of the so-called adults said, "If it were true, she would have called off the party."

"And draw attention to the scandal?" The lady in the red-beaded dress wagged her finger. "No, no."

This party? Megan's dad? Had to be another holiday party.

And then by some miracle, it finally came out. It wasn't an actual miracle; it was more like she just couldn't keep all the juicy information she had to herself any longer, even if it meant gossiping about her close, close friend. "He left last summer," Paige's mom said with the voice of authority, "with a nurse. Gwen told me everything the day it happened."

Megan's mom was Gwen. Gwen Applegate. And Megan's dad was our family doctor. Like I said, it took a minute to register, but when it did, I shot out of line, straight to Megan and the triple Ps, who stood in a huddle biting into small chocolates with their pinkies out. My head got hot like it was going to explode.

I planted my feet behind Megan and crossed my arms. "So," I said loud enough for anyone to hear, "Your dad ran off with a floozy, too."

The voice level in the room dropped.

Megan looked like she had just watched the scariest part of a horror movie.

I set my jaw. "All this time you've been bashing me at school when your dad was doing the exact same thing."

"That's a lie!" said Megan.

"Where's your dad?" I asked. "Is he here?"

A low murmur arose from the sea of party guests, who discreetly moved their eyes around the room to find him. Megan turned white as a Christmas ghost and collapsed on the rug. Someone gasped and the room went silent, except for the song *Hark the Herald Angels Sing* that the oblivious pianist began playing. In unison, Priscilla, Presley and Paige lifted their heads and sashayed away, clearly not wanting to be associated with Megan during her moment of public humiliation.

I'm the one who should have walked away, but I couldn't. I wasn't sure why I knelt down to see if she was okay. Maybe some tiny, weird part of me was still her friend. Or maybe I was the only person in the room who knew how she felt.

Megan opened her eyes and said, "What happened?"

"You fainted," I replied, helping her sit up.

By now a crowd of people surrounded us.

"Shall I call an ambulance?" someone asked. "Where's her mother?"

"I'm fine." Megan rose gingerly to her feet.

I helped her to the sofa where we sat like the two best friends we once were, completely worn out by our own drama. While the room buzzed with the news of Dr. Applegate's scandal, Megan sat in a trance with her eyes all bugged out.

Slowly, anger brewed in the pit of my stomach. I turned to glare at Megan. "Ghetto Girl? Mono? Unfaithful furniture?"

"I was just…" Megan sank into the sofa. "I'm sorry," she said quietly.

"And what's going on with you and Rafa?"

"Nothing," she said all innocently.

"Like I should believe a pathological liar?"

"Do you really think my mom would let me date a guy from a poor family?"

I peered at her sideways. "Somehow I don't think that would stop you."

"Look, he's cute and everything, but I like football players."

"Right." I said squinting. "Then who told you about our furniture? Rafa's the only one who knew."

"My mom," she said, wrinkling her forehead. "Our moms tell each other everything. That's why I thought for sure you knew about my dad."

Why do people assume mothers and daughters tell each other everything? Maybe that was normal. I wouldn't know.

"That's why I made you look bad at school," Megan explained, "so if you said anything about my dad, no one would believe you."

Rafa was right. Never piss off a crazy person.

Across the room, Mom approached Mrs. Applegate,

who immediately turned her back and strode away. Mom chased after her, which made Mom look completely pathetic. I jumped up and got over there fast.

"Gwen," Mom said still chasing her, "no one's judging you."

The problem with trying to carry on a conversation with someone who's clearly walking away is that you have to talk louder so they can hear. That's why when Mom said, "No one's judging you," she practically yelled and the crowded room hushed to an eerie silence, except for the clueless pianist who began playing *Go Tell It on the Mountain*.

With flames in her eyes, Mrs. Applegate screeched to a halt and spun on red high heels that matched her cocktail dress. I feared for Mom because I knew that look—I'd seen it on Megan. The only thing missing was a pitchfork, but then I figured out the flames in her eyes were reflections from the fireplace. I kept a steady eye on Mrs. Applegate anyway.

"I'm your friend," Mom pleaded. "I know what you're going through."

Ohmygod, Mom was oblivious to the speechless audience.

"Doreen," Mrs. Applegate said with chilling calmness, "we have nothing in common."

Mom looked exasperated. "Do you think we're the only ones who got tossed aside for younger women?"

I couldn't help but smile at my new let's-get-real Mom.

"I hate to publicly embarrass you like this," Mrs. Applegate said, "since you've had so much of that already." She actually smirked as her eyes danced around the room.

Mom's mouth dropped and stayed there. That's when I took a giant step toward Mom and squeezed her hand.

Mrs. Applegate raised her chin. "I would have sent a letter, but like a transient, you've moved three times in the last four months."

"What letter!" Mom said in the tone she used when she thought I was saying something totally ridiculous.

"We've discontinued your membership in the Society of Modern Victorian Women."

"But I'm the president," Mom said. "For God sakes Gwen, we started that club together!"

Mrs. Applegate spoke slowly, "We have a rather long list of reasons why you no longer belong in our organization."

"Do tell," Mom said, crossing her arms.

"We value p-proper—" Mrs. Applegate stuttered, "etiquette."

"Oh, we are so out of here," I said, tugging Mom's sleeve. "You don't need a friend who thinks it's polite to smile in your face while she's stabbing you in the back."

When the pianist let out an uncontrollable howl and struck up *Auld Lang Syne*, I tried not to giggle, but it didn't go very well. All night, the pianist had been listening in and entertaining himself by inserting humorous music that fit the scenario. I liked him.

"We have a list of reasons," Mrs. Applegate continued.

I took Mom's arm and pulled, but she wouldn't budge.

"Oh, please," Mom said. "Before the Victorian era,

Shakespeare wrote, 'The lady doth protest too much, methinks.'"

Dragging Mom out of the room, I added, "And don't forget, 'To thine own self be true.' Also from Hamlet."

"Ladies, you can keep your Victorian etiquette," Mom said. "I'd rather spend my days with women who have deeper values than deception." Mom touched her forehead to mine.

For our exit stage left, the pianist selected, *We Wish You a Merry Christmas*. I gave him a nod to wish him a Merry Christmas back, and I swear when he winked, I saw a sparkle in his eye.

We shut the car doors and Mom said, "Nothing like a holiday party to put you in the Christmas mood."

I snorted, trying to control myself, but when Mom busted out laughing, too, I doubled over. In my whole life, I'd never seen Mom even giggle, but that night, in Mom's car, in front of Megan's house, we laughed 'til we cried the good kinda tears.

— 23 —

On the way home from the Applegate's holiday fiasco, Mom slowed in front of a Christmas tree lot with a big sign that read, *Benefiting St. Chamuel's Homeless Shelter for Children.*

The angel of love—the curandera had asked St. Chamuel to watch over me.

"We need a tree," Mom said. "How's this lot?"

I gazed at the sign. "Perfect."

We strolled through the lot inhaling fresh-cut pine and bypassed the twelve-foot trees that we used to put in our way-too-big house.

"Over here," Mom said, pointing to the six-foot trees. "We need room at the top for an angel."

"We have a star, Mom, not an angel."

"Oh, I got rid of those decorations. We're starting anew."

A skinny old man with stubby gray whiskers hurried

over and pulled a tree out for us to examine. "This here's a fine one," he said, smiling proudly with two teeth missing.

Mom raised her eyebrows at me and I nodded.

"We'll take it," she said.

At the register, the old man pointed to a display of angels. "Need a tree topper?"

"As a matter of fact, we do," Mom said all cheery.

Every angel was exactly the same. I picked up one of the boxes and read, *St. Chamuel—Archangel of Love and Tolerance*. Goose bumps prickled my arms when I got to the small print at the bottom that read, *Made in Mexico*, like some kind of weird cosmic synchronicity thing was happening.

The old man tied the tree to the top of the car and when we got home, Mom and I dragged it in the house. That's when I started missing Rafa because he would have loved dragging the tree in and setting it up in the stand.

Mom smiled in a peaceful way I had never seen before when the tree fit perfectly in the smaller living room with a lower ceiling. Clearly, Mom planned to set up camp right here for the rest of her life.

"Won't you miss the Society of Modern Victorian Women?" I asked.

She smirked. "I thought I needed all that, but this is who we really are."

I wrapped a string of lights around the tree and hoped Mom wasn't referring to the Christmas muzak playing softly in the background when she said this was who we were. When Mom asked, "How're things at school, honey?" I nearly fell off the stepladder.

I untangled more lights and said, "Fine."

"They can't be fine if you made Megan faint and Rafa's not coming over anymore."

My heart sank. I pulled out my phone and sent Rafa a text:

Abby: I miss you.

"Abby," she pleaded.

Oh God, Mom looked all needy.

"Talk to me, Abby," she said.

I squished my eyes. "I can't."

"Why not?"

"You always think the worst of me."

"What has happened to you?" She looked perplexed and said softly, "I told everyone at the party how proud I am of you."

I rolled my eyes. "That was all show."

"Abby, come sit." Mom patted the sofa.

Not what I wanted to do. My other choice was to bolt, but that seemed childish, so I climbed down the ladder and sat at the other end of the sofa with my arms crossed.

"Honey, please." Mom scooted closer. "We can talk about anything."

"Right." I smirked. "Anything but Dad. And school. And boys."

Okay, now she looked hurt.

"Sweetheart, I know we haven't been close and I used to blame your father for that. But I've come to realize it's not his fault." She stared at her hands folded neatly on her lap. "It's my fault."

I did not see that coming.

"I told you about the painkillers I used to take, but I really shouldn't have blamed your father for that." She shook her head. "It's not like he was forcing them down my throat. I did have a choice."

I stayed quiet.

"When your father's girlfriend first appeared on the news, I thought it was just another storm we'd have to ride out. You know, as a family." Her eyes grew moist. "But when I received those divorce papers…" Mom cleared her throat.

My stomach twisted.

"I'd been off the painkillers a few years, since I filed the lawsuit against Price Pharmaceuticals, but when I got the divorce papers, I needed them again."

"You probably did for those migraines," I said.

"No, sweetie. The pills caused the migraines."

Mom calling me "sweetie" made me feel soft inside. I bristled.

"I couldn't bear to read those divorce papers. I just signed them, sent 'em back, and called my doctor." She looked at me and said, "A person in their right mind would've called their lawyer, not their doctor."

"I thought you and Dad argued over who got custody of me?"

"I didn't argue over anything. I just signed. The doctor prescribed a new painkiller that had just come on the market. After we moved into that dreadful apartment, I couldn't get enough of those pills."

For the first time ever, I could see inside Mom.

"I know I've been a terrible mother."

I wanted to tell her she'd been a good mother. The well mannered girl Queen Doreen had created wanted to say that. But really, she was telling the truth.

"When you went to visit your father for Thanksgiving, I checked myself into a rehab center." She studied my eyes. "That's why you couldn't reach me."

"You didn't have a phone?"

"It's their policy," she said. "They took away my phone and Internet so I could focus on the treatment." Mom took my hand and put her face close to mine. "I'm sorry I didn't respond, but it was the only time I could get help. I didn't want to abandon you while you were home."

"Well," I said, "I felt alone a lot when you were here."

"I know you did," Mom said softly. "That's why I'm asking you to give me another chance."

My head went all fuzzy, but I managed to nod.

Mom put her arm around me and kissed my forehead. "Now I want to hear about your dad and school and boys."

I nestled my head in Mom's neck and let her hold me. I'm not sure how long I sniffled and wiped away tears, but I felt things might actually get better.

"I'll tell you in the morning."

My mouth was dry. Mom hung an ornament on the Christmas tree when I shuffled in the living room. "Please tell me there's coffee." Saying words out loud made my head feel worse. Yes, I finished off the vodka last night and with Mom's newfound sobriety, I definitely needed to find a new alcohol and drug provider.

Mom came back with two mugs and placed them on the little table in front of the sofa and I figured that's why it was called a coffee table.

"Sleep well?" Mom asked.

I nodded and slurped the creamy coffee that tasted like mocha ice cream, except hot. Clearly, the old Queen Doreen was not in the room because she would've had something to say about the slurping. Not being constantly judged by Mom might take some getting used to. I melted back into the sofa and checked the top of the tree to make sure Chamuel was still there.

"So what happened on your visit with your dad?" Mom asked.

Ohmygod, where do I start? Surely Mom didn't want all the gory details.

And then as if she'd read my mind, Mom said, "Tell me everything."

"Thought you didn't want to know."

"It's not that I want to know." Mom nuzzled back into the sofa too. "I want us to tell each other everything so we don't have to face the world alone."

I choked on that one. When I finally stopped coughing, I said, "First of all, there's no Thanksgiving in Mexico," and then proceeded to tell her about Dad's drinking and all the mean things the Kat had said. When I told her how Dad and the Kat were either all over each other or nowhere to be found, Mom fumed a bit, but kept listening.

Finally I said, "Remember when our old Persian cat kept peeing on the Turkish rug in the dining room?"

"Oh, First Lady!" Mom rolled her eyes. "We never did break her of that habit."

"Kat's like that. An annoying creature."

"Your father used that cat's bad habit as an opportunity to teach you a history lesson."

"No way. Did you just say something nice about Dad?"

"I hope you remember some of the good things from your childhood, honey."

"Oh yeah." I boinged my palm against my forehead, which set off a new hammer-pounding episode in my brain. Oh God, please make it stop.

"I think I remember," I finally said when my brain started working again. "The Persian cat was peeing on the Turkish rug because he was pissed that a thousand years ago, the Turks defeated the Persians in some battle."

Mom grinned. "Your father's not all bad."

"Ohmygod, Mom! What did they do to you in that rehab? They must have had all kinds of personalities on a shelf, like in a clothing store, and you said, 'I'll take that cheery one.' And you took off your old personality and put on a new one, like changing sweaters or something. Maybe I should go to rehab, except they probably wouldn't take me since I'm not a drug addict or an alcoholic like you and Dad, respectively—." When I heard what I was saying, I quickly added, "and respectfully, too."

I needed to shut up or change the subject and since I couldn't shut up, I told Mom how sweet Gabby and Berta had been, and she seemed relieved, but I didn't tell her about the wine or the curandera because I wasn't quite ready to divulge anything that made me look like the bad or crazy person. I preferred pinning those labels on the Kat creature.

The whole time I blabbered on about Mexico, Mom was forcing herself to not speak. I could tell because every time she'd start to say something, she'd close her eyes and take a deep breath. But she did stay snuggled up next to me, so I guessed she wanted me to keep going.

When I finished, she said, "Sorry you didn't get to have Thanksgiving."

"Yeah, that was weird." I patted my chest. "I didn't know it meant that much to me until we didn't do it." Oh God, Mom could see my eyes welling up.

"Who says you can only make a turkey and stuffing on Thanksgiving Day." Mom slapped her leg. "Let's go to the store."

Three grocery stores later, we found a small turkey that wasn't frozen. I was busy peeling the sweet potatoes we had baked when I smelled something burning. Since Mom's hands were stuffing cornbread dressing up the turkey's butt, I grabbed a pot holder and pulled open the oven door, expecting smoke to come billowing out, setting off the fire alarm, and ruining our whole Thanksgiving by making the house smell like a crematorium. But there was no smoke or alarm or stench.

Just a bit of burned sugar from drippings of pecan pie filling that had bubbled over the edge of the crust and splattered on the bottom of the oven. I guess things had gone terribly wrong for so long, I was surprised when they didn't.

"Take it out, honey," Mom said.

The rich aroma of pecan pie swooping up my nose opened the floodgates of my saliva glands and made my stomach growl like First Lady when Mom used to lift her in mid-pee off the Persian rug. I gingerly placed the pie on the cooling rack and that's when it hit me Mom could quite possibly be the best cook in the world. Seriously, she could've had her own TV show: *Queen Doreen's N'awlins Cuisine.* She always said, "If God intended us to cook low-cal, he would've never made butter and brown sugar."

Mom's mom was a true Texan, but her dad was a jazz guitarist from New Orleans. I never got to call them Grandma and Grandpa because one day, when Mom was little, Grandpa drifted off with his guitar and never came back. A year later, Grandma died of a broken heart and Mom had to go live with an aunt in the one-stoplight town known mostly for its swap meets. Maybe that's why Mom became the Queen of Control and why it took so long for her to let go of Dad. I'd never thought of Mom as an actual human being with issues until now.

I mashed the sweet potatoes and Mom poured melted butter in the bowl. "Just a pinch of salt and cinnamon." she said. "Then we'll get started on the praline topping."

"You're finally revealing your secret recipe?"

Mom squeezed my shoulder and said, "No more secrets."

That sounded fantastic, except I still wasn't ready to tell her about the curandera or St. Chamuel. "Does this new policy go into effect from this point on?" I asked, hoping for a loophole.

Mom peered at me sideways. "You're going to be a lawyer like your father, aren't you?"

"Is that a bad thing?"

"I would be so proud."

I figured it was the perfect time to tell Mom about all the horrible things Megan had done to me at school, but complaining about it now seemed whiney and pointless. I could deal with Megan. It was Rafa who had me all confused.

Mom was pouring vanilla extract into the bubbly butter and brown sugar mixture on the stove when I said, "If you're serious about the no-secrets policy, we need to talk about Rafa."

She nearly spilled half the bottle of extract into the saucepan.

"Sorry," I said frantically. "Did I ruin it?"

"You can never have too much vanilla," she said sweetly.

I definitely needed to check out that rehab facility.

Slowly, Mom stirred the thick, brown mixture. "What's going on with Rafa?" She lowered her nose to take a whiff.

When I told Mom how suddenly, right in the middle of our normal, everyday friendship, Rafa had asked me to be his girlfriend, she didn't even flinch, so I kept talking.

"It seemed like he just felt sorry for me, though. I mean, the whole time I was in Mexico, I kept telling him how awful it was and as soon as I got back, he gave me a ring." I leaned on the counter to look Mom in the eye. "I don't want a boyfriend who feels sorry for me."

"Perhaps he missed you," Mom said. "You do spend all your time with him."

"I never looked at it that way."

"Are you going to accept?" Mom asked.

"That's the thing. I did. But from the second he gave me the ring, I stopped trusting him. A week later, I gave it back."

"You broke up with him?"

Mom looked so stunned that I was glad I hadn't mentioned the part where I threw the ring at poor Rafa like a complete lunatic. "Now he's hurt and I've lost the only friend I had left."

"Oh, honey."

"What should I do?"

"It depends," Mom said, pouring the praline sauce over the sweet potatoes, "what do you want?"

I shrugged. "I kind of want a boyfriend, but at the same time, it seems weird."

"Listen to your heart," Mom said. "You'll know."

— 24 —

After our mid-December Thanksgiving feast, Mom and I decided to make rosemary prime rib for Christmas. Cooking together had become an actual treat that we both got excited about and if anyone had told me a year ago this would happen, I would've said they were completely loco. God I missed Rafa.

Still no response to the text I sent him last week and now it was Christmas Eve. It wasn't unusual for his family to visit relatives during long holidays, still, Rafa would've gotten the text on his phone. Even though it was nippy outside, I hopped on my bike and headed over to his house to see if his Dad's truck was in the driveway. When his house came in view, I squeezed the brakes and peeked from behind a car parked on the street. The truck wasn't there, which didn't necessarily mean his family was out of town, but at least there was a fifty-fifty chance of it. More importantly, I was officially reduced to the level of a stalker.

I turned around and peddled what little bit of self esteem I had left home.

At midnight Mass, Rafa's family wasn't sitting in the section where they usually sat, or anywhere else in the cathedral for that matter. Believe me, I looked. This meant they were definitely out of town and I would have to wait until school started up again in January to see him. Clearly, he was still hurt or mad or something because he could've texted back how much he missed me too and that we should forget the whole stupid break-up thing and go back to normal. Wait, not normal. Go back to the girlfriend-boyfriend thing or whatever.

Since midnight Mass was special, we had a bishop telling us the story of Christmas instead of Father Sullivan. I checked my phone again for a text from Rafa while the Bishop wrapped it up and moved to the altar to receive the body and blood of Christ. Mom sat in a daze and didn't even notice I was checking my phone every five minutes. I knew she wasn't on drugs, so I figured she was tired. I had to nudge her when it was time for us to receive the body of Christ, but Mom said she wasn't getting in line.

"I can't," she whispered. "The divorce."

Mom closed her eyes and listened to a boys' choir singing from the balcony. When the procession of people in satiny robes headed up the aisle, I put my phone away in case it was a sin to text during midnight Mass. I wasn't sure exactly what would happen and with things getting better between Mom and me, I didn't want to blow it.

The altar boys came by first, carrying poles that dangled brass incense burners. I sneezed and instead of acting like I hadn't, Mom dug around in her purse for a tissue. Next came two girls holding huge candles. After the Bishop passed by, Father Sullivan avoided making eye contact with Mom, which was strange because he used to nod since Dad was a public figure and a pillar of the community.

On the drive home past blocks of Victorian houses set aglow with Christmas lights, I said, "You know, we don't have to go to Mass anymore. I mean, don't go for me."

Mom hesitated. "We'll see."

"Seriously, I only went to stalk Rafa."

A smile spread on Mom's face. "You're definitely my daughter."

That was the nicest thing she'd said to me, ever.

I hate to admit this, but it didn't occur to me 'til Christmas morning that I hadn't gotten Mom a gift. When she handed me a shiny gold package with a beautiful silver bow, I turned red as the two Christmas stockings hanging on the hearth.

"I hope you like it," Mom said, while my mind was busy conducting a brainstorming session on what to give her.

The Pancho Villa T-shirt was the only recent purchase I'd made and I'd already worn it several times just to annoy Kat. Other than that, I had nothing. My eyes traveled up the tree and focused on St. Chamuel. Even a simple Christmas ornament would've been nice. I was the worst daughter ever—the slimiest worm beneath the dirt.

I must've gone into a trance because when Mom said, "Aren't you going to open it?" my eyes came back into focus and I heard the muzak version of the song about the little boy who had no gift for Jesus, so he played his drum instead. Not a bad idea.

"Wait!" I said to Mom, making a dash for my room. "Lemme get your gift!"

My only talent was writing, but I couldn't think of anything gift worthy I'd written, other than a poem that came to me late one night in Mexico. I'd scribbled it down somewhere, but wasn't sure I'd even kept it. Flipping through the stack of stories I'd written in Mr. Oliver's class, I hoped at least one would work. I only needed one.

Hurricane? No. A homeless person's right to steal food? Maybe. King leaving a queen for a younger princess? Definitely not. Suddenly the poem flashed in my mind and I scribbled it down again:

Luz de la Luna (Light of the Moon)
Moonlight rides dark winds
Through gusty treetops unscathed
And slips inside my window
To laugh in my crazy dreams.

Too short and barely gift worthy, but it would have to do. I tore the edges of the paper to make it look artsy, rolled it up, and tied a piece of ribbon around. Not bad for a worm.

Mom was poking the fire when I returned to the living room with my poem in hand. "Found it!" I said, feeling guilty about lying in front of the Archangel of Love and Tolerance who was watching over me from the top of the tree.

Mom took the scroll and said, "Thanks, sweetie."

After Mom read it, her eyes got all watery and it took me by surprise since really, the poem wasn't that good.

"You have a gift for writing," she said.

Actually, I had a gift for pulling a present out of my butt on short notice.

"Open yours," she said, handing it to me again.

The box contained a stack of gift cards to restaurants, movies, amusement parks and all the other cool, touristy stuff to do on Galveston Island. In years past, Mom and Dad had always given me clothes I didn't like and jewelry I'd never wear, but this was like a year's worth of fun in a box.

"It's for you and Rafa," she said with a sparkle in her eye. "I'll volunteer to be your taxi service 'til you get your license." Mom gave me a squeeze and I had a feeling she was forgiving me for stealing her car and going on that, ahem, joy ride.

Rather than stalk Rafa's house every day, I decided to be mature about it and only go every other day. The truck reappeared in the driveway on New Year's Eve and even though I'd been waiting and waiting, I couldn't knock on the door. Maybe I'd wait 'til school started back. With more people around, talking to him would be less intense.

Who'd of thought I'd ever be nervous about talking to Rafa, but I needed time to plan a strategy for this messy situation I'd gotten myself into and that's why I turned my bike around and pedaled home.

At the magical hour of midnight on New Year's Eve, Mom said, "To new beginnings."

We clinked mugs of hot apple cider, which by the way were unspiked, only because Mom had stopped buying anything mind-altering. As if there was something wrong with that.

Mom had made "new beginnings" sound like a good thing, but I wasn't so sure. Dad was probably married to the Kat by now and sometime next summer, I'd have two half brothers or two half sisters or maybe half of each. You'd think that would've been the biggest thing in my life, but all I could think about was Rafa.

— 25 —

I arrived at school with one goal: Get Rafa back.

I didn't exactly have a plan, but sitting next to him in Mr. Oliver's class would at least put him within chatting range and I'd worry about the rest after I got there.

But even before then, everywhere I went, I searched for him, my boyfriend, feeling a rush of freedom in finally admitting it. Getting out of Mom's car, I scanned the area, hiking up stairs, I kept looking back, maneuvering through hallways, I checked every face. And just when I acknowledged how truly pathetic I was, he appeared right in front of me and my heart stopped. Without a word, he squeezed by.

"Rafa!" I had practically screamed, but he disappeared in the swarming hallway and my eyes darted everywhere, hoping to keep him in sight among the droves of fast paced kids.

He was gone.

With my head hung low and my hands shoved deep in the pockets of my jeans, I trudged to my locker, exactly eight lockers down from Megan's. The tip of my finger felt a tiny object in the deepest crevice of my pocket. Megan was there, the traitor. She was too busy rummaging through her locker to notice me and just when I was about to open my mouth and go off on her, I rolled the little thing in my pocket between my fingers. A beautiful flash of light filled me inside—a painkiller! If I swallowed it now, I'd feel euphoric in about ten minutes and then I could handle Megan, Rafa, anything. I dug the pill out, but it was only the tiny, hand carved wooden heart the curandera had given me in Mexico.

My shoulders slumped. "She's worried about your heart," Gabby had translated for the curandera. I groaned.

At this point, I pretty much hated everyone, especially Mom for getting all clean and sober at the worst possible time in my life. Okay so I didn't hate Rafa, but he thought I did and that was just as bad. Maybe there was something wrong with my heart. I wanted to hate Megan, but when my eyes rose from the tiny heart in the palm of my hand to Megan's droopy face staring blankly in the locker, it hit me: I knew exactly how she felt.

When Priscilla and Presley sashayed by and sneered at Megan, I stuffed the heart back in my pocket and drew a deep breath. Megan gently shut the locker and kept her head down.

"Weird, huh?" I said to Megan, approaching slowly.

She didn't respond.

I leaned against the lockers. "Your dad wants you to hate your mom and your mom wants you to hate your dad."

Megan lifted her eyes and cocked her head, with that why-are-you-being-nice-to-me look that I knew too well.

"Kinda like being a double agent," I said. "You have to please both of them without the other one knowing." I scanned the crowded hallway. "No one understands, so you keep it all inside."

Megan's eyes got all watery.

"Look at them." I squinted at the kids rushing by. "They go home and everybody's still speaking to each other."

Megan sniffled and said, "We go home and can't say anything because everyone's so angry."

I made Megan look in my eyes. "The air's so thick you can't breathe."

"I'm still in trouble for telling Mom I liked the necklace Dad gave me for Christmas." Megan touched the silver and gold chain draped around her neck. "I have to take it off before I go home."

"That's crazy," I said.

The bell rang and kids scattered through doorways. That's when it hit me. "We're not the only ones," I said to Megan before heading off to history class.

While Mrs. Goldstein went on about the criminal court system, I began devising a plan to break out of prison. Megan and I had been handed life sentences for crimes we didn't commit and it was obvious no one was going to save us. By the time I got to Mr. Oliver's English class, my plan had taken shape.

Rafa slid down in his seat, sulking, but cute, having gotten better looking over Christmas break. His brown eyes seemed rounder, those lips, fuller and that dimple on his chin, deeper. After not seeing him for two weeks, he looked hot.

"I'm sorry," I whispered. "I'll wear the ring."

Rafa's eyes slid sideways to me then back to Mr. Oliver, who was lecturing the class on a book we had to read about the civil rights movement since Martin Luther King Junior's birthday was just around the corner. Even though it was truly pathetic, I placed the tiny hand carved heart on Rafa's desk. He stared for a moment and flicked it off like an annoying piece of lint. Getting Rafa back was going to be harder than I thought.

"Martin Luther King dramatically changed the course of history in the United States of America," Mr. Oliver was articulating, British style. "But is it fair to say he changed the world?"

Someone actually raised their hand. She went on about how Martin Luther King could have inspired people in other countries to stand up for their rights, but her voice sounded vague because quite frankly, I had bigger things to think about.

"If you could change the world, what would you do?" Mr. Oliver paused, like he was deep in thought or something. He swallowed some tea and said, "This is your writing assignment today."

Oh, please. No way could I wrap my brain around that topic, but with Rafa so angry, I needed something to do that would help pass the time. I started writing whatever.

How I Would Change the World

I would stamp out hate and try to bring peace to every country in the world. A bumper sticker once said, "Be the change you wish to see in the world." I agree. The world can only be as good as the people in it. I do not believe it is possible to change the world from the outside in. The world must be changed from the inside out.

If people want to change the world, they have to make sure they are not fighting with the people in their own families first. Gandhi once said, "If we could change ourselves, the tendencies in the world would also change." (yes, Mr. Oliver, I used my phone in class. When are we getting internet access???) Gandhi changed himself first by getting inner peace. After that, he changed India, which inspired Martin Luther King to do the same thing in America. Martin Luther King was also spiritually enlightened before he tried to change anything in the world around him.

Both Gandhi and Martin Luther King changed the world from the inside out. That means if I want to change the world, I have to get inner peace first. Then and only then can I help the rest of the world. Therefore, the only way to change the world is from the inside out.

Thank God for the stupid bell. My writing has gone from progressively worse to making practically no sense at all. This paper is proof that journal writing destroys creativity. I started to write a note to Mr. Oliver about that, but stopped. I truly didn't care about the stupid Teen Fantasy Writers novel writing contest anymore. I passed the paper forward and analyzed my real world.

Rafa hated me, Megan's whole amazing persona had been demolished, and my family had elevated dysfunctional to a whole new level.

At this point, I could use a little inner peace. Perhaps this paper would somehow magically come true and one morning I'd wake up feeling all enlightened. I could, you know—stranger things had happened. Like the two stories I wrote at the beginning of the year; they both came true. First the hurricane story, then the one about getting a bunch of money for a new castle. If those things happened, it's entirely possible that whatever magical powers I possess could cause me to change the world from the inside out. But truthfully, I would be happy with a little inner peace.

On the way to lunch, my idea started taking shape. I ran the plan past Megan and she was in. But I warned her it wasn't going to be easy convincing other kids to participate and if no one did, we would definitely be super embarrassed.

"We're already embarrassed," Megan said.

She was right. We had nothing to lose.

The text message Megan blasted to every kid at school went like this:

Megan: Student poll by Abby Alexander and Megan Applegate: If your parents are divorced, wear your clothes INSIDE OUT on FRIDAY. This is IMPORTANT!

We sent it exactly one minute before school got out,

since practically everyone checked their messages the instant the bell rang. That night, I posted the message on *friendworld*, but no one added any comments.

I laid in bed obsessing about it for hours, mostly thinking how stupid Megan and I would look as the only two people wearing our clothes inside out tomorrow. I envisioned a lot of pointing and snickering, which I was certainly used to, but somehow self inflicted humiliation was ten times worse. It's not like I could blame my parents for this.

The second my alarm blasted, I checked *friendworld* one more time. Nothing.

I called Megan.

"You're still in, right?"

"Why wouldn't I be?" she asked.

Clearly, Megan had slept.

"I was up 'til midnight," she said, "calling all the kids I could think of with divorced parents. They're all in."

"How many?"

"Fifteen."

I kept my mouth shut. At least she had done something. "See you in an hour."

Friendworld still had nothing. I turned a sweater inside out and pulled the arms through, then did the same with a pair of jeans. With every inside seam showing and pockets flaring out, my fashion statement definitely reflected how my parents' divorce made me feel: Exposed—ugly side out. I flung the backpack over my shoulder and headed to the living room where Mom was sitting on the sofa, waiting.

With her eyes glued to me, she set the cup down, completely missing the coaster. "New trend?"

"Apparently," I said, not wanting to explain.

She grabbed her keys. "Nice pun."

I had no idea what she was talking about and was too tired to figure it out.

Usually I jumped out of the car the second we got in the drop-off line, but I squeezed the door handle and glared out the window instead. A group of guys walked by wearing their clothes the regular way, like sane people would do. Behind them, a group of girls dressed normally, too.

"Bad idea," I mumbled.

"What?" Mom said.

Mom's Mercedes crawled up another car space and two girls strolled by chatting. Not just two girls, two seniors—the two prettiest and most popular seniors—and their clothes were inside out. I finally started breathing again and got a panoramic view of the swarms of kids coming from every direction. Counting those with their clothes inside out, I stopped at a forty and let out the biggest sigh of relief.

I shot a text to Megan:

Abby: You seeing this???

She didn't answer and when I got closer to the building, I could see why. Megan was holding court on the steps, surrounded by dozens of kids wearing their clothes inside out. Passing by, I gave her a nod. She winked back and in that moment, our friendship was fully restored to the place where we could read each other's minds. Big smile…

In my morning class, I got fist bumped by countless of kids of divorced parents. A few girls actually grabbed me for quick hugs and told me stories that were almost identical to mine, except for the part where they broadcast my Dad's affair on TV. The bell finally rang and I was out in the hallway enjoying my natural high until Priscilla got in my face and in a monotone voice said, "Your boyfriend had boy sex behind the curtain in the auditorium." She held up her phone and showed me a photo of Rafa and some older kid looking all shocked. And then she walked away.

By the time I got to Mr. Oliver's English class, I'd heard it again and again. The more I heard it, the madder I got. Unable to sort it all out, my brain went fuzzy, but one thing became clear: Rafa and Dad were exactly alike and I wished I'd thrown that ring a lot harder at Rafa.

— 26 —

I sat in my seat, stewing, while Rafa stared at the top of his desk. Kids whispered to one another, but this time it wasn't me they were snickering at; it was Rafa. My anger shifted from Rafa to the other kids because I knew how it felt to be publicly humiliated, to feel lower than a worm.

Mr. Oliver paced through the aisles, bouncing a tea bag in a cup. Some kids searched for their journals while others stood in line at the pencil sharpener. I was thinking about how nobody really cared when girls had sex with each other, but for boys it was different. Mr. Oliver must have been reading my mind because after everyone got settled, he said, "Today I want us to think about two words: double standard. Raise your hand if you know what this means."

I really didn't feel like joining in on this public discussion. Rafa was, after all, my ex-boyfriend, which somehow made me feel humiliated all over again. At the beginning of the year, I told myself that if this ever happened, I would stand up for Rafa. But I didn't know Rafa and I would end up falling in love and even so, I never in a million years thought he would ever cheat on me. As I sat in silence, waiting to get out of this annoying class, someone finally raised their hand and said, "I think double standard means…um, like you have bi standards."

The whole class burst out laughing. I turned to Rafa, who still sat like a statue without even a teensy flinch. I knew that stoic look because that was me on the first day of school. The notes, the gossip, the mean pranks, all the things that plagued me in the first semester flooded my mind, but the worst betrayal of all had been Megan's. In my darkest hour, Rafa had been the one person in the world who was on my side.

I scooched my desk over and bumped it up against Rafa's. Then gently, I reached for his hand and held it through the rest of the class period. Rafa never moved and Mr. Oliver left me alone since I had found a more important use for my hand than writing. When class was over, Rafa stood up and that's when I saw the purple bruise around his eye. Without a word, he walked out the door. Rafa was in safe mode.

After school, Megan was the last person I wanted to hang out with. The events of the day stirred my anger toward her all over again. Oh bloody hell; she was coming right toward me. I took a deep breath and smiled for one reason and one reason only. Megan still had access to alcohol.

"Want to come over?" Megan asked.

"I absolutely do," I replied. That was easy.

When I called Mom, she seemed happy that Megan and I had rekindled our friendship, even though her own friendship with Mrs. Applegate was pretty much over. As we walked down the sidewalk, Megan said, "Poor Rafa— and you. Ohmygod."

"It's not like I didn't know he was gay," I said.

"You knew?"

I put on my most nonchalant face. "I figured it out at the beginning of the year. He's the one who didn't know."

"Why didn't you tell me?"

Sometimes Megan needed time for her mind to catch up with the words that came out of her mouth.

"Nevermind," she said. "Hey, I'm really sorry about all that stuff at the beginning of the year."

"You owe me," I said with a smirk.

Megan took off the necklace her father had given to her for Christmas and stuffed it in her pocket, but Mrs. Applegate wasn't even home when we walked into the foyer. My eyes went straight to the well stocked liquor cabinet in the parlor.

"Come on, let's go to my room." Megan pulled my sleeve and trudged upstairs.

I followed her, trying to figure out if Mrs. Applegate would notice that a whole bottle of vodka was missing.

Megan turned on the song that we used to sing together about being bad and not caring about anything. We immediately started singing at the top of our lungs and at the end of the song, we both fell back on the bed, laughing.

"Let's drink some vodka and orange juice," I said, like it was a random thought.

Megan's eyes got wide and then a smile crept over her face.

Scrambling downstairs, we giggled all the way to the liquor cabinet. Megan picked up a half empty bottle of vodka and lifted it high like she'd won a trophy. I had my eye on the full bottle that stood right behind it. While casing the rest of Mrs. Applegate's supply, I told Megan about my method of refilling the bottle with water so her mom wouldn't notice we'd had some.

"Please," Megan said, "she'll think she drank it. My mom gets annihilated like every night."

With a glint in my eye and pep in my step, I followed Megan to the kitchen. While she filled two glasses with ice, I grabbed the orange juice and vodka and led the way back to her room.

She set the glasses on the nightstand and I filled them half full of vodka. Megan poured orange juice on top and we sprawled out on our stomachs across the bed. I took a big gulp and closed my eyes. The liquid went down sending feelings of warmth through my entire body. Like a fire breathing dragon, alcohol fumes burned out my nostrils. My inner dragon was hungry and I needed to feed her. I touched the glass to my lips and swallowed more fire.

Megan was making a sour face when I opened my eyes. "Clearly you're a vodka virgin." I grinned. "Try it again."

Megan finally got used to the taste and it didn't take long to finish off the bottle since it was only half full. I may have had more.

"So what was with you and the triple Ps?" I asked.

"I dunno." Megan furrowed her brow.

"You're name doesn't even begin with a P." I nudged her. "That should have been your first clue."

"At least my boyfriend's not gay," she said.

"You have a boyfriend?"

Megan reached for her pad and touched the *friendworld* icon. "I'm just saying, if I did have a boyfriend, he wouldn't be gay."

Someone had posted photos of newly spray painted lockers on *friendworld*. The one next to the science lab definitely belonged to Rafa and in huge letters they had written: FAG. There were no context clues to identify the locker in the second photo, but since they'd written FAG HAG on it, I knew the locker was mine.

"Oh," said Megan. "That is so wrong!"

My halfhearted smile must have told Megan what I was thinking.

"That wasn't me," she said. "The triple Ps took that photo and painted Ghetto Girl on your locker."

"Yeah, but you were on their side."

"Well, yeah but now I'm on your side."

"Alright," I said. "Prove it."

Megan stared at me, waiting.

"Help me stand up for Rafa."

She looked me square in the eye and said, "Done."

I didn't exactly have a plan, but whatever we were

going to do, it needed to be magnificent. "Let's have a rally," I said, "a massive school rally."

"A stop gay discrimination rally," Megan said.

"No, turn it around."

"You mean don't stop gay discrimination?" Megan looked perplexed. "Why would we do that?"

"No, no," I said. "Instead of anti-discrimination, we'll be pro-love."

Megan's face lit up. "We'll have it on Valentine's Day!"

"Holy crap, that's perfect," I said, "but it's not enough."

"Huh?"

I peered sideways at Megan. "I'm gonna need that other bottle of vodka so I can think about it."

Downstairs, the door slammed.

Megan rolled her eyes. "Mom."

I tossed the empty vodka bottle in the trash and flung my backpack over my shoulder.

"That vodka bottle," Megan stuttered. "My mom, she'll see it."

I retrieved the bottle from the trash and zipped it in my backpack. "I'll smuggle it out," I said with a grin.

Mrs. Applegate pretty much hated everyone in my family, which was fine because it was mutual. While Megan distracted her in the kitchen, I sneaked out the front door, and on the way out, I stuffed the full bottle of vodka in my backpack, too. All the way home, I beamed like a hunter who had sacked her prey. A day that had started off horribly was ending quite nicely.

Back in the safety of my room, I sat on the bed and

tilted the vodka bottle up against my lips. The sweet fire burned going down and left an afterglow of pure inner peace that made me feel whole. I don't know whether it washed away my stress or just made me not give a crap, but either way, I could focus on being a productive, living, breathing human again. I took another swig. If Megan and I were going to pull off a gay rights rally at Marconi High School, it had to be big.

The one thing Megan did exceedingly well: public relations. Never make an enemy of a person like that. I really wanted to forgive her completely for what she had done to me at school. And half of my heart did forgive her because I truly understood how she felt when her father just packed up and left. But the other half, no. The old saying, "keep your friends close and your enemies closer" made perfect sense.

Okay, that was settled. Megan would be in charge of public relations.

Now for my part—the leader. We needed a celebrity, someone really famous. I swallowed more vodka. God I was brilliant. But who could I get? When Dad was here, famous people paraded in and out of our lives, like…like…oh bloody hell, I can't even think of a comparison right now. But they came to promote Dad's causes. Dad was a frigging celebrity magnet. I picked up the phone and called Dad.

"Hey baby cakes," Dad said as if no time had passed since the last time we talked, which I couldn't even remember when that was.

"I need your help," I said and then realized I probably

should have said "hello" first. Oh well.

"Sure baby," he said with his usual confidence. "Whatcha need?"

"I need a celebrity."

Silence.

"Are you there?" I asked.

"I'm listening," he said. "Go ahead."

I'm not sure what I said next—something about how my boyfriend got caught having backstage boy sex and how Megan had proven her knowledge and expertise in the field of public relations at my expense, and how I was going to take these two negatives and make a positive by organizing the biggest gay rights rally the state of Texas has ever seen. "And that's why I need a celebrity," I said.

After a brief pause, Dad said, "I'll see what I can do."

And then he said something about how he loves me. And then he hung up.

I'll see what I can do??? I needed to know definitely, not I'll see what I can do. I mean, God! I took another swig. I never could count on Dad.

With music playing, I scrolled through *friendworld*, but it was boring, so I sent Megan a text.

Abby: getting a celebrity for the rally
Megan: who?

My head melted into the pillow and closed my eyes.

Since the pounding in my head the next morning was less than usual, I poured some vodka into a water bottle and stuffed it in my backpack. I knew Megan would interrogate me endlessly, wanting to know the identity of the celebrity, but I was still in shock over the fact that I had even called Dad in the first place. Part of me said, "what were you thinking, you idiot!" and the other part said, "glad you finally got some balls, girl!" I decided to listen to person number two.

I was right about Megan hounding me all day for a celebrity name. And Rafa became even more hostile after I told him about the rally. I'd said I was doing it anyway—for all gay people. "Everything's not about you!" I'd shouted. Good thing I'd brought the vodka.

As Valentine's Day drew near, the whole celebrity thing really started stressing me out. Either Dad was in or he was out. Late one night—after I drank a six-pack of courage that I'd talked some man into buying for me on the way home from school—I called Dad.

"Hey baby cakes," he said. "How's my favorite girl?"

He forgot. That's just friggin' great.

"You were supposed to get me a celebrity," I said. "Remember?"

"I did. I told you, I got Phillip Gentry."

"Phillip Gentry, like the Houston Pistols Phillip Gentry?" My voice cracked.

"Yeah, baby. I told you last week,"

Okay, Dad must have been drunk and thought he'd called me because I would have remembered that.

"You don't remember talking to me about it?"

"Oh, yeah, I remember now." Dad was totally tripping.

"You have the time and place yet?" Dad asked.

"Valentine's Day," I said, "at Marconi High School."

"I know that, sugar. What time? Where are y'all havin'

the rally?"

I hadn't thought of that.

"I told you I need to know ASAP." Dad sounded impatient. "He has a busy schedule."

"Okay, um, after school," I said. "Three-thirty on the front steps of the school."

"Gotcha," Dad said. "He'll be there. I'll make the call now." And poof he was gone.

I had to give Dad some credit. He may be an irresponsible alcoholic who forgot to call me, but at least he came through with his promise. I sent Megan a text.

Abby: I got a celebrity

Megan: Who???

Abby: Phillip Gentry

Megan: The basketball star???

Abby: Yup

Megan: Omg omg omg

I tossed the phone aside—a slam dunk. I polished off the inch of beer that remained in the last bottle and got under the covers. Damn I was good.

— 27 —

The hardest part about not being old enough to drink is one, getting the alcohol, and two, not getting caught. So far, I was pretty good at both. Every morning I put whatever empty bottles I had from the night before in my backpack and tossed them into the recycling dumpster at school. Fortunately, Mom got some new friends and had stopped being so needy, which was fantastic because I needed more time to drink in peace.

Megan and I spent the two nights before Valentine's Day in my garage getting all the signs and banners ready for our pro-love rally. It seemed weird doing all this stuff without Rafa. I missed him. I shouldn't have told him this rally wasn't about him, when really it was.

"Everything's ready," Megan said at her locker on Valentine's Day. "TV news stations, check. *Friendworld*, check. Text blast at two-fifty-nine, check."

"What if no one comes?" God, I sounded panicked. I

needed a drink.

"Um, that's not possible," Megan said in her snobbiest, know-it-all voice. At least she had confidence.

By three o'clock I had a good buzz from drinking vodka out of my water bottle between classes. At the top of the steps, two varsity football players Megan had recruited carried a lectern, while the president of the drama club tested the mic. Dozens of kids gathered at the bottom of the steps and in no time, there were hundreds. While Megan flirted with one of the football players, I moved through the crowd, handing out the heart shaped signs we'd made and searching for Rafa. If he didn't come, I was personally going to kill him.

Just as I finished handing out the signs, a black SUV exactly like Dad's pulled up in front of the school. The passenger door opened and Phillip Gentry stepped out wearing a Pistols jacket and jeans. Dad had introduced me to him at a basketball game once, but I seriously doubted Phillip Gentry would remember. Ohmygod. Was that Dad's car?

My heart stopped when the door opened on the driver's side, but the person who stepped out wasn't Dad. Did I actually think Dad would leave the Kat creature long enough to be with me for something this important?

I stood all sad and droopy when Phillip Gentry, who was a giant, walked right up and said, "Abby?"

I flipped the switch to fake-happy mode and looked up. "How'd you know?" I asked all cheery.

He flashed a photo of me on his phone. "Your dad sent this."

Judging by all the pointing and staring, it didn't take long for everyone to recognize the basketball superstar. I grabbed hold of his giant hand and led Phillip Gentry to the top of the steps toward Megan, who was suddenly speechless.

"Cough, cough."
Mouth. Dried paste.
Light—too bright.
The walls of my bedroom spun like a wobbly top. I gripped the bed to brace myself. Oh God, getting seasick. I rolled on my side and tons of puke blasted out, over and over, until my stomach had completely emptied itself on the rug below. I reached to wipe my mouth with the sheet, but my hand shook uncontrollably. I collapsed.

Vague sounds of people talking. My eyes finally opened. This time Megan and Rafa and Mom sat in chairs in my room. Softly, my breath moved in and out. I was alive.

Mom got up and stretched her hand toward me.

"Don't touch me," I said with only half my mouth. Drool glued the other half to the pillow. I was able to prop myself up like a cobra and look around. "I think I puked my guts out," I said to them.

"We cleaned it up, Sweetheart," Mom said. "Are you okay?"

"What happened?"

"You passed out after the rally," Rafa said, looking all worried.

239

"You came to the rally?"

The room went quiet. Six eyes stared at me like I was from outer space. My head pounded like a big bass drum as I shifted around, trying to sit up.

Mom mumbled something indecipherable, and then Megan and Rafa left. Oh God. I was in trouble.

"Honey, what were you drinking?" Mom asked.

Holy crap!

"Where did you get alcohol?"

"I don't know what you're talking about," I lied.

Mom closed her eyes and sighed.

I don't know why I couldn't tell her. Actually I did know exactly why. Mom would take it all away. No more vodka. No more beer. And I would probably die.

"Look," I said. "It was just this once. I was nervous about the rally. It won't happen again."

For a long time, Mom stared at me without saying anything. I picked up a glass of water and shakily took a small sip. My head swam over big ocean swells and I had to lie back down.

"Where did you get that much alcohol?" she asked.

"God, you're relentless."

Finally she gave up and left. "Are Megan and Rafa still here?" I asked before she closed the door.

Megan came in and sat on the bed next to me. "Rafa went home," she said.

"What happened?" I asked.

"You passed out."

"Like before the rally even started, I passed out?"

"No," Megan said. "After the rally was over."

I tried to think, but my brain couldn't process any memory of the rally whatsoever. If I couldn't remember, I was probably drunk and made a complete fool of myself. "Oh God," I said, "how bad was it?"

"Well, Mr. Baldwin called the paramedics and when they came, one of them was really cute."

Okay, she was talking about the passing out part first.

"Anyway, the paramedics said you were fine, but you had too much to drink, so Mr. Baldwin called your mom to come and get you."

"Great." I said.

"Your mom was already on her way though, because she saw you on the news."

"What!" More water. Head swimming. A million questions. "Okay, so how did I get to my mom's car? Please tell me the Pistols basketball player didn't have to carry me."

"You walked," Megan said, looking all perplexed again.

"Weird." I held my pounding head.

"You really don't remember?"

"Yeah, I remember. I'm just messing with you." A total lie. "The rally's still kind of fuzzy in my brain," I said carefully. "What happened exactly?"

"See for yourself." Megan got my pad and said, "The local news streamed it live."

The video was loading. Holy shit.

"Here we go," said Megan, handing the pad to me.

Okay, the TV camera scanned the crowd, which was much bigger than I remembered. "Look, our signs," I said. Some kids made their own signs that read *No Place*

For Bullying or *Kindness is Kool.* Suddenly, my face appeared on the screen and underneath, it read, *Abby Alexander Daughter of Former Senator John Alexander.*

"God! Why didn't they just keep writing," I said.

"Huh?" Megan leaned in to get a better look at the video.

"Why didn't they go ahead and finish that sentence, *Daughter of Former Senator John Alexander, who's currently shacked up in Mexico with some weird Kat creature.*"

Megan's face got all twisted. "Your dad's not in Mexico."

As much as I wanted Megan to finish that thought, I needed to hear what I had said on live TV.

"He—"

"Shhhhhh. Jeez!" I slapped her arm without taking my eyes off the video. The news guy was talking into the mic like he was getting ready to ask me a question.

"You're so cranky." Megan crossed her arms and pouted.

"If that's what it takes to shut you up!"

Megan looked stunned. "You used to be nice," she said and gathered up her things.

"Yeah, well, things have changed."

Finally, she was gone and I could hear myself talking. I slid up the volume button. "This issue is important because of the bullying that goes on after people find out that you're gay." Oh, thank God I sounded normal. I didn't even look drunk.

"Are you gay?" the reporter asked.

"No, but my boyfriend is."

Ohmygod. Please tell me I didn't say that.

"I see." The reporter smiled devilishly. "So let me get this straight." He turned to the camera and winked. "Pun intended." Then he looked back at me and said, "You're fighting for your boyfriend's right to be gay?"

Then in my most sarcastic tone, I replied, "That's right, 'bleeeeep.'"

What! They bleeped me. I rewound the video to figure out what I had said. I watched my lips this time. Oh, lovely, I'd called him an asshole on live TV.

The news man turned to the camera and said, "We'll bring you the rest of this story later tonight."

"Yeah, when you can censor it!" I shouted and pushed my head into camera view, making a funny face.

I cracked a smile that made my head hurt more, if that was even possible, but it was kind of funny.

"Reporting live from Marconi High School, this is Mark Thomas." And the screen went black.

"Where's the rest of the rally?" I shouted at my computer pad.

That's when Dad walked in my room. I stared at him for I don't know how long, until a deep sigh filled me with relief at the realization that this was all a bad dream—a super weird dream.

"Hey sugar dumpling," Dad said in his usual Texas drawl.

I slapped my face to wake up. Bad idea. Bass drum. Beating harder.

"Hey," he said, sitting down next to me. "Don't do that."

"What are you doing here?" I asked, wrinkling my forehead and hurting my brain.

Dad seemed surprised.

"Don't tell me, we've already had this conversation, right? I seemed to be getting a lot of that lately."

"We have," he said, nodding his head.

Great. More bits of deleted memory from my brain.

"When you told me you were organizing your first civil rights rally, I got so proud." He put his arm around me and squeezed gently. "That's one of those things in life you just don't miss—your daughter growin' up and all. It brought tears to my eyes just thinkin' about it."

"Why didn't you tell me you were coming?" I asked.

"I did."

"No you didn't. I would have remembered that."

"Seems like there's a lot you don't remember," Dad said softly. "Your mama says you've been drinking."

"And?" I said to the total hypocrite.

"And I'm concerned," he said.

"That's funny because you're the one who's an alcoholic, not me."

"Now hold on, there," he said. "Yes, I used to have a problem, but I got it under control. I haven't had a drink since my plane landed in Houston last night."

Visions of Dad in that bar in Mexico—drinking tequila with the Kat creature crawling all over him—played in my brain like a tacky scene from a low budget movie. Why could I remember that, but not what happened today?

"What happened at the rally?" I asked all bewildered.

"You had a blackout," Dad said, but it was more like

he was thinking to himself.

"Thank you for that diagnosis of my mental state, but that's not what I'm asking. I need to know what happened, like exactly."

Dad took my hand. Then he let out a deep sigh and closed his eyes. Oh God, he was getting all emotional and reflective, like he was going to impart some words of wisdom on me or something.

"Please!" I said. "Don't think, just talk."

"Well, baby," he said, "it went just fine. I was proud of you." He spoke slow and flat, like he was delivering bad news.

"You'd better tell me the truth," I said. "I'm sure a gazillion kids already posted videos on *friendworld*." Why didn't I think of that sooner? My brain was so not working.

"When you got up there and started talking to that crowd in the microphone, my smile was as wide as a Texas summer sky."

He still sounded sad, but at least he was talking. I gave him the keep-going stare.

"You said you knew what it felt like to be bullied, something about Ghetto Girl?"

"U-huh, what else?"

"Well, let's see, you took a poll of the audience." Dad voice started perking up. "You told them to raise their hand if anyone's ever talked bad about them behind their back. And they all raised their hands! I mean you were a natural." Dad grinned and made big gestures with his hands. "You had your audience fully engaged and I was standing there shaking my head, wondering how I got so lucky to have a child as smart and as caring as you." He squeezed me again.

"What about Phillp Gentry," I said. "Did he talk?"

"He sure did. You introduced him all professional like and I stood there wondering when my little girl grew up to be such a fine young lady." But then Dad's expression changed. I assumed I showed my not-so-fine side at some point during the rally. Or maybe he was thinking of the TV interview, which wasn't exactly lady like.

"Okay, so I introduced Phillip Gentry. Then what happened?"

"You really don't remember?" Dad asked. "It was huge news. In fact, they're still talking about it on all the channels."

"What, what!" This was worse than interrogating a criminal.

"He came out of the closet. He's the second professional basketball player to ever do that."

"No he didn't!" I perked up.

"Oh yeah, he asked if anyone in the crowd had an issue with it. Everyone got real quiet."

"I bet they did."

"He went on about how kids need to respect each other and to stand up for people who are being bullied."

"Was Rafa there?"

Again, the look of total disbelief. Whatever.

"Rafa was standing with me, watching," Dad explained. "He was really happy to see me."

Rafa was probably hoping to see the Kat creature in

real life. Ohmygod, the Kat creature. "Is she here?"

"Who?"

"Kat." My tone clearly expressed that I hoped the answer was no.

"What? No. I wanted to spend time with you." Dad stood and rubbed his head. "Why don't you get cleaned up and I'll come back and pick you up. We'll go have some dinner."

"Why didn't you tell me you were coming?"

"I did, baby girl. I told you on the phone."

"Whatever." Dad turned to leave, which stirred up my abandonment issues, but I reminded myself he was coming right back. "I can't believe Mom let you in the door," I said.

"She called me at the hotel and told me to come over—that it was urgent."

I couldn't even picture that in my mind.

— 28 —

The fact that Dad left the Kat and their unborn children in Mexico on Valentine's Day to hear me speak at a rally blew my mind.

After Dad went back to Mexico, I still had a lot of unanswered questions about my little episode of amnesia. Fortunately, it was all on *friendworld*. If there's any part of your life you may have missed, you can find it there.

I studied all the videos and I hadn't slurred my words or stumbled and fallen, like Mom that time she got drunk after finding out she was going to have to get a job. The only weird thing I found was the censored TV interview, and with the fifty-thousand-plus likes it got on *friendworld*, I was practically a legend. After that, it was a big joke around school that Rafa was my gay boyfriend.

"Where do you want to go for spring break?" Megan's eyes went back and forth between Rafa and me. Yes, we were eating lunch in the cafeteria now and I'd stopped smuggling vodka into school in my water bottle. After all the confrontations about my drinking, it was time to prove once and for all that I was not a teenage alcoholic. I mean seriously, how lame is that?

"Panama Beach," I said randomly. "And who will be Megan's boyfriend of the week?"

"I'm not taking a boyfriend," Megan said. "I mean jeez, it's spring break."

"How about Key West?" Rafa said. "Lots of cute guys there."

"Cute gay guys," Megan said, giving Rafa the look. "This is about me."

I took a bite of pizza. "How did I get stuck with not one, but two divas?"

"Because you're lucky." Rafa winked.

Megan sat up straight and tilted her head. "Okay, it's settled then: South Padre Island."

"Why did you ask if you already knew?" I threw a napkin at Megan.

Megan's mom had offered to take us to a beach for spring break. Even though my mom was still not speaking to Mrs. Applegate, she'd somehow miraculously agreed to let me go. Okay, so she didn't exactly glow like a festival of lights at the thought of me going off to some beach for spring break after my little episode of drunken amnesia. There had been a fight—a major fight. But I'd won after convincing Mom that I'd learned my lesson and there was no way I'd ever drink alcohol again for the rest of my life.

"Let's hit the mall after school," Megan said. "I need a

bikini, some dresses, a purse, makeup, sandals—"

"I only need three things," I interrupted, "swimsuit, sunscreen, flask."

"What's flask?" asked Rafa.

"For alcohol," I said. "To fit in your pocket."

"What's wrong with the water bottle?" he asked.

"That's for school, when you don't want people to know." I looked at Rafa like he was a Martian. "On the beach, you want people to know."

Rafa grinned.

"Shorts, tees, tanks, tote bag," Megan's list continued, "phone case, shades, toe nail polish, did I say makeup?"

"Yes!" Rafa and I said in unison.

The obnoxious bell finally blasted, putting an end to Megan's never-ending shopping list.

"I can't go to the mall," Rafa said quietly.

Even though our relationship status had changed three times this year, Rafa and I could still read each other's minds. I slung my arm over his shoulder and whispered, "Mom's paying your way. That includes shopping."

A beautiful smile spread across my gay boyfriend's face.

Rafa and I climbed out of Mom's car in front of consumer paradise: The Galveston Mall. "Be back here at seven," Mom said.

Megan thought of the Mall as her kingdom and all the people in it, her subjects, but to me it was pure chaos. When we stepped inside, Rafa's eyes widened, like Dorothy in Oz.

Megan had said she'd be at the sunglasses booth at four o'clock and when she tried to explain where it was located in the mall, I told her I already knew. But somewhere between February and March, the sunglasses booth must have taken a fertility pill because now they were everywhere.

"Great," I said to Rafa and started texting Megan.

Right after hitting send, I heard Megan's voice say, "If you want to see this pair with a bikini, come to South Padre Island for spring break." When I turned around, Megan was modeling a pair of shades to a guy on the football team she hadn't kissed yet. The guy she held captive wasn't even looking at the shades. Megan glanced at her phone, then dropped it back in her purse and continued modeling.

"She ignored my text!" I nudged Rafa. "Did you see that?"

"Are you kidding," Rafa said. "I'm taking notes."

When Megan spotted us, she flattened her palm against the guy's chest and pushed him away. "Go tell your friends," she said, smiling at us. By the pleading look on his face, the poor guy was not finished gaping.

Rafa raised both arms and bowed three times to Megan.

Megan lifted her chin and grinned. "Watch and learn, little boy. Watch and learn."

Three purchases later, we scratched shades off our list. Megan chose wire rim, I got big, black sunglasses that covered half my face, which Megan totally disapproved of, and Rafa selected bright green. They actually looked cool, but he's so cute, all the shades made him look like a fashionista.

I picked out a swimsuit quickly, and in the mirror, I noticed how unevenly my hair had grown back out since fairy girl whacked it off. Meanwhile, Megan had to try on every bikini in the store and Rafa was encouraging her supermodel fantasy. I decided to venture out on my own in search of flasks, even though I had no idea where to look. I started to ask the first sales person who walked by, but it was like asking someone's mother where they kept the flasks. Finally, I ran into a young girl with a department store tag pinned to her shirt.

"Men's department," she said, like it bored her.

Great, the man in the men's department was old enough to be my grandfather. "It's a Father's Day gift," I said. "For my dad." Ohmygod, when is Father's Day? It had to be coming up soon because the man seemed unfazed by my explanation and led me straight to the flasks.

They were beautiful. Sleek and silver, or chrome, or whatever. I picked one up and unscrewed the little lid. How cool was that? I imagined sipping vodka from my flask on the beach at night, with live music playing, and me all golden brown. "I'll take three," I said.

Clearly, I'd stunned the old man, but I owed him no explanation. I mean what could I say at this point? My father's a drunk? This was true, but it was none of his business and obviously there was no age requirement to buy a flask. When I returned to the bikini section, Megan had just finished making her purchase.

"Flasks? Check," I said, holding up the bag. Megan and Rafa fist bumped me and we moved on to junior clothes.

I'd been X-ing out the days until spring break like a prisoner counting down to freedom. Finally, the day to start packing arrived.

"Megan, it's me," I said on the phone. "Why do you always answer like you don't know who it is?"

"You sound cranky," Megan said with no emotion.

"Well God, doesn't it say Abby on your phone when I call?"

"No," she said, still uninterested in the conversation.

"What are you doing?" I asked.

"Painting my toes."

"Well, what does your phone say when I call?" Now I sounded cranky.

"My Besty."

I waited in silence while Megan painted her toenails. Really, my heart was sinking. Sometimes I didn't like myself very much and this was definitely one of those moments.

"Why are you so crabby?" she asked. "You better be in a good mood by tomorrow morning."

"I know." I paced around my room. "Have you been stashing away bottles of your mom's vodka?"

"Well, yeah, I got like one."

"You mean one each, right?" I had a super bad feeling that's not what she meant.

"Um, like one total," she said. "You want me to get

another one?"

"Ohmygod. Seriously?"

"Okay, chill," she said. "I'll go see what's down there. Call you back. Jeez."

I stared at: Call Ended. Unbelievable. I'd waited a whole month for this. And no way was she going downstairs right now with her toenails wet. I threw the phone on the bed. Since Megan wasn't calling me back anytime soon, I went on *friendworld* to see what everyone else was doing for spring break. Priscilla wrote a weird post about the triple Ps going to Florida. At least something was going right.

Rafa and his whole family stood on the porch when Mom and I pulled up in front of his house. He kissed his mom and dad goodbye and loaded a duffle bag in the trunk of our car. I had no idea how much alcohol we had for the week and I did not like surprises. Rafa rolled down the window to wave goodbye to everyone and they all waved back. Why couldn't I have a sweet, little perfect family like that?

When we pulled up to Megan's, she was loading something in her mom's car. Instead of pulling into the circular driveway, Mom parked on the street to keep plenty of distance between herself and Mrs. Applegate. Rafa and I grabbed our bags out of the trunk.

"Have fun, kids," Mom shouted from the window.

Kids? I blinked slowly.

"Abby," Mom said. "Abby, come here."

"What! God, I'm on vacation." I rolled my bag over to Mom.

"Be careful," she said, looking all worried.

I shook my head and dragged my bag up the driveway. Mom was so out of touch with reality.

Megan was already back inside when Rafa and I stashed our bags and climbed in the back seat.

"What is wrong?" Rafa said. "You should be happy."

I didn't realize I was scowling. I tried to relax my face and forced a weak smile. When Megan finally got in the front seat, I said, "Well?"

"Well what?" Megan asked while Mrs. Applegate locked the front door of the house.

"How many bottles did you get?" I whispered loudly.

Megan held up two fingers.

I let out a frustrated sigh.

"Stop worrying about it," Megan said. "There'll be plenty on the beach."

Megan was right. There would be plenty.

Mrs. Applegate got in the car and all conversation virtually ceased. I slid down to stare out the window while Rafa listened to music.

Six and a half hours and two not-so-funny DVDs later, we were in South Padre Island. Actually, Rafa thought the movies were hysterically funny. Megan slept in the front the entire way and I envied her because I had been in excruciating pain during the whole trip. Not physical pain, more like restlessness. I wanted to be there already.

"Why didn't we just fly?" I asked Megan inside an enormous, glass rotating door that deposited us in the hotel lobby.

"All the flights were booked," she said.

While Megan and her mom went to the counter to check in, Rafa and I rummaged through brochures of fun stuff to do. I definitely wanted to go parasailing, purely for the adrenaline rush, not that I'd ever done it before, but it had to be a rush. Rafa picked up a water park brochure.

"That's lame," I said, having been to a gazillion water parks already.

Rafa looked hurt.

"It's for kids," I explained.

In the elevator, Rafa studied the water park brochure all the way up to the ninth floor.

"Can you find your room, Megan?" Mrs. Applegate asked.

"Yeah, we got it, Mom."

Thick, metal doors closed tight in front of Mrs. Applegate and the elevator whisked her away to the top floor, hopefully to be seen nevermore—or at least for a week. Megan and Rafa and I jumped around in the hallway, shrieking like girls.

Megan squished her face and squealed, "We're here!"

"I can't wait to see the room." Rafa was still jumping up and down.

I was just glad to be free. And I was thrilled Mrs. Applegate wanted to be free. I mean God, Mom would have gotten an adjoining room and set a curfew every night. And then she'd be bored and want to hang out with us all day. Fortunately Megan handed us our own key cards and pushed open the door, because I couldn't stop obsessing about how horrible it would have been if Mom had come.

Our room was huge, with a living room area, a small kitchen, and another room with two big beds. "Rafa honey," Megan said, "you get the sofa bed."

Rafa's eyes lit up. "I have my own room? My own TV? This TV is huge!"

Megan spun around and gave Rafa the look. "Okay, first of all, if you're going to be a diva, you have to be a lot more high maintenance than that."

Rafa had that half excited, half scared look.

"A diva," she said slowly, "would complain that the TV's not big enough."

Rafa grinned.

I threw my bag on the bed next to the window because I knew diva number one wanted to be next to the bathroom, close to her makeup and hair supplies. I stared out the window and counted how many years I still had to wait to be free from all bossy adults. A little over three years seemed like forever. I wasn't sure I could make it.

Megan threw her arms around my shoulders and screamed. "Ohmygod! Look at our view!"

I pushed her away and rubbed my ear. "You broke my eardrum."

"That's it!" Megan said. "You're not going to be crabby all week."

"Well, if you weren't so annoying, I wouldn't be crabby."

This time Megan didn't look mad, she looked hurt.

Rafa came in and glanced at each of us, his brow

furrowed. "What did I miss?"

"Megan's being annoying," I said firmly.

Megan rolled her eyes. "No, Miss Crabby needs a drink." Megan stormed to her bed, unzipped her suitcase, and pulled out a bottle of vodka. "Rafa, check the fridge for some orange juice. Oh wait, I forgot, she drinks it straight." Megan set the bottle on a table and gave me a hard look.

Rafa came in carrying a tray with three cartons of orange juice and three glasses. My eyes zeroed in on Megan's. I lifted the vodka, unscrewed the cap, and chugged straight from the bottle.

"No, no, no," said Rafa. "You spit in it."

"It's okay." Megan pulled out the second bottle. "We'll share." She poured vodka in two glasses, looked at me and said, "Alkies need their own bottle."

While Rafa diluted their vodka with orange juice, a wave of comfort washed over me. I didn't know if they were being mean or funny, and I didn't care. I took another swig. Alcohol burned through my nose and warmed my cheeks. Out of nowhere, a huge smile seized my face. I shouted out, "God that's good!" The fire breathing dragon was back.

Megan and Rafa started laughing and I was relieved because I thought they'd never lighten up. To show that I was a team player, I poured some vodka in a glass and held it up to make a toast. "To the best spring break ever!" We clinked our glasses and drank the fire.

Just as I was getting all relaxed, Megan looked out the window and said, "Everyone's at the beach."

Rafa took the cue and went straight to his end of the room and rummaged through his duffle bag. Meanwhile, diva number one went into the bathroom with her makeup kit. I assumed all this meant we were going to the beach.

I took my time unpacking, since diva number one would be in the bathroom for awhile. When I uncovered the shiny flasks, my heart lit up like a child unwrapping a present on Christmas morning. After lining up the three flasks and admiring them for a moment, I carefully filled mine from the bottle that contained my spit. For a boy, Rafa sure got grossed out easily. I filled the other two flasks with the germ free bottle they were sharing.

Rafa danced over wearing a black T-shirt, white swim trunks, and his green shades. I pulled the buds out of his ears and said, "They have live music on the beach every night. You don't need these."

"How do you know?" he asked.

I showed Rafa a flyer next to my bed that had the lineup of live music for the week.

"We need music in our room." Rafa started dancing again to whatever imaginary music he had going on in his head. I picked up the remote and found a good music station.

"Ahhhhhh, I love that song!" Megan screamed from bathroom and began singing.

I tilted my flask. The vodka flowed with the music through my body.

"Which flask is mine?" Rafa asked.

I smirked. "This spit free one."

Rafa pulled out his pocket knife. He was actually carving his initials in the bottom of the flask.

"Okay, you do know that you kissed me once and probably got some of my spit."

Rafa looked up from his engraving project. "I will always remember our kiss. You are the first and only girl I have ever kissed." He said it so sweetly.

"Did you know you were gay?"

He stared at the floor and quietly said, "I was trying to be straight."

I guess I should have felt insulted that he didn't really mean it, but I smiled and said, "Straight is overrated." I let Rafa carve our initials on the bottoms of all the flasks. It really was a good idea. While he did that, I changed into my orange bikini and threw on a pair of shorts.

Megan finally came out of the bathroom poised like a model and said, "How do I look?"

"Like a total sex goddess," I said, knowing it was exactly what she wanted to hear, but it was also true. Megan was a boy magnet. It really didn't matter what she was wearing since most of her magnetism came from her attitude, but looking like that, she'd just doubled her magnetic force. Maybe I should try to be more magnetic. I stuffed my flask in my back pocket and we headed to the beach.

— 29 —

By the time our flip-flops hit sand, the bright orange sun disappeared and multi-colored lights reflected on palm trees along the beach. We passed a sign that read, *No Glass on the Beach* and I reached around to feel the metal flask in my pocket, as if I would forget to bring it. Megan's magnetic force immediately turned three boys' heads and she stepped out in front, leaving Rafa and I to walk behind like peasants. I pulled out my flask and took a sip.

"Look at that," Rafa said, pointing to an outdoor buffet of shrimp and crab legs. I was starving, but Megan obviously had other priorities, so Rafa and I paid and loaded up our plates. We found a couple of chairs where we could eat popcorn shrimp and watch Megan hold court with a couple of guys.

"This reminds me of the movies." Rafa tossed a shrimp in the air and caught it in his mouth. I must have needed food because I tore through my shrimp and then sipped on my flask while Rafa finished eating.

When music started blasting from a stage not too far down the beach, Rafa and I tossed our plates in a bin and headed that way.

"Wait!" Megan shouted out from behind. I grabbed Megan's hand and pulled her through swarms of people to the stage until it was impossible to get any closer, but at least we could see the stage. The Backstage Boys belted out a song that Rafa loved and he was already lip synching, completely lost in his own little dancing world.

Megan had at least a half dozen boys in her magnetic field who were feeling her pull, but she clearly had her eye on one: tall and tanned, with a clearly defined six pack—and not the one in his hand. Megan licked her lips like she wanted him for dinner.

I folded my arms and checked him up and down. The guy had more curves in his arms than a rollercoaster. "Getting hungry?" I asked.

"I am," she replied deliciously.

I pulled out my flask and took another sip. When I turned around, Megan was already talking to the guy. He popped opened a can of beer and handed it to her, and then they laughed until their lips accidentally bumped into each other. Ohmygod, they were already making out! It was too weird to watch. Rafa was still lip synching his heart out, so I bent my knees and bounced up and down with the music, pretending like I was dancing with him.

In front of us, a group of guys had a funnel, the kind Rafa's brother used to put oil in his truck. A clear plastic tube, about an inch in diameter, was duct taped to the narrow end of the funnel. The tubing was about three feet long and I could not figure out why they needed oil changing stuff on the beach when there were clearly no cars anywhere. Eventually, one guy put the end of the tube in his mouth while another held the funnel above his head. A third guy reached up and poured a whole can of beer into the funnel and within seconds, the first guy with the tube in his mouth had downed an entire can of beer. It was insane.

"Ohmygod, I would never do that," I said to Rafa, who wasn't even looking at them. I was thirsty though, and a cold beer sounded pretty good. By all their laughter, they seemed harmless. "Go ask them for a beer," I said to Rafa.

"Who?"

"Those guys, over there." I nodded my head toward them.

"You go ask," he replied timidly.

"We are truly pathetic," I said. "Megan has more guts than the two of us put together." I slung my arm over Rafa's shoulder and moved in the direction of the boys with the weird contraption. "What's that?" I asked, like it was a random conversation.

The cute boy grinned and said, "Beer bong. Here, try it." Another boy held the funnel in front of me.

"No thanks. I was just curious."

"Oh, come on," the cute one said. "You have to try it."

I looked at Rafa, who was smiling and shaking his head

no.

"I'm Daniel," the cute one said. He looked half Asian.

"Abby," I said, "and this is Rafa."

Daniel introduced the other two guys, Bobby and Brad, but I wasn't paying attention. I had my eye on the ice chest.

"Have a beer," Daniel said.

"Oh thanks," I replied as unexcitedly as possible.

"Sure you don't want to give it a go?"

"Huh?" I said.

"The beer bong," Daniel said. "Try it."

I looked at Rafa, who shrugged.

"Sure," I said, "why not."

Daniel took the beer I was holding and handed me the end of the three-foot tube. Bobby and Brad operated the funnel end.

"Okay, put the tube in your mouth," Daniel said, "and just let the beer go down."

Bobby and Brad lifted the funnel and poured in the whole can of beer, which came through the tubing fast and I'd downed it within a matter of seconds. Daniel put his hands on my arms. "How does it feel?" he asked.

"Ohmygod," I said. "My stomach feels ice cold. It's crazy. Rafa, you have to try it."

Rafa was grinning. "No, I don't think so."

"That's cool," Daniel said and signaled the other two guys to pour a couple of beers in the bong for themselves.

After they all had a turn, we hung out and listened to the music. Daniel was cool. He didn't try to kiss me or anything, we just talked. He asked if Rafa was my boyfriend and when I said yes, my gay boyfriend, Daniel laughed and fist bumped Rafa.

After awhile, Daniel said, "Want another beer?"

"Absolutely," I said.

I downed another through the bong and before I could savor the ice cold feeling in my tummy, I heard Megan's voice say, "Ohmygod, you didn't! And I thought I scored tonight!"

I threw my arms around Megan and said, "I'm so glad to see you." I may have sounded drunk. "And these," I said, waving my hand all over the place, "are the beer bong boys."

"Hi beer bong boys," Megan said hurriedly. "Rafa, honey, let's get her back to the hotel."

"Bye Daniel." I waved my arm through the air. "Bye Daniel."

"She needs coffee," Megan said on the way back.

"No coffee." Rafa pulled my arm tighter around his neck. "Mamá says if you give a drunk man coffee, all you get is a wide awake drunk man.

"No coffee," I said. "Bad idea, coffee. Bad coffee. Ha, ha, ha. Bad coffee. Get it?"

"Jeez, she's ripped." Megan struggled to hold me up. "How did you let this happen?"

"I didn't know," Rafa replied.

"He didn't know," I said, totally sticking up for Rafa.

I didn't remember going through the rotating glass doors or riding up the elevator, but we must have because Megan was sticking her card in the slot and opening the door of our hotel room. I stepped on a paper just inside the door. "Oopsie," I said, and headed straight for bed because it felt like the floor was moving.

"What's this?" Megan picked up the paper.

"Someone must have slipped it under the door," Rafa said.

I propped up some pillows and sat on the non-moving bed.

"It's a test," Megan said, reading the paper. "Oh, this is funny! Let's take it."

"God, I hate tests." I reached around and tried to pull the flask out of my back pocket, but it was wedged between my butt and the bed.

"No worries," Megan said, giggling. "You're gonna ace it."

I lifted my butt and finally got the flask out.

"Number one," Megan said. "Are you unable to stop drinking after a certain number of drinks?"

"Oh God, it's the alkie test!" I screamed. "Lemme me see that!"

Megan kept reading. "It's from some treatment center. Guess they figured all the teenage alkies came to South Padre Island. Okay, number two: Do you need a drink to get motivated?"

"Absolutely not. Whoops, I slurred. Absolutely not."

"Do you repeat yourself?" Rafa chimed in.

Megan snorted and laughed, "They should have that on here!"

"I missed something. Huh? What…" and then I forgot what I was going to say.

"Okay, this is a real question. Number three: Do you often forget what happened while you were partying?"

"No," I said.

"What!" Megan and Rafa shouted in unison.

Megan gave me the look. "You are such a liar."

This was getting all confusing. Megan had her hands on her hips. "You had to watch videos to find out what you said at the rally." She sounded far away.

Smell of bacon. Bacon and eggs. Eyes glued shut. Maybe they'll open in a minute. People talking. Rafa. Now Megan.

Eye popped open. First one, then the other.

"You slut," Rafa said in a complimentary way.

"You're only a slut if people know," Megan argued.

"Ohmygod." My mouth barely moved. "You had sex."

"Well what do you know," Megan said. "It's alive."

Rafa, the kind one, came over and helped me sit up. "Would you like some breakfast?" Rafa asked. "Megan ordered room service."

"Part of your diva training?" I scanned the room. "My mouth feels like a desert. Death Valley, to be exact."

"What do you want?" Rafa said. "I'll get it for you."

"Water. God I love you right now." I made my way to the table and Rafa brought a glass of ice water. The ice gave me a headache as the water quenched my thirst. I watched them talk and eat, but I didn't participate. I figured they were lucky I was sitting there at all.

"Abby, did you even hear me?" Megan said.

"Huh?"

"I ordered this for you." She was pointing at some things on the table. "It's what my mother drinks to cure her hangovers." Megan pushed a large glass of tomato juice closer to me and set a bottle of Worcestershire sauce next to it. "Oh, and this." She plopped a bottle of hot sauce next to it.

I stared.

"God you're pathetic." Megan shook some hot sauce in the tomato juice and then added a few dribbles of Worcestershire sauce.

Rafa picked up a spoon and stirred.

"Oh, and black pepper." Megan sprinkled some in, while Rafa kept stirring.

"You want me to drink this?"

"Mom stirs it with a big stalk of celery, but the room service people said they didn't serve celery for breakfast."

I smelled it. My body didn't scream for me to reject it, so I took a sip. "Not bad," I said and took another swallow. "It's actually good."

"It's a virgin Bloody Mary," Megan said.

"A virgin?" I said. "Like a drink without alcohol?"

"It normally has vodka in it, but my mom drinks the virgins for breakfast."

My brain tried to process that, but it couldn't. I took another swallow to make room for the vodka I was going to add later when I could stand up. Finally, I made eye contact with them. "I think it's working."

About an hour later, Megan got in the shower. Rafa had already showered; I could tell by the stiff hair gel lines in his black hair. The no-longer-a-virgin Bloody Mary had kicked in and I was finally able to put a coherent sentence together. I ordered breakfast and turned up the music.

When Megan got out of the shower and opened the door to let the steam out, I was eating a stack of pancakes soaked in butter and drenched in maple syrup.

"What are we doing today?" Megan asked. "I vote for hanging out at the beach."

"The water park," Rafa said.

I swallowed a mouthful of pancake. "Parasailing."

Megan rolled her eyes. "I'm not doing that."

Rafa picked up the brochure. "Looks dangerous."

"Hey, you're supposed to be on my side," I said to Rafa.

"It's settled then," Megan said, "we'll go hang out at the beach and figure out what we want to do from there."

"No, we'll go parasailing and figure it out."

"No, no." Rafa was laughing. "We'll go to the water park and from there we'll know exactly what to do."

Rafa was so cute. He made me smile.

"I bet the big, bad, beer bong boys are basking bare butted on the beach," Megan said. Betcha can't say that ten times!

Rafa's face lit up. "I bet the big, bad, beach bong boys—"

Megan had a silly laugh, like a xylophone going up. "Nice try, diva number two."

"Those guys were geeky." I tried to remember their names.

"They were funny!" Rafa said, and then his voice dropped. "—until you got too drunk. That was not fun."

Okay, awkward silence. "I'm sorry," I said, and I truly meant it. "I'll pay more attention to how much I'm drinking."

Megan studied my face. "No worries," she said. "It's spring break."

"Look!" Rafa pointed at the brochure. "The parasailing is on the beach."

"Looks like we're going to the beach," I said.

"Yes!" Megan beamed.

— 30 —

Amid gusty winds, it took two of us to get all three towels laid out on the sand. We got Diva number one set up first and she sat poised on her towel, texting someone, while Rafa and I struggled to get the other two towels spread out evenly.

Rafa picked up the sun block. "You do me and I'll do you."

I smeared cream all over his back and then sat on my towel and watched parasailers float over the Gulf of Mexico while Rafa returned the favor. I took a sip from my flask. "That's where I wanted to be," I said, "floating in the sky."

"Megan, here." Rafa tried to hand her the sun block.

Megan flipped hair off her shoulder and leaned back. "No thanks," she said. "Someone's coming to do that for me."

"Ahhhh," Rafa and I said simultaneously.

"Lemme guess," I said. But then I couldn't think of his name. "Wait, I can see him, the guy with a six-pack tummy and rollercoaster arms." Rafa and Megan stared, waiting for me to produce a name. Finally, it occurred to me. "You never told me his name."

"You never asked," Megan said bitterly.

She was right. I hadn't even asked. And just when I was feeling like the worst friend ever, Rafa intervened. "Jax, with an x."

"Cool name!" I said in my most interested voice.

"He's very cool," Megan said with a curly smile.

And right at that moment, Jax with an x appeared.

"Hey." Obviously Megan wanted to sound only half interested. She held up a tube of sun block and he took it.

Jax turned Megan over on her tummy and straddled across her butt. I stood up to go walk around and signaled Rafa to get up and go with me. While Jax squeezed sun block in the palm of his hand, Megan reached around and unsnapped her bikini top. Rafa's mouth dropped when Jax started rubbing lotion on her back with his tanned arms glistening in the sun.

"Dude," I said all aggravated. Rafa's eyes would have popped out from behind those shades if I hadn't pulled him away.

We zigzagged through a maze of people on the beach until we reached water. The waves felt cool on my feet and I drew in a long breath of salty air. "I love it here," I said to Rafa. Not that we didn't have a beach at home, but here the water seemed bluer and you didn't have to worry about bumping into adults who knew your parents.

With the sun warming my face, I took a sip from my flask. "Megan had that guy's number," I said to Rafa and wiped my mouth with the back of my hand. "I should've gotten the number of those beer bong boys. What was the name of the guy I liked?"

"Daniel," Rafa said. "You have his number. You let him put it in your phone last night."

"I did?" I scrolled through my contacts. Dad, Daniel. "There it is!" We walked along the shore toward a big banner that read, *Over the Rainbow Parasailing*, with a multi-colored parachute swaying in the wind above.

"Are you going to call him?" Rafa asked.

"I dunno," I replied. "Are you going parasailing with me?" Even though his heart wasn't in it, Rafa said he would. He probably didn't want me to run off with Daniel and have no one left to hang out with. "I promise I'll go to the water park with you tomorrow."

Rafa's big, beautiful smile reappeared.

We stepped into the harnesses of a tandem parasail and two big, burly guys got the parachute all full of wind. One of the guys waded out and grabbed a line from a boat that was backing in toward the beach. He clipped the line to our parasail and signaled the boat to take off, and within seconds, we were airborne. While Rafa white knuckled the harness, I threw up my arms and let out a cry of freedom.

We moved out over the Gulf of Mexico and below, in turquoise water, the boat shrank into a miniature toy, until it was nothing more than a speck with a long whitewater tail. At last Rafa loosened his grip and scanned the horizon. It was as if we were actually flying, except for the tug of the harness from the line that connected us to the boat like an umbilical cord. I resented the cord because I wanted to be free from everything on earth, completely free. No more Mom, who wouldn't let me drink or do anything else I'm clearly old enough to do. No more Dad, who was entirely too old to be reliving his teenage years with the Kat creature. No more poverty for sweet, loving families, like Rafa's. I pulled out my flask and took a swallow. The world wasn't fair.

"Hand me your pocket knife," I shouted to Rafa.

"Why?"

I took another swig. "I want to cut this stupid umbilical cord so we can be free."

Rafa peered at me sideways. "You are drunk."

I punched him in the arm, which made us sway to the side and he tightened his grip on the harness again. I took one more swig and stuffed the flask in my back pocket.

We began dropping down, closer to the water. The guys on the boat were reeling us in, like fish on a line. That's all we were to them, just two fish on a line that they were reeling in. It wasn't fair, but really life wasn't fair. I was getting woozy.

"The ride is almost over," Rafa announced, as if he'd just figured that out.

"Why is it only a ten minute ride? Why can't we stay here all day if we want?" Rafa was right. I sounded drunk. I reached for my flask and pulled, but the flask slipped through my fingers and fell through the air to the water below. I pulled out my phone and Mom's credit card, and handed them to Rafa.

"What are you doing?" Rafa asked.

I unclipped the harness and pulled my legs out as fast as I could and jumped.

"Stop! No!"Rafa's voice trailed off.

Gravity had snatched my flask and I wanted it back. The fabulous feeling of free-falling ended too soon when I made the splash. The deeper I sank, the darker the water became and the colder it felt. I wasn't about to close my eyes. Not that I could see anything. Finally, I slowed enough to start making my way back up and paddled toward the light. I burst through the surface and blew out all the air I'd been holding underwater.

I treaded water, looking around, breathing hard. No flask in sight. Swells blocked my view. I dropped underwater and catapulted straight up to see over the swells. Still, no flask.

Duh! I had jumped *after* the flask fell, which meant it would have hit the water way behind me. To get my bearings, I located land, which was on my right. I needed to face land and swim to the right.

I swam a good distance, but still no flask. Surely it would float since nearly all of the vodka was gone and it had mostly air inside. Ohmygod, double duh, the current would have carried it closer to shore. I watched the swells. They moved at an angle toward land. I swam in that direction and looked around for something shiny—a beautiful metallic container for transporting a magical serum that made me feel normal.

Just when the idea flashed in my mind that it was

entirely possible I may never find the flask, something had found me. It was a fin. A big, triangular fin. And it was moving toward me. My heart raced. Even though I'd been treading water naturally, now it was something I had to focus on. My breath was short and my muscles tensed. Oh, God. I was actually going to die. There were times in my life I didn't care if that happened, but this was not one of them.

No point in swimming; sharks swim. I could catapult into the air again, or kick the shark, or dodge off to the side just before it attacks. When I visualized jumping or kicking, I saw the shark chomping down on my leg. Only one thing to do: I had to dodge it.

The shark was moving in, thirty more feet. I tightened my muscles to dodge its strike. Was it slowing down? It turned. It actually turned off to the left. I felt myself breathe again. Holy crap, it moved around me, circling. Oh God, circling its prey. Something banged the back of my head and splashed. I screamed like a girl.

"Grab the life preserver," a man's voice yelled out.

When I turned around, a bright orange thing bumped my face. A boat with *Over the Rainbow Parasailing* written on the side rocked back and forth in the swells. Not the same boat that was pulling us, a smaller one. I wrapped my arms over the orange donut and the man pulled me in. Suddenly, I was glad to have a cord connecting me to someone. That's when the fin came back into view.

"Shark," I said to the man. "Look, shark."

"That's a dolphin," he said, and pulled me up to the boat.

I climbed over and looked out at the dolphin. My whole body relaxed. "From up here, it looks like a dolphin, but when you're at eye level and all you see is that fin, it looks like a shark."

"Grab a towel," he said. "Let's get you to shore."

Captain Bob, at least that's what it said on his shirt, pushed the throttle forward and hauled ass back to the parasailing place where Rafa and I had launched. Rafa was there, with that same worried look on his face his mother gets when she sees my mother. Kind of funny, but weird. I climbed out of the boat and another guy came over. This was Captain Ray, according to his shirt.

"This young man over here says you jumped." His mouth twisted. "Is that right?"

"Yes, sir," I said and saluted him, being a captain and all.

He squinted and said, "Don't ever come back here again."

"Yes, sir!" I saluted again and headed toward Rafa, trying hard to not bust out laughing.

As soon as I got within earshot of Rafa, I said, "I'm expelled from parasailing." He started going off on me in Spanish. "Dude, you ratted me out," I interjected, but he went on and on, all the way back to where we'd set up camp on the beach. Megan and Jax were baking in the sun when we got back. Fortunately, Rafa had calmed down by then.

Megan shaded her eyes. "Where have y'all been?" They both rolled over on their tummies and looked up.

"Parasailing," I said.

Rafa crossed his arms and didn't say anything.

"Oh, sick!" Jax propped himself up on his elbows.

Megan propped herself up, too. "How was it?"

"Insane!" I said with as much enthusiasm as I could muster. "We killed it!"

"Let me translate," Rafa said sarcastically. "Abby went insane and almost killed herself jumping out of the parachute."

"How high were you?" Megan asked.

"At least three hundred feet," said Rafa the rat.

"I dropped my flask," I explained.

"Oh!" Jax beamed. "You are totally badass."

I smiled. It warmed my heart that I had just been promoted to the highest rank possible. It's way higher than captain of some lame parasailing boat. Ghetto Girl was once the ultimate BA. Maybe I wasn't faking it when I was Ghetto Girl. It could be that all that coolness was real. And just when I started feeling good about myself for the first time in my life, Rafa said, "I don't want to be around you when you are drinking." He picked up his towel and pushed off through the sand.

I didn't argue with Rafa, or chase him down and try to change his mind. A BA does not make an enemy of a friend, does not fight with a friend, and is always true to herself. Rafa needed time to cool off. I decided to sit my badass self down and let him. People don't realize it, but the title of BA carries with it huge responsibilities. Now that I had a clear picture of who I was, I needed to live by the code.

Megan and Jax got up and brushed sand off each other

while I stretched and yawned in the warm sun.

"We're going out in the waves," Megan said.

"Wanna go?" Jax asked.

"I'm good, thanks." A BA is polite and kind to others who are kind.

"Cool," Jax said and escorted Megan toward the shore.

Megan glanced over her shoulder at me. By the look on her face, she seemed genuinely happy that Jax had respected her besty. I stretched out on my tummy and buried my forehead in the fold of my arm. Life was good.

— 31 —

Rafa was not in the hotel room when Megan and I got back, but judging by the wet bathing suit hanging in the bathroom, he had already come back and showered. "I hope wherever he is, he's at least having some fun," I said to Megan. "Poor kid needs to lighten up."

"You scared the bejesus out of him when you bailed from that parachute," Megan said. "He cares about you."

"I doubt that," I snapped back and then I ordered a pizza. While Megan showered, I rummaged through Rafa's bag to see if he'd left his flask behind. No such luck. Now how was I supposed to drink on the beach?

After I showered, the pizza arrived, and Megan and I didn't talk the whole time we were eating. Just as we finished off the pizza, Jax showed up.

"See ya," Megan said. Jax fist bumped me and as they walked out, I spotted the other flask moving up and down in Megan's back pocket.

I let out a frustrated sigh. I bought all three flasks, so technically, they were all mine. You'd think one of them would figure that out and give me their flask. I sat and stared at the vodka on the table. Since my bottle was lower than theirs, I poured some of their vodka into mine to make up for the fact that they were being extremely selfish with their flasks. And then I took a swig from their bottle. My second night of spring break and I had no one to hang out with. Rafa was making me choose between drinking and him. "This is who I choose," I said out loud and took another swig. That's when I remembered the beer bong boys. I picked up my phone and called Daniel.

"Sup," Daniel said.

"Hey, this is Abby."

"Oh, psych. I was lookin' for you."

"You're at the beach?" I asked.

"By the stage," he said. "Where are you?"

I gathered up my key and credit card. "Hey, you guys have beer, right?" Probably a dumb question, but I needed to ask.

"Yeah and we scored a bottle of Mexican tequila."

I grinned and headed out the door. "On. My. Way."

The elevator took forever, and then that slow rotating door finally released me out into open where I was free to walk as fast as I wanted. I jogged along the outer edge of the crowded sidewalk because with the kind of luck I was having tonight, something better could come along and the beer bong boys would take off with their tequila and beer. Not that I'd ever tried tequila, but it was definitely on my to-do list. I picked up my pace and made it to the beach where people wandered aimlessly or huddled with their friends. Since I hadn't found my friends yet, I decided to look like I was wandering aimlessly, and finally, there they were: the nerdy, hilarious beer bong boys, but Daniel was much cuter than I remembered.

"Hey," I said without looking at him.

"There she is." He said it like we'd known each other forever.

The two other guys smiled, but I couldn't remember their names. And then as if they'd read my mind, or maybe it was the lost look on my face, they said, "Bobby. Brad."

"Bring your friends?" Daniel asked.

"Nope, just me." I shrugged, like I was apologizing. Maybe he was disappointed that I hadn't brought Megan the boy magnet, or Rafa the rat.

"Alright, let's head out," Daniel said all cheery.

Bobby and Brad lifted the ice chest.

"Head out?" I said.

"We can't stay here," Daniel explained. "With glass being totally illegal on the beach and all." He reached in the pocket of his baggy shorts and pulled out a bottle of tequila.

Bobby opened a button down shirt to reveal what was underneath. My mouth dropped. Over a Pancho Villa T-shirt almost exactly like mine, two black straps loaded with shot glasses crisscrossed his chest.

"Pure Velcro," Bobby said proudly.

"Don't laugh," Daniel added. "We might actually be engineers if we ever grow up."

Okay, that explained the duct taped beer bong. They were inventor geeks. Somehow that made me feel comfortable and since they were all staring at me, waiting for my reaction, I smiled and said, "Lead the way."

We found a place in the sand dunes where we were sort of hidden, but had a great view of the full moon rising over the Gulf of Mexico.

"And then there's that ridiculous law about how old one has to be to drink, like sixteen isn't old enough." Daniel flipped open the ice chest. "It's wack. Who makes these laws?"

"My dad," I said. "Well, he didn't make that law, but he was a lawmaker." I'm so not telling them I'm fourteen.

Brad pulled out the bong. "Our guest of honor can go first," he said and handed me the tube.

"Wait!" Daniel said. "Your dad's a politician?"

"No, no." Bobby wagged his finger at Daniel. "Once the bong is removed from the ice chest, all serious conversation must cease."

Bobby popped open a beer and poured it through the funnel. The ice cold liquid filled my stomach. I handed the tube to Daniel and closed my eyes. And then I let out an enormous burp that I didn't even know was coming.

"Yes!" Bobby and Brad high fived each other.

Okay, that was kind of nerdy. I mean nobody high fives anymore except old people. But it was their nerdiness that made them kind of cute and definitely real.

"Wait, who's your dad?" Daniel asked.

"Nope, you know the rules, Danny boy," Bobby said with a smile. "Drink first, ask questions later."

After everyone had downed a beer, we all got quiet and mellow.

Brad eventually broke the silence. "Oh beautiful one, Sir Daniel over here really wants to know: Who's your daddy?"

"Yeah, is it him, him or me?" Bobby asked, cracking up.

"You'll have to excuse my poor judgment in friends," Daniel said, half kidding.

"No, no, they're hysterical!" I said, staring at the beer.

"Well alright then," said Daniel, cocking his head. "Who's your daddy?"

"He's not a senator anymore," I said dismissively, "so it's no big deal." They all stared, waiting. "Oh crap, whatever. John Alexander."

This time it was their mouths that dropped.

Bobby peeled off his shirt and pulled four shot glasses from the arsenal strapped across his chest. Daniel pulled out the bottle of tequila.

"Damn," Daniel said. "I did not see that coming."

Bobby cleared his throat and Brad just sat there with his eyes bugged out.

"Seriously?" I said. "Give me the frigging tequila. Let's get this over with." I filled the four shot glasses and passed them out. I looked Daniel in the eye, lifted my shot glass, and in my most sarcastic voice said, "To scandal."

Brad smiled first. "To scandal!"

Daniel stared in disbelief.

"Wait!" Bobby said. He unstrapped a salt shaker and a

lime from his chest and cut the lime into four pieces. "Have you ever had tequila?" he asked me.

I shook my head, but I wasn't really thinking about the question. I was relieved we were actually having a normal conversation again.

Bobby licked his hand, sprinkled salt on it and then licked the salt off. He signaled me to do the same. After I had, he threw back the shot and downed it all at once. His whole face puckered up, and then he stuck the lime in his mouth and sucked as hard as he could. I immediately downed mine and sucked on the lime. Tequila tasted completely different than vodka and honestly, it wasn't very good, but I immediately refilled my glass.

"Come on!" Bobby said. "We're getting sober sitting here waiting for you guys to catch up." He moved the glasses closer to Daniel and Brad.

Once everyone got caught up and could handle reality, I said to Bobby, "I have that shirt. Pancho Villa. I like that guy."

"Liked," said Brad. "He's dead you know."

"Yeah, but he went out in a blaze of glory," Bobby said.

Daniel grinned. "If you fight for what you believe in, you get a T-shirt after you're dead."

"How can you get a T-shirt if you're dead?" Brad asked.

"Pancho Villa stood up for something," I said. "That's important."

"Damn right that's important." Bobby poured another round of tequila. "To Pancho Villa."

After we spit out our limes, I said, "Let's go stand up for something. You know, wrong a right."

Daniel laughed. "You mean right a wrong."

"That calls for another shot," Bobby said. "To righting wrongs!"

Together we licked, swallowed, sucked, and spat.

"What's a wrong we need to right?" Brad asked.

"I can't think of anything right now," said Bobby.

"I can think of a hundred things," Daniel said.

"Name one." I didn't know who said that. They all sounded drunk.

"I have one," I announced, fully aware that I sounded drunk too, but proceeded anyway. "Look at that dumb sign." I pointed in the general vicinity of the sign. "Why can't we bring a glass bottle to the beach? Isn't glass made of sand?" I sifted sand through my fingers. "If it breaks, it just goes back to being sand."

"How are you gonna get rid of the signs?" Brad asked. "Run for city council?"

I got up and staggered over to the sign, which was not easy. "We need to change the signs," I said. "All of them."

"Change to what?" Daniel asked.

"Betcha all didn't know I'm really a badass." I could tell by their puzzled looks they didn't believe me. "No seriously, people actually call me badass."

"I did not know that about you," Daniel said.

"Here's what I think." Then I forgot what I was going to say.

"We're listening," said Bobby.

Finally, my brain started working again. "We could change these signs," I patted the pole with my hand. "Right now it says, *No Glass on the Beach*. We paint over the *No* and the *Gl* so it just says *ass on the beach*."

Bobby's face lit up.

"Then write *Bad*, so the sign says, *Badass on the Beach*."

Bobby and Brad howled.

"We'll hit every sign from one end of the beach to the other." I opened my arms to be more dramatic.

Daniel got up and dug around in his pocket. He dangled some keys in the air and said, "I'll go get my truck!"

— 32 —

I awaken in a room with no color. A small room with walls made of concrete blocks painted an ugly shiny beige. I am on a cot. Across the narrow room, a big steel door with a small window reveals that someone is outside. I shuffle to the door and pull the handle. The door is locked. I knock on glass. The person on the outside is wearing a uniform, a policewoman. She turns around to look at me, but does not open the door. I bang the glass. I am weak. Can she hear me?

The officer opens the door.

"Where am I?"

"Stop knocking on the window." She shuts the door.

The badge on her arm says something, something juvenile detention center.

"Wait!" I scream. "You've made a terrible mistake!"

She scowls at me.

"I'm not the kind of person who belongs here!"

The officer walks away.

"They made a mistake," I say quietly.

I go back to the cot and rest my head on a blanket. I am too weak to freak out.

I am looking down at myself. At the ceiling, someone is beside me. I don't know who. Far below, my body is in a bed and it is unconscious. But I am not unconscious. I am here, above, awake.

At the ceiling, I feel peaceful, wise. I gaze at myself below. I appear sickly. I feel a deep sadness for the person on the bed. The person is me.

The person below stirs. There is panic. She pulls.

I go back.

I hear a siren. Lights too bright. Bed is bouncing. Someone holds a plastic mask over my face. I am in an ambulance.

— 33 —

I bolted up. A plastic mask smashed itself against my face. I grabbed for the mask, but my hands were stuck. Not stuck, shackled. My hands were shackled to a rail on each side of the bed like a crazy person or a prisoner. Tubes projected from my arms and connected to an I.V. drip bag. I was in a hospital.

I almost died. I left my body and went to the ceiling. I was pretty sure that qualified for almost dying. I needed to stay awake. Falling asleep could equal death. I would force myself to stay awake, no matter what—keep my eyes open, concentrate.

I shivered in the cold. The room was gray. I didn't notice that until a light peeked in. Someone pushed the door ever-so-slowly. It felt eerie and I wished they'd hurry up and come on in. I didn't see how things could possibly get any worse, unless the person sneaking in the door was a serial killer. I blinked slowly, waiting. It was Rafa.

"Help me get these things off." I rattled the handcuffs on the metal side rails.

Rafa's eyes grew wide like I was a ghost or something. "You're awake," he said.

"There has to be a key around here." My voice cracked. "Turn on the lights and find it."

Rafa ran out of the room, screaming, "She's awake, she's awake!"

Ohmygod. Was I the only sane person left on the planet? My eyes scoured the room for a key, but every tabletop looked like sterilized gray Formica, untouched by human fingerprints, and then my eyes stopped and zeroed in on Rafa's duffle bag that was draped over my suitcase in the corner of the room. Before I had time to finish saying WTF, the lights came on and three medical people in scrubs surrounded me. One shone a flashlight in my eye.

I squirmed. "If you're looking for me, I'm right here!"

Without a word, he looked inside my other eye. When he finished, he said, "Follow my pen with your eyes."

It's not like I had anything else to do. My eyes wandered around in my head, following the stupid pen wherever it went.

"Can you hear me?" another one asked. And then he said it loud and slow. "Can. You. Hear. Me?"

The man was living proof that I was the only sane person left on the planet. "If I couldn't hear you," I said patiently, "I wouldn't have been following the pen with my eyes." But the mask had muffled my voice, which explained why they were ignoring me and talking to each other.

A wave of dizziness washed over me and I closed my eyes. My mind melted into the pillow and my breathing slowed. I was drifting back to sleep and I couldn't make myself stop.

The memory of looking down at my body floated into my head. My eyes thrashed open. Rafa stood next to me and the medical people were gone. I forced my eyelids open as far as possible and refused to even blink. "Stay awake," I said inside the oxygen mask, "I'm awake."

Rafa took my hand. His puffy eyes gazed down at me. Thin lines of tears glistened on his cheeks. I squeezed his hand tight, afraid to let go.

With my other hand, I pointed to the mask. "Take it off, please."

Rafa lifted the mask enough for me to ask, "Why am I pinned down like a wild animal?"

He gently put the mask back into place. "They said you are under arrest for many things. Your mom, she is almost here. I promised I would stay with you."

"Arrested for what?" I shouted. "Get this mask off!"

"I can't," he said. "You need it to breathe. Just listen and I will tell you."

I squished my eyes to hold in the tears that were coming. Whatever it was, it was bad. I'm not the kind of person who gets arrested. Maybe I was in a car accident. But why would I get arrested for that?

"The police, they will not tell me everything." Rafa stroked my hand softly. "They will only tell your parents. I told them your dad, he lives in Mexico." His voice was weary. "They, they called your mom. She can tell you more. All I know is they said multiple charges. This is all they would say to me. There is a police lady sitting outside the door."

Warm tears slid down both sides of my head and creeped into my ears. Because I was being held captive, I couldn't wipe them. I couldn't even ask for a tissue because of the stupid mask on my face. Maybe it was some kind of weird water-in-the ears torture system they used to get people to confess. But how could I confess? Wait, how could I deny everything? I had no idea what I'd done.

Rafa hunched over me and wiped my tears. "You almost died."

That was true. It was the only part I remembered.

"How?" I muffled weakly underneath the mask.

"They said you have alcohol poison."

"Huh?" With the mask muffling my voice, I said, "Maybe the policewoman outside the door can tell me what happened."

Rafa lifted the mask and I said it again.

He nodded. "I'll get her."

When Rafa opened the door, Queen Doreen's voice came bellowing in from the hallway. "Your daughter needs a lawyer!" she was screaming in the phone as she blew in the room.

My stomach twisted. My eyes followed the clear plastic tubing from my arm up to the IV bag. If I could get an IV bag of vodka, one drop at a time, that would be perfect because then I wouldn't over drink.

"Thank God you're all right." Mom tossed everything in a chair and wiped my tears, which I'd completely forgotten about. She lifted the mask and placed it on my forehead. "How did this happen?"

She was definitely asking the wrong person. I looked away. "I was hoping someone could tell me."

"She does not know anything," Rafa said. "I do not know anything. I was not there." Rafa said it like he felt guilty. Hurting myself didn't bother me nearly as much as hurting Rafa. He was so sweet, unlike me. "Do you want me to leave now?" Rafa asked Mom.

Mom's eyes examined both of us, sizing us up on her bull crap meter.

"No honey, sit down. I told them you were her brother so they'd let you stay in the room until I got here." Mom clenched her jaw. "I still can't believe Gwen Applegate left you here like this."

"She was poisoned with alcohol," Rafa said. "That is all I know."

"Someone poisoned me?" I asked.

"No one poisoned you," Mom said calmly. "You overdosed on alcohol. That's called alcohol poisoning. They weren't sure you were going to make it." Mom's voice was shaking.

Who knew you could overdose on alcohol? I thought that only happened to druggies. I closed my eyes. The beer bong boys. Tequila. It must have been the combination of beer and tequila. I might have had some vodka that day, too.

I heard my ringtone. Rafa pulled my phone out of his

pocket. He read the screen and silenced the phone. With eyes squinted, he snarled at the phone and said something in Spanish.

"Who is it?" Mom said. "Give me that."

"Excuse me, but it's MY phone." I turned my palm up and raised my hand the maximum six inches allowable by law.

"You are no longer in charge of your life." Mom took the phone and read the screen. "Who is Daniel?"

Daniel. I closed my eyes and smiled. Whenever I closed my eyes, waves of blurriness washed through my brain and made me sleepy. I kept my eyes closed anyway. I wanted Mom and Rafa to go away.

I don't know how long I slept, but when I awoke, they were still there. My mouth was dry and gritty like beach sand. I needed water. Rafa and Mom weren't looking at me, which was good because I needed a break from them more than I needed water. The last thing I remembered was sitting on the beach with the Beer Bong Boys. More than anything, I wanted to talk to Daniel. He wanted to talk to me, too.

Without moving my head to tip off my captors that I was awake, I slid my eyes around the room, searching for my phone. The Queen of Control probably had it in her purse. With my hands cuffed, I had zero chance of getting the phone. The handcuffs definitely had to go and if anyone could get them off, it was Queen Doreen.

"I need water," I said in a raspy voice that was totally real.

Mom jumped up. "Of course you do." She poured

water from a Styrofoam pitcher into a plastic cup. "The doctors said you're dehydrated from all that alcohol." She tipped the cup to my lips and my tongue absorbed the water, like dry sand absorbing a cold ocean wave.

"More," I said. My tongue had hogged all the water and there was nothing left to swallow. Mom tilted the cup again. This time, cold water passed through my raw throat. I took several swallows. What I really needed was Daniel's beer bong to get the whole pitcher of cool water into my stomach.

"Slow down, honey."

She pulled the cup away and I wanted to say something totally smartass, but my body let out a huge sigh of relief instead. I needed to know why I was under arrest, but I really didn't want Mom to be the one explaining it to me. I rubbed my eyes and that's when I noticed my hands were free.

Maybe it was all a bad dream—the mean prison guard, dying and going to the ceiling, the handcuffs. I lifted my hands to check for any marks on my wrists. The red marks were real, but what bothered me more was the fact that my hands were trembling like I had some kind of weird neurological disorder.

"Lovely," I said. "Let's add Parkinson's to the list of reason I'm having the worst day ever."

"You don't have Parkinson's," Mom said.

Again, the big door opened slowly and I was tired of guessing who was going to come in next. It had to be a doctor or a nurse since Rafa and Mom were here.

"Hey, sugar dumpling."

"Ohmygod, Dad!"

Mom rolled her eyes and stood up. Dad nearly knocked Mom over making a beeline for me. Mom hastily gathered her things and headed for the door. Rafa stayed put for the drama that was about to unfold with the arrival of Dad. It was the diva in him.

Mom turned back. "Don't expect any father-of-the-year awards, John. If you had supervised your child in Mexico, she wouldn't be here."

Sometimes Mom was a real witch. Clearly, she was having a relapse from that nice, new personality they'd given her at the treatment center back in November.

Dad lowered the jail bar that I had been shackled to earlier and sat on the edge of the bed. He squeezed my trembling hands and then pulled me into his arms. "You don't have to do this alone, sweet baby. We're gonna do this together."

I had no idea what he was talking about. "Are you my lawyer?" I guessed. "Do I need one?"

"Yes and yes," Dad said. "I've already talked to the police and we're working on a deal."

"Will someone please tell me what's going on!" I screamed.

"Calm down, baby. I'm fixin' to tell you everything I know."

Rafa moved to the other side of the bed and lowered the railing, too. He pulled a chair up close.

"What do mean, 'a deal?' Are they trying to give me the death sentence?"

Dad looked sad as he gazed down at me. It was eerie

because I knew how he felt. I'd felt the same way when I was at the ceiling looking down at myself.

"Metaphorically speaking, you do have a death sentence to deal with. But that doesn't have anything to do with the police."

"Now I'm totally confused."

"Let's take one thing at a time," Dad said. "They have four charges against you."

I held my breath.

"Public intoxication. That's number one." Dad had that professional lawyer tone. It was the tone he used to explain super emotional things in a matter-of-fact way. It put me at ease because I was getting sick of my feelings.

"Now, we can't argue with that," he said. "Your blood alcohol level was point three nine. A point zero eight is legally drunk."

It took a minute to process the numbers in my brain. Meanwhile, Dad's eyes welled up and his tone changed. "Baby, a point four o is legally dead. I almost lost you."

Rafa sniffled.

No, no, no, it was not time to cry. I wanted answers. I needed Dad to get back into legal mode and stay there.

"I have no intention of arguing with the fact that I was drunk," I said. "What else?"

Dad cleared his throat. "Number two, vandalizing state property."

"What!" I bolted up.

Rafa's eyes got big, like he was watching a horror movie.

"They have photos of the signs you allegedly painted.

Badass on the beach." Dad raised his eyebrows like he was trying to keep a straight face.

Something clicked in my brain. "I remember talking about painting the signs, but not actually doing it. How do they know I did it?"

Dad stayed in professional lawyer mode and said, "There's a video of you on You Tube, sitting on a boy's shoulders painting the sign."

"I do not remember that," I said.

Dad shrugged. "Doesn't matter. They have the video. The boy was arrested, too."

"Daniel? Was it Daniel?"

Dad scratched his head. "I think that was his name."

"Well, it could have been Bobby or Brad," I said.

Rafa cleared his throat.

"What were you doing drinking with a bunch of boys?" He was clearly in dad mode now. Rafa bristled while Dad unfolded a piece of paper. Completely exasperated, I opened my mouth to speak when Dad said, "Daniel."

I let out a guilty sigh. The whole thing was my idea and Daniel had been arrested, too. Now I was the one getting teary. No. Stop. "Let's finish this," I said. "What else?"

Dad took a deep breath. "Resisting arrest and assaulting a police officer."

"What?" I shrieked. "I do not remember that!"

Dad and Rafa got quiet. I got quiet, too. Obviously, the police had made a huge mistake. I'm not the kind of person who goes to jail.

— 34 —

No longer illuminated by sunlight, the outer edges of the hospital curtain appeared dark. A few dim lights from the beeping medical equipment surrounding me left gray shadows here and there. All at once, a sea of rats made their way up the walls, crawling to get to the ceiling. Within seconds, they reached the top, and then more came, so many they had to crawl over each other to climb higher. I think I stopped breathing. Hundreds, maybe thousands of rats climbed the walls, but none came near the bed. The fact that they weren't climbing on me felt odd, like somehow, in the midst of all the rats, I felt safe.

Like a dead person sitting up in a coffin, someone emerged from the shadows. With arms stretched forward like a zombie, it moved toward me, and when it touched my face, I screamed.

"It's all right honey," Mom said.

The thump of my heart pounded my ears. Sweat bled

from my pours. Mom pulled me close and wiped my forehead with a cool wash cloth. I checked the walls. The rats were gone.

"It's OK," she said. "You're detoxing."

I tried to speak but couldn't. A nurse appeared and gave me a shot. My eyelids grew heavy and the world went black.

When I awoke, the sun streamed through the window. Mom, Dad and Rafa sat in chairs, scattered around the room. Dad texted someone, probably the Kat, Rafa played a game on his phone, and Mom stared at me, worried. I'd never been so thirsty in my life. Before I could say that, Mom held a cup if ice water to my lips and it soothed me, but I shivered in the coldness of the damp sheets.

"How long have I been here?" I asked in a raspy voice.

"A week." Mom combed my hair with her fingers. "How do you feel?"

Dad and Rafa stood on the other side of the bed and stared as if I were a two headed freak in a traveling circus.

"Exhausted. When can I go home?"

"Soon," Mom replied, but then she looked at Dad, as if waiting for him to say something.

Dad pulled up a chair and leaned in. "Baby, you're not going home from here."

Oh yeah, all those charges. Dad was busy organizing in his brain exactly how he was going to deliver some news that I wasn't going to like. Too weak to rush him, I waited. Truthfully, I didn't want to even hear it.

Dad placed his hand gently on my head and looked

straight into my eyes. "As soon as you're released from here, the police will take you into custody."

My nose tingled and my eyes welled up. I fought back tears as hard as I could, but when I tried to speak, my lips trembled. Warm tears crawled down both sides of my head and filled my ears with water again. This time it wasn't annoying because I had bigger problems than water in my ears. Mom handed me a bunch of tissues and pushed a button that raised my back until I was sitting up.

Dad continued in his lawyer tone. "They will take you to an alcoholism treatment center."

My heart stopped. "What!" I said.

Dad cleared his throat. "After twenty-eight days in treatment," he continued in a complete monotone, "you'll serve three months in the Galveston County Juvenile Detention Center.

It took a minute to process that one in my brain. I remembered being at the ribbon cutting ceremony with Dad. "You mean that new building you got all the credit for?"

Dad shook his head yes, but it was more of a circular motion, like he was confused.

"How ironic," I said sarcastically.

"Look," Dad said in a stern tone. "I'm trying to get them to agree to three months of community service in lieu of time served, but they're not going to agree to anything until you change your attitude."

I decided to shut up. Everything coming out of my mouth was obviously going to be used against me in a court of law.

A nurse came in and everyone scattered back to their chairs, as if they were just as relieved about the interruption. While the nurse checked my vitals, I opened my mouth to ask if I would live, but realized dying wasn't such a bad alternative. I closed my eyes, hoping to drift back into a comatose state, but thoughts streamed faster through my mind and it got dark and scary in there, so I lifted my heavy eyelids open again.

After the nurse left, a doctor came in and talked to Mom and Dad over in the corner of the room. Rafa stayed in his seat and looked at me like I had some kind of disgusting disease. My eyes moved toward the window and I wondered if there was any way to escape. If there was a way, I would figure it out. Life as a criminal on the lam sounded pretty good. After all, it was kind of a family tradition, since that's what Mom had called Dad when he moved to Mexico. Ohmygod, Dad could smuggle me into Mexico and I could go to school with Gabby, and we could leave this whole mess behind, like it never happened.

After the conference of the adults was over, Mom immediately began going through my suitcase and holding up clothes for inspection. Clearly, we were leaving.

"Dad," I said, "can't I just move to Mexico with you instead of going through all this drama?"

Dad furrowed his brows. "You don't have a choice."

"You mean you don't want me."

"No," Dad said calmly. "You have to stay here and take responsibility for the things you did that were wrong."

"Oh, I see," I said. "Like you."

Dad got all tongue tied. "I didn't break the law."

"You broke our family law," I said, my anger stirring deep inside. "Why don't you have to take responsibility for that?"

The room went silent. Dad's head dropped and he mumbled, "I'm paying for it now." And for the first time in my life, I watched my dad cry. Mom looked just as stunned. No one said a word as Dad lowered himself into a chair with his face buried in his hands, sobbing. It went on for a few minutes and no one tried to stop him, or comfort him, but somehow, his pain comforted me, like a huge weight had been lifted—maybe because Dad was finally carrying some of the emotional burden.

After Mom helped me shower and get dressed, a policewoman came in with a zip tie and pulled my hands behind my back. "Seriously?" I said.

Mom pursed her lips and didn't even argue on my behalf. Neither did Dad, who was standing in the doorway. I glared at my parents and said, "I see how it is."

The bumpy van ride on the filthy gray vinyl seat seemed endless. I turned around to peer through the caged back window and saw Mom's car following behind, but Dad was driving. I was surprised they were still there since neither of them wanted me. My life as I knew it, was pretty much over.

The Corpus Christi Juvenile Detention Center wasn't as beautiful as the one Dad cut the ribbon for in Galveston. Fortunately, I didn't have to stay there. After I got fingerprinted and they took my mug shot, I was released into the custody of my parents. I sat in the back seat with Rafa on the long drive back to Galveston, rubbing my wrists from where the zip ties had pressed a mark into them and wondered if that was how people came up with the idea of cutting their wrists. It seemed like a pretty good idea, unless there was a lot of pain involved, but probably not as much pain as trying to go on with your life after completely screwing it up. I closed my eyes, not caring if I died again. If my soul were to leave my body, I wouldn't panic. I'll just let it happen, say goodbye, and never come back.

Unfortunately, that didn't happen. Five hours later, somewhere in Houston, we pulled into a driveway with a small sign next to a long, brick building that read, County Youth Alcohol and Drug Secured Treatment Facility, and yes, there were bars on the windows.

"John!" Mom shrieked. "I'm not leaving my daughter here!"

"Dad put the car in park and said, "It's either here or the Juvenile Detention Center in Galveston. If they put her in J.D., a criminal record follows her for life. This place will just show up on her medical record, saying she was treated for alcoholism. Y'all need to trust me on this one."

"Trust you," I said. "That's funny." I thought Mom would at least crack a smile on that one. "Did your treatment center look like this?" I asked Mom, hoping for some reaction.

Both Mom and Dad pushed open their car doors and

got out. Mom opened my door and I got out, too, but she brushed me aside and said to Rafa, "Honey, wait here." Clearly no one was speaking to me anymore.

Mom and Dad checked me in at the front desk and somewhere between the entrance and the desk, I shut down. When the lady behind the desk asked me a question, my mind wouldn't process whatever she was asking and my mouth refused to move. It was exactly the way I felt after seeing Dad on the news with the Kat creature for the first time. I think Dad answered the lady's questions, while Mom cried, and then they left. They might have said goodbye. I don't remember.

Some man escorted me down a long hall and then opened a door to what I assumed was my room. He put my suitcase on a cot. On the other cot sat a girl who looked like she was actually dead, but still in her body. A druggie.

"I'm not a drug addict," I said to the man. "I just drank too much. There's a big difference, you know."

The man handed me a schedule that I assumed he wanted me to follow, and then he left me alone with the druggie.

The rutty faced girl stared. I opened my suitcase, so I wouldn't have to deal with her. "Must be nice to go through life with no real problems," she said. "What'd you do? Drink some wine in one of them fancy glasses?"

I ignored her and rummaged through my suitcase for my phone. I needed to call Daniel. No phone. Mom. The witch. "Do you have a phone?" I asked the druggie.

She smiled and said, "Is that what you're looking for? I

thought maybe you smuggled something good in here."

I stuffed everything back in the suitcase. "Do you have a phone or not?"

"No phones allowed," she said. "No communication with the outside world. You may as well put your clothes in the drawers. You're gonna be here awhile."

I sat on the cot and stared at the schedule. The creepy drug addict brushed her split hairs and then announced, "We have a meeting in ten minutes."

"I can read." I studied the schedule, but didn't understand all the acronyms, except the one that said, AA. That was the meeting we had in ten minutes.

"What's your name?" Creepy Girl asked, obviously not getting the message that I wanted to be left alone. I pulled clothes from my suitcase and stuffed them in a drawer. "Kayla," she continued. "I'm Kayla. And you are—?"

God, she was relentless. "Well," I finally said, "since you were here first, I'll be Prisoner Number Two."

Creepy Girl gave me the look.

"Learn that from your mother?" I asked.

Her stare turned cold. "I don't have a mother."

"Lucky you. Where's this meeting?"

She got up and walked out the door, so I followed. We ended up in a room with rusty folding chairs, set up in a circle. Creepy Girl plopped down next to a big girl with a Mohawk. "I got a debutante," Creepy Girl said to The Mohawk right before some lady, who obviously worked at the treatment center, started the meeting. It was one of those kum ba yah things where everyone shared their pathetic feelings. I wanted to scream that everyone needed to get a grip, but decided against it because I just wanted to do my time and get out. After an hour of agonizing boredom, the professional lady asked me why I was there.

"To become a better human being," I replied, hoping that would satisfy everyone, but I don't think it did, because they stared at me like I was the pathetic one and then the meeting was over. I sprang from my seat to get out of there fast, but Creepy girl grabbed my hand and then someone else took my other hand. They chanted something about serenity, which sounded vaguely familiar, and then the meeting was really over. The whole thing made me want to drink.

From there, Creepy Girl led me to the cafeteria, where we ate processed chicken in mushroom soup and some canned green beans and corn. I spoke to no one and from there, went straight to my room.

"It's movie night," Creepy Girl said. "Come on."

"I'm going to bed early." I shut the door behind her and then curled up on the cot, pulling my knees all the way up. I needed to be held, but there was no one to hold me. I grabbed a blanket from the foot of the bed, pulled it over my shoulders, and gently rocked myself, pretending someone was holding me in their arms and loving me.

— 35 —

By the end of the first week, I felt like a rat in a science lab, doing the same things over and over, while people in white coats observed and took notes. They started letting Creepy Girl and some of the other inmates go somewhere at night, but I was not invited. They loaded them in a van, and two hours later, brought them back. "Where do y'all go every night?" I finally asked. "Bowling or something?"

"I wish," Creepy Girl replied, acting like it was no big deal that I'd finally spoken to her. I stared, waiting for an answer.

"It's my last week, so they make us go to AA meetings out in the real world." She made it sound like torture.

"You're getting out?" My voice got all excited. "Aren't you happy?"

True to her name, Creepy Girl didn't say anything.

"I'd give anything to get out of here." I said it like she was totally wack.

Her eyes got all moist, and then she ran out, crying down the hallway.

All I said was that I'd give anything to get out of here. I'd just mastered the art of not saying what I really thought in my out loud voice. This, in and of itself, was a big deal. Yesterday for example, the therapist, Dr. Drake, had pointed out my magnificent progress in this area and had written about it on her clipboard. So why did Creepy Girl run away? I was starting to get pissed off about it when a shadow darkened the doorway. I turned around. The Mohawk girl from the AA meeting squinted and clenched her fists. Holy crap.

Just when I thought my life was finally over, two men appeared and escorted The Mohawk maniac away. That was close. Clearly, I did not belong in this place. I made a decision right then and there to escape. Ohmygod.

That afternoon, Dr. Drake asked me what had happened. I explained that I had done nothing wrong and that I needed to be placed in solitary confinement because the oversensitive crazies were planning to kill me. She wrote it all down on the clipboard.

I waited patiently while she finished writing and then she cocked her head and let out a long sigh. "I want you to try something new," she said. By the tone in her voice, I could tell I wasn't going to like it. She handed me a journal and a pencil, and said, "It's time for you to start writing."

"First of all, no." I pushed it away. "I don't do journaling. You can ask Mr. Oliver."

"Who's Mr. Oliver?" She crinkled her forehead.

"Nobody. My English teacher. Hey, shouldn't I be in school?"

She wrote some more stuff on the clipboard and said, "I don't want you to write in a journal. I want you to do something else."

I swallowed my words and put on a big, faux smile. "Right now, I'm not saying anything that's actually going through my head, just like you taught me."

"Excellent," she said. "Now I want you to listen."

I took a deep breath and concentrated on only listening, nothing else, just listening.

"I want you to reflect on your relationship with Kayla."

"Who?" I asked.

"Kayla, your roommate."

"Oh, yeah." I'd called her Creepy Girl in my mind for so long that I'd actually forgotten her real name. "We're not roommates; we're cellmates."

"Let's turn off the committee of sarcastic voices in your head and go back to listening."

I had no idea what she was talking about, until I heard them—a committee—talking about Creepy Girl and how unfair it was that they were letting her out and making me stay. The more they talked about it, the madder I got.

"How do you know what's going on in my head?" I asked.

"You're not as unique as you think. Everyone in here has the same negative committee in their head telling them what to say and do. My job is to help you fire the committee."

I must have looked stunned because she smiled for the first time ever. Not wanting to appear weak, I casually lobbed one leg over the other, and with my hand, gestured for her to please continue.

"Alcoholics are wired differently than most people," she said. "Our first instinct is to look at everything from a negative point of view."

I raised one eyebrow. "Our?"

"Believe it or not, I do know what I'm talking about."

"I'm intrigued, but just because you're an alkie, doesn't mean I'm one. How do you know my fascination with drinking wasn't situational?"

She frowned, like she'd lost her best friend. "Do you still think about drinking?"

"I do," I said. "Considering everything I've been through, I think that's perfectly normal."

"And what exactly have you been through?"

"Seriously?" I said. "The arrest, the hospital, and now this insane asylum? Ohmygod, it's perfectly normal to need a drink."

"That's enough for today," she said. "Think about the committee and we'll talk again."

As far as I was concerned, the committee was still out on whether we would even talk again. It was getting old listening to her blame me for all the things my parents had done. I went back to my room, where Creepy Girl stretched out on the bed with her head resting on a duffle bag stuffed with whatever she'd brought to prison.

"Leaving?" She didn't even acknowledge my presence, so I shrugged it off and went outside to sit on a bench and stare at the ugly building surrounded by a moldy brick wall. This proved I wasn't an alcoholic with a committee of naysayers hardwired into my brain because getting ignored by Creepy Girl didn't upset me in the least. When I returned to my room, she was gone. I just hoped my next cellmate had a dentist.

I froze. That last thought sounded horrible, like another person had said it. Was it me? Had I become that mean of a person? Or was it that committee Dr. Drake was talking about—the thoughts in my head that made me view everything from a negative point of view. I gazed in the mirror and I loathed the person staring back. "No!" I shouted and tried to shake it off. Dr. Drake was wrong. I was too young to be an alcoholic. I'd simply overreacted to my parents' divorce.

That evening, in Café a la Can Opener, the girl with the Mohawk pointed her middle finger right between her eyes and stared me down. Obviously, her committee was working late, but my non reaction was once again living proof that I was nothing like them. I swallowed a plastic spoonful of Spaghetti Os. I could deal with Spaghetti Os, but that tinny tasting spinach, no. Even though it was pointless, I picked up the plastic fork and twirled the Spaghetti Os in the spoon, like I used to do with long strings of spaghetti at home. How did my life get to this point? I wasn't even fifteen. A tear landed in the middle of the Spaghetti Os and I tried to stop the next one before anyone noticed, but a sea of tears followed and I sat there, gasping uncontrollably right in front of everyone.

Two people put their arms around me, but I couldn't tell who they were because I had the napkin bunched up in my eyes. Maybe they would take me back to my room and let me cry in peace now that my roommate was gone. Someone rubbed my back, but I couldn't stop sobbing long enough to see what was going on. Finally, I caught my breath. Whoever sat next to me handed me another napkin and I blew my nose. When I looked up, I expected to see Dr. Drake, but instead, five or six girls I didn't know were telling me everything was going to be all right. "This is all my fault," I said through jerky tears. "My parents didn't get me arrested. I did."

A few of them grinned, but not in a mean way. "I think she's ready," said one girl. Two others nodded in agreement and somewhere in the midst of my complete emotional meltdown, I started feeling better, like I didn't have to hide or fight anymore. I think I might have actually hugged someone. At our AA meeting that night, I found out what they meant when they said I was ready. "Abby's gonna tell us her story," a girl named Jasmyn announced after the meeting began.

My eyes got big. "I don't know what to say."

"Start with your first drink and how it made you feel," someone suggested. "Then end with how you got here."

Weird—no therapists in sight—just us. I scanned the room again and wondered why I didn't know anyone's name. A deep breath filled me with strength. "My first drink," I said, trying to remember.

I must have been silent for a whole minute, thinking back over the past year. No one said a word; they sat and waited patiently. Finally, I said, "My first drink was vodka and orange juice." Their eyes lit up and they smiled reassuringly. "I was watching Hurricane Ike on TV and my parents were going through a divorce." Even though my voice kept quivering, I continued. "So how did it make me feel?" I took a deep breath. "The vodka felt relaxing and melted all my anxiety away. I remember pouring water back in the vodka bottle so my mom wouldn't notice any was missing."

A wave of giggles erupted in the room and some of the girls nodded like they had done the same thing, so I continued. I told them about seeing Dad on the news, and when I described the Kat creature in detail, they hooted and hollered. It never seemed funny to me until that moment when I found myself laughing and crying at the same time. When I told them about Megan's betrayal to cover up her own family's dirty secrets, one girl snapped and shouted, "Uh-huh. When you point a finger at someone, you got three pointing right backatcha." And they loved the part about my knight in shining armor turning out gay. "In the end," I said, "Rafa and Megan were there for me, as loyal as two friends could possibly be. But alcohol had changed me into someone I didn't even like anymore."

The room got still and everyone listened intently, so I continued. "I'd already had a few blackouts, but the one that got me here was the worst." I told them about spring break and the beer bong boys and the tequila. And when I got to the part about changing the signs to read, Badass on the Beach, they totally cracked up. "Unfortunately, I don't remember painting the signs because I was in a blackout. And when I woke up, I was in a hospital, handcuffed to a bed with a police officer sitting outside the door. Later, I found out I was under arrest for public intoxication, vandalizing state property, resisting arrest, and assaulting a police officer. I didn't remember any of it."

For the first time, the girls looked truly stunned. Hearing it come out of my mouth made it real for me, too. This was who I had become. "But that wasn't the worst part," I said. "I almost died. And no I did not try to kill myself. Alcohol was doing that for me."

I looked around the room and the tough street girls I'd felt so superior to a few hours earlier, looked back at me with the sweetest, most loving eyes I'd ever seen. They knew how humiliated I felt. Suddenly, I was no better and no worse than anyone in the room. We were all the same.

"I guess I am an alcoholic and… I may need some help here."

They all clapped for a long time and then lined up to give me hugs. Even though I felt emotionally exhausted, I stayed and helped clean up. When I got back to my room, a new girl sat on the cot with her jaw set and fists clenched.

"Hey, I'm Abby," I said.

She rolled her eyes and turned away.

I smiled because I knew she was going to be all right.

The next week, while chewing on a piece of Spam and canned pineapple, Tiara asked if I'd heard from Kayla.

"How is that even possible?" I asked. "No phones."

"I was hopin' she wrote you," Tiara said. "I been thinkin' 'bout her."

"You get mail?"

"You don't?" Tiara scrunched here eyes. "Everyone gets mail, 'cept Kayla, 'cause she ain't got no mama."

My heart landed in my stomach with a soft thud. All this time, Mom could've been writing. Not a word from Dad or Rafa, not even Megan. I laid down the plastic fork, and let out a deflating sigh. I was sick of me, too.

"I worry 'bout that girl," Tiara continued. "Goin' to some new foster home after what happened at that last one. People are crazy. Guess I don't need to be tellin' you all this, since y'all shared a crib."

My eyes welled up and my nose tingled. Kayla's problems were a zillion times more painful than mine and I'd made her feel even worse. It was official: I was lower than a worm.

That afternoon, I asked Dr. Drake if she knew how I could get in touch with Kayla. "That's confidential information," she replied, "although it warms my heart that you're asking."

"But—that doesn't even make sense. She has no family. You'd think it would be a good thing that someone wants to get in touch with her."

Dr. Drake studied my eyes for a long time. "I'll see what I can do."

The day finally arrived when I could go to meetings out in the real world. All the girls who had checked in that same week, climbed into the van with caged windows that let the outside world know we were dangerous prisoners. I sat next to a window and Tiara scooted next to me. About ten of us settled in the van and even though we usually talked a lot, the van was silent, perhaps because our predictable lives were about to become unpredictable again. It was only a meeting, I told myself, and then we'd go right back home.

We drove down a bumpy street and turned onto a smooth one. I didn't bother keeping track of where we were going since I wasn't familiar with that part of Houston. The sun shimmered like glitter through green leaves that wiggled in the wind. The drive would have been enough for me, just to get a glimpse of nature, but the blinker ticked at a light and we turned into a rundown strip center, and then parked in front of a window with a triangle that looked like the AA logo. The driver turned around and in a stern voice, gave us instructions about how to exit the van and stay in a single file line, while the guy from the passenger seat slid open the side door. No one said a word as we filed into the meeting and filled up the back row of seats.

At our meetings back at the treatment center, we sat in a circle, but here, the chairs were arranged like an audience. I looked up at the clock. One minute 'til eight. People drifted in alone, mostly older, like in their thirties and forties, and they filled up the middle part of the room. A guy sitting in a chair facing the audience announced, "A van just pulled up, so we'll get started in a minute." He flipped through a book and waited.

When the door opened, a line of boys filed in exactly the way we had and since most seats were taken, a man herded them to the front. Tiara squeezed my arm and whispered something that I couldn't hear because Daniel had come in, and I was busy having a heart attack. He looked sad, and while the other boys scoped the room, Daniel kept his head down and quietly took a seat. I couldn't breathe.

— 36 —

We were instructed to close our eyes and say the Serenity Prayer, but I couldn't take my eyes off Daniel. While everyone murmured the part about accepting things they couldn't change, I wondered if Daniel had spotted me when he first came in and if that was why he had kept his head down. Clearly, he had reason to hate me. If I hadn't painted the signs, he wouldn't be serving time in the boy version of the treatment center.

The guy leading the meeting went on and on about himself, but none of it registered in my brain because my committee was busy obsessing about Daniel. Finally, he stopped talking and one of the older people in the middle of the room said she realized her life had become unmanageable when she woke up in jail. "I'm not the kind of person who goes to jail," she said. I nudged Tiara and whispered, "I said that, too." Tiara rolled her eyes and the guy leading the meeting called on someone else.

"What's the topic?" I asked.

"Step one," Tiara whispered back.

Everyone who shared admitted all the crazy things they'd done while they were drunk and that made me feel normal. I'm not so sure that was a good thing, but it was the truth. Then the guy up front called on Daniel.

He sat up straight and cleared his throat. "I'm Daniel, and I'm an alcoholic."

"Hi, Daniel," everyone said.

It was weird to hear him admit he was an alcoholic after all the fun we'd had on the beach. Seeing his face would have helped, but I had to look at the back of his head, kind of like texting, when you can't see the other person's facial expression to know if they're being serious. "I didn't know I was an alcoholic when I was drinking," he said, "but now that I've been sober for a month, I can see how it made my life unmanageable." Daniel squirmed in the chair. "I not only messed up my own life, I messed up someone else's, too—someone I really cared about, I mean a lot."

"You all right, girl?" Tiara whispered.

I swallowed hard and nodded.

"You don't look all right," she said.

"Shhhh…" Ohmygod.

"Because of me, she's in a lot of trouble with the law, and like that other lady shared, she's not the type of person who goes to jail."

Tiara shook her head and mumbled, "People keep saying that. Not the type, my ass."

"I may never see her again," Daniel continued, "but I

know when I get to that step where I have to make amends, I'll find her and I hope she'll forgive me."

"Thanks for sharing," the guy leading the meeting said.

For some reason, my hand shot straight in the air and they guy pointed to me. I felt like Queen Doreen had taken over my body and was getting ready to set everyone straight. "My name is Abby and I'm an alcoholic," I stated firmly.

"Hi Abby," everyone in the room said in unison. Daniel whipped his head around and his eyes met mine.

"Okay, first of all, no one is to blame for the trouble I'm in, except me." I looked right at Daniel and said, "I was drinking vodka at school and having blackouts way before spring break. Nobody forced me to drink; I wanted to." I rubbed my sweaty palms on my jeans. "I used to blame my parents, but it's not their fault. A few days ago, my roommate left to go live with strangers and I realized how lucky I am to have parents." When I raised my eyes back up to Daniel's, he gazed at me so sweetly. "Anyway, I don't blame anyone, except myself, just so everyone's clear on that."

Daniel half smiled and had a starry look in his eyes. Ohmygod.

Finally, someone else began sharing and everyone stopped staring at me, except Tiara, who had reared up in her chair and was giving me the look. I shrugged my shoulders and said, "What!"

She furrowed her brows and pointed at Daniel. "I can't believe somebody actually likes you."

"Shut up!" I slapped her arm, but Tiara shook her

head and chuckled until the meeting finally ended and everyone got up to hold hands in a big circle and pray. Normally this bothered me, but with Daniel in the room, it didn't matter what we were doing. Once that thought registered in my mind, I didn't want to be around him anymore. And then, when all the praying and chanting ended, they herded us back to the van before I could even say hi to him.

On the way out, I glanced over my shoulder and Daniel made a hand signal that he would call me. Obviously, he meant after our release from captivity, when we've returned to civilization where they have real food and modern technology. I slid into a seat next to a window and stared out into the darkness. That was my future—dark and uncertain. Had I ruined my life forever? Fortunately, Tiara started teasing and poking me about Daniel—otherwise, my committee would have obsessed about my ruined life all the way home. Not home, whatever.

The next night, the same group of boys filed into the AA meeting, but Daniel wasn't there. A wave of panic hit me. While everyone else said the Serenity Prayer, I closed my eyes and tried to think. He probably didn't have to be chained to a hospital bed for God knows how long, so he would have started treatment before me. He was already out.

The leader decided to talk about step two—something about getting restored to sanity. People began sharing things that qualified them to be legitimately classified as insane. I did my best to not make eye contact with the leader, since I couldn't think of anything that proved I was insane. Other people, yes. Me, no.

Then someone shared that once they started drinking, they couldn't stop, even if they wanted to. Night after night, they drank against their own will. I could totally relate, but did that make me insane? No. It just made me a pathetic teenage alkie.

Next, someone shared that they had killed someone while driving in a blackout. Ohmygod. I couldn't imagine having to live with that. Yes, I'd had a few, okay more than a few blackouts. Did I hurt anyone? No. And just when I was feeling totally grateful that I wasn't insane, someone shared that they drank so much, they almost died. "Committing suicide, while telling myself that I'm not committing suicide is pretty crazy," the girl said.

Great, now I'm crazy. As if I didn't have enough problems already.

For some reason, the AA meetings at the treatment center were better. Maybe it was because we knew each other so well. But when the day came to say goodbye, my personality changed. I became rude and sarcastic to pretty much everyone, until I realized I didn't want to say goodbye to the band of misfits who had become my friends. I needed them. In my most vulnerable moments, they'd made me feel safe. It was easy to not drink in the treatment center, but could I do it out in the real world? Tiara had said I could, and since she was the most honest person I knew, I tried to believe her, but there was sadness deep inside me and alcohol had always been the only thing that could make it go away. I packed my bag, while my committee continued this lovely conversation about how I was going to fail, once I returned to the real world.

I dragged my bag to the lobby, where Mom stood, eagerly smiling, with her arms stretched out. She squeezed me tight, but I felt distant, like I wasn't even there. I peered over Mom's shoulder and spotted Rafa standing by the door.

"Let me look at you," Mom said, all mommy-like, fussing with my hair. "How do you feel?"

I had no idea how I felt. I couldn't even speak. And then, out of nowhere, some angry voice inside of me blurted out, "Don't act like you care now. You didn't even write!" Mom's eyes got big. An all-too-familiar look of disappointment covered Rafa's face as he turned, pushed the door open, and walked out. I stared at the aftermath of my anger.

Someone pulled my shoulders and guided me off to a corner. It was Dr. Drake. "Remember," she said in a quiet voice, "your insides are not going to match your outsides for a while. Try not to blurt anything out until you see things the way they really are."

Tears streamed down my cheeks. I thought I had seen things the way they really were. It totally sucked to be me.

Outside, Rafa leaned against the car with arms folded and eyes down. Mom clicked open the trunk and I threw my bag inside. When I climbed in front, Rafa slid in the back seat, pushed in ear buds, and closed his eyes. "Thanks for picking me up," I said to Mom as she climbed in, even though it sounded corny. I just hoped it matched the reality of the situation.

"We have so much to talk about," Mom said, "but let's get you settled first."

Well, yeah. I had questions, like when do I get my phone back? Is Dad still here? Is my next stop jail? I decided to practice step three and let go of all those questions. I'd let God surprise me. Not that I believed in God, but whatever.

"Rafa and I cooked a welcome home dinner for you," Mom said. "All your favorites."

"Anything that doesn't come from a can will be yummy," I replied, hoping that sounded positive. I turned around to see if Rafa was still ignoring me. He was, so I climbed between the seats and practically landed on his lap. I finally squirmed my butt over on the seat and squeezed him tight, but he didn't respond. "I love you bro," I said, wondering if it had sounded sarcastic or real. He still didn't respond, which made my committee wake up and call a meeting to order, but Dr. Drake had told me to stop trying to guess what other people were thinking, so I adjourned the committee until further notice. It was actually easier than I thought.

Rafa finally relaxed and rested his head on my shoulder. I decided to sit still and hold him, but not say anything, so I wouldn't mess things up. When we finally made it to Galveston Island, I praised myself for not pushing those three big questions. I'd wait until we were enjoying the fabulous meal Mom and Rafa had prepared, and then ask all my questions in a civilized manner over dinner. It wasn't easy being normal, but at least I knew what it was supposed to look like, thanks to Queen Doreen's insistence that her daughter grow up overly well mannered.

Mom hit the garage door opener as we turned into the driveway. I couldn't stand it any longer. I needed answers. "Is Dad still here?" I asked nicely.

After Mom pulled into the garage, we all got out. While Rafa grabbed my bag out of the trunk, Mom said, "He went back after he got all your legal issues settled."

"Ohmygod!" I screamed. "Will someone please tell me what's going on!" It's too bad you can't rewind how you've said something and try again. Once it's out, it's out. I stood there like an idiot, listening to my words echo around the garage while Mom and Rafa stared at me, totally shocked.

"I'm sorry," I said.

"I know you have a lot of questions, sweetheart. Let's go in and get you settled. Then we'll talk."

A flood of sadness washed through me again and my eyes and nose welled up. It wasn't that I was afraid of the legal consequences for my actions; it was because I didn't know how to love or show kindness. Before I could stop myself, I began sobbing uncontrollably, gasping to breathe. Mom led me to the living room and sat down with me on the sofa. Rafa brought a box of tissues and sat on the other side. I wondered if the girls at the treatment center had people who cared about them like this, too. I doubted it. As much as I hated sappy moments, I couldn't stop saying "thank you" to Mom and Rafa.

"You're going to be fine," Mom said, stroking my hair.

"Always listen to your heart," Rafa whispered. "It will make you stronger."

Okay, that opened my floodgates. Ohmygod. "So tell me about this fabulous meal you've prepared," I said, smiling through tears.

Rafa sat up and his voice got all girlie. "Well," he said, waving his hand in the air for emphasis, "we made rosemary-lemon chicken with lightly caramelized sweet potatoes, and a spring mix salad with goat cheese and roasted pears."

My eyes widened. "Ohmygod. Mom's been teaching you how to cook."

For the first time all day, Rafa lips widened into a cute smile, making the little dimple in his cheek appear. "We had to do something while you were gone," he said.

This was my family. The people I loved. I got all teary again. Ohmygod. "Okay," I said, like I'd had enough. "This is way more sappiness than I can handle." I stood up and grinned. "Let's have dinner and you can tell me how many years of hard time I'm doing."

Mom smirked and shook her head. "And I thought Rafa was a drama queen."

The smell of real food made me woozy. My mouth began watering before they put the last salad on the table. Of all the roasted chickens I'd devoured in my lifetime, none ever tasted that good. "I wonder if this is how Jesus felt at the last supper," I said.

Rafa looked at me all quizzically. "I don't get it."

"My last meal before I go to prison."

"You're not going anywhere," Mom said. "You have to do a hundred and twenty hours of community service."

"What is that?" Rafa asked.

"She has to volunteer at a nonprofit organization over the summer." Mom passed me the chicken platter. "Oh, and you need to get a job. You owe me two thousand dollars. I paid your fine."

I took the chicken platter and set it next to my plate. "No more incarceration?"

"Nope," Mom said, "you're a free woman."

It took me all of two seconds to figure out where I wanted to volunteer. "Do I get to choose where I do community service, or do they assign something?"

"You choose," said Mom.

"I want to serve food in the kitchen at the treatment center," I said. "Do you think they take volunteers?"

"You can call and ask," Mom said. "By the way, Mr. Oliver came by last week for a visit. Apparently, he's very fond of you."

"Mr. Oliver was here? That's totally weird. Here at our house?"

"You never notice when people care about you," Rafa said. "You have always been his favorite one."

Okay, first of all, Mr. Oliver hated me. He wouldn't even let me write a novel in place of that stupid journal assignment. The committee of negativity had convened and was calling a meeting to order. "Um, like no," I said, getting ready to unleash the committee right at the dinner table. But did I really want to go there? Already my stomach was twisting. Fire the committee. Don't let them speak. With a positive tone, I asked Mom, "What did he want?"

"He wanted to know if you were okay." Mom took a sip of iced tea. "I really liked him."

"Of course you did. He's all English and proper. I can see the two of you sipping Earl Grey and eating biscuits."

Mom smiled. "He offered you a job at his book shop downtown, just for the summer, for tourist season."

I looked at Rafa. "Oliver's Book Shop? I always thought Oliver was somebody's first name, like Oliver Twist, not Mr. Oliver."

"How does he do that?" Rafa looked puzzled. "He is always at school."

"His sister manages it during the school year, but she goes back to London in the summer. Anyway, I told him yes."

I was trying to picture Mr. Oliver with a sister, when it finally registered that I would be working in his book shop this summer. "Are you sure he likes me?"

Mom threw her linen napkin at me and Rafa seized the opportunity to wad up his and bombard me, too. "One day you'll know how wonderful you are," Mom said.

That did not make sense in my brain, but I decided to keep my mouth shut and let it go. Mom gathered our plates and piled the silverware on top. "Mr. Oliver said he'd talk to you about it on Monday."

I lifted the chicken platter. "Monday?"

"At school." Mom took the pile of plates to the kitchen.

School—it seemed a million miles away. I followed

Mom into the kitchen and set the platter on the counter next to my phone that was plugged into a charger. Daniel. I unplugged the phone and stuck it in my pocket. With a worried look, Mom shifted her focus from me to the dishwasher and hurriedly assembled the plates inside.

"I'm responsible for me now," I said to her reassuringly. "I'm the only one who can keep me sober."

"I know," she said, keeping her head down.

— 37 —

I went to my room to call Daniel, but after clicking the door shut, a strange feeling came over me that was hard to describe, like danger was near. Perhaps calling Daniel was a bad idea. I sat on the bed and stared at the bookshelf without actually focusing on anything. The feeling of impending danger probably wasn't real. I mean, when have my feelings ever been appropriate to the situation? I was shocked that Mom hadn't deleted the eight text messages from Daniel, mostly saying to call him, oh and three from Megan that just said, "???"

I curled up on the bed and sent Megan a text:

Abby: r u there?

Ten minutes later, my committee convened to discuss all the reasons Megan hadn't replied. *She hates you. If she betrayed you once, she'll betray you twice. You're lower than a worm and don't deserve friends.* I turned over on the bed and hoped the committee would stop, but it didn't. "Fire them," Dr.

Drake had said. "Just fire them." I wish it were that easy.

When I figured out why my eyes kept wandering back to the bookshelf, the wave of fear returned—I'd hidden water bottles full of vodka there. I leapt out of bed, reached over the books and scoured the empty space behind them. Ka-ching! I pulled out the first bottle and tossed it on the bed. Ka-ching! Bottle number two. As I pulled out bottle number three, Rafa opened the door and his bright spirit transformed into pure loathing.

"Don't get your panties in a wad," I said. "Help me dump all this vodka."

Rafa's spirit recovered nicely and he started at the bottom shelf while I worked my way up to the top. We found two more bottles and carried them to the kitchen where Mom had just finished cleaning up. "Mom—" I started to explain, but her face lit up and she said, "A vodka dumping ceremony!"

"Yes, indeed," I said. "It's time to say goodbye to my not-so-loyal friend, Ms. Vodka." I unscrewed one of the plastic caps. "She seemed sweet at first, luring me with the warmth and comfort I craved; but she destroyed my relationships with everyone I loved." I took a moment to acknowledge Mom and then Rafa. "I won't miss you," I said, raising the bottle high. And then, ceremoniously, I turned it upside down and the clear liquid danced its way out of the bottle to the sink below. I held my breath to keep from inhaling any fumes, but by the end of the second bottle, I needed air and sucked in another breath. Magically, no fumes entered my nasal passages, which surprised me at first, but then I remembered that vodka didn't have much of an odor, which was why I'd chosen it as my constant companion in the first place. I took another sniff. Nothing. Finally, I sniffed directly into the bottle and found no trace of alcohol whatsoever. I shrieked, "This is water!"

Mom had the guiltiest look, ever, and just as I started to unleash my rage, Rafa laughed. "She loves you," he said, grabbing me in a headlock and swaying back and forth. "Don't be mad because someone loves you."

I didn't trust my feelings, but I trusted Rafa's. His first instinct was to see the positive side, unlike mine. "Okay, okay." I tickled his belly and he released me from the headlock.

"I'm sorry," Mom said. "I just—"

"Hey, fair is fair," I said. "I filled your vodka bottles with water, too."

Mom's eyes got big. "I had no idea."

A surge of pride rushed through me. "Anyway, you have to trust me."

She gave me a sideways hug. "I know."

"It's late," Rafa said. "I must go home."

Mom gathered her keys and her purse. "I'll drive you, honey."

After they left, I went back to my room to sort out all my mismatched feelings. Thank god a message appeared from Megan because I'd had enough emotional trauma for one day.

Megan: Hey badass! R u out of the slammer???
Abby: Yes!!!!
Megan: With the parental unit. C u at school??

Abby: Yup, c u

Instead of calling Daniel, which kept crossing my mind, I drew a hot bath and poured in lots of jasmine scented bubble bath. After lighting a few candles, I stepped in and let the warm water soothe me. At some point, Mom peeked in and said goodnight, but I kept my eyes closed and let myself completely relax. Finally, I would sleep in my own bed.

Sunday was uneventful, which was perfectly fine with me, because I'd had enough drama for one lifetime. Mom and I went grocery shopping and then chilled on the sofa and watched a few movies, romantic comedies, which kept reminding me of Daniel. That made no sense, since there was nothing romantic between us. Yet he'd said something at the meeting that made it sound like we were more than friends. I tried to not remember, but I couldn't stop going there. I think he'd said I meant a lot to him, or whatever. By not calling him back, I gave my feelings a rest and chose to have a drama-free day.

Just when I'd changed my mind again and decided to actually call him, Mom said, "It's time for a meeting." I looked at my phone. Seven-thirty. "Ninety meetings in ninety days," Mom said in a sing-song voice. That's what they'd prescribed when I checked out of treatment. Quite frankly, I was relieved, because a meeting was exactly what my rollercoaster of emotions wanted. Surprisingly, the meeting, right down the street by the way, wasn't any different than the ones I'd already attended. Well, different faces, different location, but the same topics of discussion. I felt at home.

The next morning when the alarm went off, it felt weird to have to get ready for school. Rafa arrived on his bike at the usual time and when we rode up to the school, it looked different, smaller maybe. We locked our bikes and I got a couple of weird looks, but mostly kids smiled as they passed by. For some reason, it didn't seem important to me.

"See you in English class," Rafa said and took off.

In the hallway, other kids acted childish, hiding each other's binders, saying silly things that sounded shallow. I felt distant, like I didn't belong anymore, until I spotted Megan at her locker, smiling at me down the hall.

"Hey BA, how's my favorite detoxed alkie?"

I threw my arm over her shoulder. "I can always count on you to be real."

After the bell rang, Megan said, "Okay, here's the thing. Mom's forbidding me to be friends with you."

"What!" I studied her eyes.

"Don't worry about it. She's just threatened by your recovery. You know how much she drinks. Anyway, don't call or text. I'll contact you."

I grinned. "A forbidden friendship, I like it."

"You really think I'd give up a chance to be best friends with the only badass girl at Marconi High School?" Megan gave me a hug. "I really admire you. I know it's hard."

Good thing she ran off, because I still hadn't mastered the art of mushiness.

In English class, Mr. Oliver never said a word about letting me work in his book shop in the summer. Later, when I mentioned it to Mom, she said he probably didn't want to discuss it in front of the other students, which made sense. I wondered what it must be like to be perfectly appropriate at all times—to know what to say and what not to say in every situation. I tried to imagine myself all overly appropriate like Mr. Oliver, but I couldn't see it, which was probably a good thing. I mean yes, I definitely needed to change my personality to stay sober, but please, that was a bit extreme.

I somehow managed to get through the end of the school year without a drink, which in and of itself was a miracle. Dad had called from Mexico every single night, just to check in, since we were both trying to get sober at the same time. We mostly talked about AA and how to apply its basic principles in our everyday lives. All those words of wisdom he'd given me as a child now had a strong sense of urgency, probably because it was a matter of life and death, literally.

And speaking of literally, while spending way too much time with Mr. Oliver at his book shop over the summer, he kept insisting that I base my first novel on the events of the past year. "That's not possible," I'd said repeatedly. "There's no happy ending."

Daniel disagreed. Yes, I finally called him. Every afternoon, he collected me (I learned that from Mr. Oliver) at the book shop and drove me to the treatment center to fulfill my hours of community service, slopping canned food on plastic trays for juvenile delinquent girls. Daniel did the same thing at the boy treatment center where he had detoxed.

One day, I asked Dr. Drake if I could bring in real food and she explained that the treatment center needed to remain somewhat punitive, otherwise some girls would relapse just to keep coming back to a place that was better than home. She never would give me Kayla's phone number and I thought maybe it was because Kayla had run away again. I got all sad and wished I could redo everything I'd ever said to her.

That day, while Daniel was driving me home from community service, I asked how he saw this story Mr. Oliver wanted me to write with a happy ending. Daniel went on and on about how we couldn't control anything, except ourselves, which by the way I was still having trouble with, and that we had to let go of problems like Kayla's that we didn't have any control over. Again, I tried to let it go, but it still didn't work. I'd probably always wish I'd been nicer to Kayla.

Freeway traffic came to a standstill and I closed my eyes to try to let go of everything around me, so I could focus on only the things I could change within myself. That's when Daniel kissed me. His soft, warm lips melted into mine and instead of pushing him away, I pulled him closer. We would have kissed forever if the car behind us hadn't honked after traffic started moving again. I didn't say a word the rest of the way home, but I totally liked how that letting go thing worked.

By the end of summer, Daniel and I had completed our community services hours and instead of seeing each other every day, we were down to once a weekend. It sucked that he lived halfway between Galveston and

Houston, but since his dad was an engineer at NASA, it wasn't very likely they'd be moving to the Island. Anyway, Daniel spent most of his time working on an invention, the details of which he refused to discuss. On some days, this infuriated me because I thought we were close, but most of the time I could see it rationally: inventors had to keep their ideas a secret until they got a patent.

With Daniel busy creating his invention, I decided it was time to write that novel. Not the fantasy novel I'd envisioned, but the one Mr. Oliver wanted me to write. "Truth is stranger than fiction," he'd said. When I had trouble getting started, Mr. Oliver told me to be honest and the story would write itself. He'd winked and said, "Change the names, of course, to protect the guilty."

On my laptop, I typed: *This is not the story I wanted to write when I turned fifteen.* That was the freaking truth.

Megan appeared in the doorway and I slammed the laptop shut. "Your mom let me in. She was on the phone." I rolled over and Megan sat next to me on the bed. "It sounded like she was talking to your dad."

"Just what I need, more drama."

Megan stretched out and propped her head up with her hand. "Isn't your birthday on Saturday? We need to do something fun."

"I thought you were forbidden to have fun with me."

Megan grinned. "That makes it more fun. Jax and I broke up, by the way. Thanks for asking."

"Let me make a note of that character defect. Self-centeredness, I wasn't aware of that one." I rolled my eyes and smiled.

"You're lucky Daniel lives here. Long distance relationships never work out."

I stared at the ceiling. "I wonder if Dad called Mom because the Kat finally had kittens." Just then, Mom's voice came up the stairs. She stood in the doorway and clicked off the phone. After taking a deep breath, Mom said, "Your father and Kat are coming here to have the babies. She's due in two weeks. Your father wants to be here in time for your birthday. They're arriving tomorrow."

That was a lot of emotion-packed info for my committee to process. Separate birthday celebrations: one with Mom and one with Dad. Would the Kat creature come? Why couldn't I just celebrate with my friends and have a parent-free birthday? I kept myself on mute and continued staring at the ceiling. Fortunately, Megan picked up the conversation in a perfectly normal tone. "So where's the party?"

"That's what I came to ask," Mom said.

I turned my head sideways to look at her.

"We can have a dinner party here, or your father can make reservations at the restaurant in the San Luis Hotel where they're staying."

Was she freaking serious? One party with Mom and the Kat creature in the same room? Slowly, Megan got up and walked to the door. "We need a minute, Mrs. Alexander." Mom nodded as Megan closed the door. When Megan turned around, her eyes were huge. "We're so having it here," she said.

I bolted up. "What difference does it make? It's still a

formula for disaster."

"Oh, it makes all the difference in the world." Megan peeled her eyes at me. "You don't want to feel like the guest at your own birthday party. Make the witch come here. Make her the guest."

I didn't know if it was politically correct for my so-called spiritual program of recovery, but I totally agreed.

— 38 —

Saturday afternoon, Mom and I struggled to get two cumbersome leaves inserted in the dining room table so everyone who was coming could have a sit down dinner prepared by Mom and her new protégé, Rafael. "One leaf is big enough for eight people," I said to Mom, after counting the guests in my head. "We're setting a table for ten," she said. I started to ask who else was coming when a visual image of the pregnant Kat creature sitting at our dining room table appeared in my brain. Let's add raging hormones to the witch on wheels I met at Thanksgiving and this whole birthday extravaganza was more than my committee could handle, so I fired them again and turned everything over to my higher power, whom I'd chosen to call, Ohmygod.

That worked for about ten minutes. To keep my mind occupied, I counted the people who were coming again: Mom, Dad, the Kat, Rafa, Me, Daniel, Megan, her date du jour, and that was eight. Rafa didn't know who the other two were and when I asked Mom, she said, "I'm doing twenty things at once—I can't think about it now."

Finally, Rafa finished ironing all the table linens and I helped him spread the ivory table cloth over the longest table ever. That's when it hit me. "Do you have a boyfriend?" I asked.

Rafa smiled. "I wish."

I was truly the worst best friend in the world since it took me this long to ask. With peach colored napkins, we pitched ten tiny tents along the table's edge and I wanted to crawl into one of those little tents and stay there until the party was over. Since that was impossible, I went to my room to get ready, while Mom and Rafa rustled around in the kitchen creating some magnificent meal that smelled a lot like rosemary.

Little jasmine bubbles blossomed in the bathtub as I slipped into the warm water and closed my eyes. My plan was to store up a massive amount of serenity ahead of time, if that was even possible, and hope it could last through the evening so everyone would come out of tonight's situation alive. But thinking about absolutely nothing was harder than I thought. It would be a lot easier if I had some vodka. My eyes flashed open.

Okay, letting my mind wander was obviously a bad idea. It had walked straight over to the bar and ordered a drink. Was AA a way to reprogram your brain so it would stop wandering over to the bar? If it was serenity I wanted, then supposedly I just needed to say the Serenity Prayer. I closed my eyes. "Ohmygod, grant me the serenity to accept the things I cannot change, like the fact that the Kat creature is on her way over, the courage to change the things I can, like keeping my mouth shut, and the wisdom to know the difference." I kept my eyes closed to make sure it really sank in. Since my mind didn't wander back over to the bar, I assumed it had worked and I opened my eyes. For the first time in a long time, I felt present in my body and focused on the moment, which only included me taking a bath and nothing else. That was amazing.

I pulled myself up and out of the tub with new strength, wrapped myself in a terrycloth robe, and stepped into the closet. When I moved my hand to slide clothes over, they slid so easily, as if I had more muscle, but it wasn't really muscle, it was the way I felt inside. Out of respect for all the hard work Mom and Rafa were doing to make the night special, I chose something semi-elegant to wear—a trim-fitting, blue dress. When I finished getting ready, I caught myself smiling in the mirror.

Out in the dining room, Rafa arranged peach colored roses in a vase at the center of the table. His lips curled into a cute smile. "Beautiful," he said and yes, he was talking about me, not the roses. That's when the doorbell rang. Rafa went back into the kitchen, which left only me to open the door. I grabbed the handle, sucked up a deep breath, and pulled open the door. It was Daniel, looking all hot in a silk shirt and jeans, holding a gift. I must have been staring because he finally asked, "May I come in?"

"Of course!" I pulled him in the house and took the

present over to a table in the living room.

"Wow!" he said, looking me up and down, and then he kissed me on the cheek. I think I actually blushed and that led to a heart melting kiss on the lips that came to an end when the doorbell rang again. This time it was Megan with a boy I didn't know.

"Remember, Clyde," she was telling him, "it's not a real date, so just relax." She handed me a gift and rolled her eyes. "It was the only way I could get a ride over here without my mother suspecting anything. Hi, Daniel."

"Clive," he said, "not Clyde, and why would your mother care if you came over here?"

Megan turned on her high heels and wrapped her arms around me. "We have a forbidden friendship," she said to Clive, who looked stunned.

"You're a lezzie?"

"Yes, Clyde, tonight I'm a lezzie." Megan sat on the sofa and crossed her legs. "Remember that."

Daniel nearly choked trying not to laugh. "You're only making it worse."

With a big smile on his face, Rafa set a tray of lemonade on the coffee table and the doorbell rang again. Who was left besides Dad and the Kat? Before I finished counting how many people were already here, Rafa had opened the door and in stepped Mr. Oliver. He handed me a brown bag with a book inside and said, "Cheers," and then stood awkwardly and nodded at everyone else in the room. "Is your mum around?"

"In the kitchen," I said slowly.

Mr. Oliver hurried off while we each grabbed a glass of

lemonade and I sat on the sofa next to Megan. "It's weird having Mr. Oliver here," I whispered to her.

"I know, right?" Clive came toward Megan and she pointed to a chair across the room where she wanted him to sit. "You get to tell people we had a date," she said to him. "That's it."

I patted the sofa for Daniel to sit with us. When he put his arm around me, I got goose bumps. I acted like it wasn't a big deal, but Megan smiled because she knew it was. Even though Mom was all the way in the kitchen, we heard her burst out laughing and the louder Mr. Oliver talked, the more she laughed.

Megan raised her perfectly trimmed eyebrows and said, "Mr. Oliver's trying to get in your mom's pants."

"Shut up! He's just been helping me a lot this summer."

"Uh-huh." Megan took a long sip of lemonade. "By Christmas you'll be calling him Dadsy or whatever they say in England."

Fortunately, the doorbell rang and I didn't have time to obsess about Megan's madness. Rafa opened the door and with a big smile, shouted, "Mr. Alexander!"

Dad's voice boomed, "Hey, Rafa! How's my favorite son?" He'd always said that when we were kids. Dad stepped in and hugged Rafa, and waddling in behind him with a snarl on her face, entered the Kat. Holding her bulging belly, she scanned the room and said to Dad, "I told you we should've had it at the San Luis."

Megan made a hissing sound and swiped her claw through the air. Poor Daniel cleared his throat, as if trying to make sense of Kat's rudeness. Rafa smiled nervously and motioned for them to come in. "Please," he said, "have a seat." Within five seconds, the witch had insulted my home and made all of my friends uncomfortable. No.

I was about to open my mouth and insist someone drive her back to the hotel, when Mom walked in with Mr. Oliver and said, "Welcome, I'm so glad you're here."

Seriously?

Megan put her hand on my leg to calm me down and Clive smiled at Megan, nodding like he had it all figured out. I took a big swallow of lemonade and wondered if I still had a bottle of vodka somewhere in the house.

Dad helped the Kat creature to a chair, where she plopped down and went into her own little Kat world, as if we had all disappeared, and in the corner of my eye someone else had come in the door.

"Gabby!" I leapt from the sofa and threw my arms around her. "I'm glad you came!"

Gabby grinned and handed me a gift. "I have been looking forward to it," she said. "Happy Birthday."

Fortunately, Rafa introduced himself to Gabby because I was getting teary, but in a good way. Rafa said, "I feel like I already know you."

"And you, too," Gabby replied. "Abby spoke of you in Mexico."

I tried introducing Gabby to Megan, but Megan was distracted by the scene developing across the room— Mom had introduced Dad to Mr. Oliver, and while they were carrying on a conversation, Mom straightened Mr. Oliver's bowtie. Dad stuttered for a moment and then kept on talking. I smiled at Mom because she was nobody's fool.

The Kat creature stirred and pointed to the glasses of lemonade Rafa had placed on the coffee table. I would have handed her one if she had asked nicely, but Gabby obviously didn't have any feelings about it one way or the other because she picked up a glass and handed it to her. I definitely needed to lighten up, which was why I needed some vodka in my lemonade to make me feel like everyone else. How could I sneak out to get some? When I realized what my committee was saying, I panicked and rushed to the bathroom, locked the door and slid down to the floor.

If I drink, I could die—I'd already established that. I imagined hovering over my dead body, shackled to a hospital bed, only this time I couldn't get back, so why was I craving vodka? It made absolutely no sense whatsoever. Out of desperation, I closed my eyes and asked Ohmygod to please remove my obsession with alcohol, like they told me to do in the AA meetings. I waited and waited, but nothing happened. If someone handed me a bottle of vodka, I'd still have swallowed it.

I needed to try this for real. I closed my eyes again and pleaded desperately. "God, please, remove my obsession with alcohol." This time, I meant it. I'd never felt so desperate in my life. I waited. Slowly, my eyelids opened, and while they were opening, a tingling sensation began in my feet and moved up my legs, through my body and out of my head. Afterwards, I was at peace. The kind of peace I felt when I was at the ceiling looking down at my body—a centered kind of peace—only this time I was still in my body and the last thing I needed was a glass of crazy. "This stuff really works." I stood up, brushed myself off, and went back to my birthday party.

Dad was talking to Megan when I pulled him aside and explained what had happened in the bathroom. His face lit up and he squeezed me tight for a long time. "You're gonna be just fine, little girl." He gripped my arms and looked me in the eye. "Now listen to me," his voice deepened, "alcoholism is a sneaky disease. It doesn't go away. But when it comes back, you know what to do."

I didn't care how or why that praying thing worked; I was just glad it did. A little bell rang in the dining room, which was Mom signaling everyone to come in and sit at the table. Dad winked and said, "Guess we better do what she says."

I went to find Daniel while Dad helped pull the Kat creature to her feet. Daniel squeezed my hand and as we walked into the dining room, Dad was asking Mom why there weren't any name place cards. "Oh, I don't do that anymore," she said, sitting down at one end of the table. "Sit wherever you'd like." Dad grinned and took a seat at the other end of the table with the Kat beside him. Since I was the guest of honor, I sat in the middle with Daniel.

Everyone else was busy finding a seat, except Rafa, who brought a huge bowl of salad to the table. "Sit here," I said, patting the chair on my other side. Megan had taken a seat next to the Kat and I could see the wheels turning in her head.

"Pass the salad around." Mom raised her hands in a

welcoming manner. "We're eating family style tonight." With his long, skinny finger, Mr. Oliver slid his glasses up his nose and smiled for the first time ever, which instantly made him look ten years younger.

Rafa leaned into me and said, "This is what you wished for. Remember?"

It took a moment to figure out what he was talking about—yes, right after Hurricane Ike. Rafa had said, no matter what happens, you still sit down and eat with your family. I'd said in my family, that would never happen. I squeezed his hand. "Thank you."

Rafa blushed and said, "You're welcome."

While the salad bowl made its way around the table, Dad stood up and raised a glass of tea. "I'd like to make a toast to my daughter." After everyone else's glasses were raised, I was the one blushing. "I'm so proud of her—." Dad got all choked up. "Today she turns fifteen, and I've had the privilege—no, the honor—to watch her grow into a young lady with inner strength and wisdom beyond her years." That's when the Kat creature screamed. Not a little scream, but a big, huge scream, like someone was killing her.

Megan looked under the table. "Yuk. Her water broke, or whatever."

Dad's eyes got big. He dropped the glass he was toasting with to dig around in his pocket and pulled out keys. Daniel stood up and held out his hand. "I'll drive," he said, looking Dad square in the eye. Dad put the keys in Daniel's hand, scooped up the Kat creature, and headed for the door. Rafa and I must have been in shock because Megan had to practically push us out the door to go with them.

At the street, Daniel opened the door to the back seat of Dad's rental car. Dad put the screaming Kat creature inside and shut the door. After we all got in, Daniel sped toward the hospital and the Kat screamed the whole way there. Whatever tiny morsel of serenity I'd found on the bathroom floor was pretty much gone.

Daniel called nine-one-one on the way to the hospital and they had a wheelchair waiting by the curb for the Kat creature when we pulled up. They probably heard the screams in the background and knew it was for real. When the medical people whisked her way, Dad followed them and disappeared. Someone in scrubs told us to go to the waiting room on the fourth floor, which we did.

The nearly empty waiting room had comfortable chairs and we plopped ourselves down in the corner.

"We were this close to eating," Rafa said, pressing his finger and thumb together.

Daniel rubbed his stomach. "I know, and I was hungry."

I looked at Rafa. "You worked hard on that dinner. I'm sorry this happened."

"No, I did not mean it like that," he said. "This is more important."

Of course Rafa would make that correction. "You always see the big picture," I said. "Wish I could do that. I still think the world revolves around me."

Daniel winked. It was cool that we both had the same flaws to overcome and that we understood each other.

Over the summer, we'd decided if we had to do all this AA stuff, we'd have to be the most badass recovering alcoholics ever. If anything good came out of the trouble I'd gotten myself into, it was Daniel. I was busy gazing at my badass boyfriend when Megan's voice said, "Here they are." She stood across the waiting room with Gabby.

Rafa bounced up. "Please forgive us, we ran out so fast—," and finished whatever he was saying to Gabby in Spanish.

The five of us sat in the corner and waited. "Where's your date?" I asked Megan.

"When he dropped us off, I gave him a kiss on the cheek and told him our date was over."

"You're so getting grounded."

"I don't care. I want to be here."

After a long silence, I let out a heavy sigh. "You know, when we first got here, I was furious at the Kat creature for ruining my birthday party."

Daniel twisted his face. "I'm not trying to defend her or anything, but you can't control when you go into labor."

"Oh, believe me," Megan snapped, "that witch would have found another way."

"That's true," said Daniel.

"Anyway," I continued, "whatever the Kat creature does, she does." Daniel squeezed my hand. "I'm not letting her get to me anymore."

Megan rummaged through her purse and shook her head. "If I were you, I would have already slapped her."

Gabby let out a yelp and clamped her hand over her

mouth.

For some bizarre reason, an image of the curandera's wrinkly face popped in my brain. I smiled. My heart was fine now.

Slowly, I scanned my friends' faces. "Look, I always have two choices. And the way I see it, I'm getting a brother and a sister for my birthday. That's pretty amazing."

"Yes." Rafa's eyes sparkled. "It is a gift."

About the Author

Born on the border of Mexico to a U.S. Army family, Tina Laningham traveled the world before settling in Galveston, Texas. After a few intellectually stimulating years as a political journalist, followed by an outrageously fun time as a political speech writer, Laningham fell in love with the art of writing fiction.

Made in the USA
San Bernardino, CA
18 March 2014